T0323807

Economics of the Firm

This volume presents an interdisciplinary, critical perspective on current issues surrounding the economics of firms. The contributions largely depart from traditional approaches and stress the importance of interdisciplinary study of the firm as a dynamic evolving organisation.

The chapters emphasise the themes of change and evolution, and explore issues arising from the history and organisation of firms. This combination of economics and history is the characteristic setting for interdisciplinary analysis of evolution and change.

The contributors include Bart Nooteboom, Stavros Ioannides and Sue Bowden.

Michael Dietrich is Senior Lecturer at the Department of Economics, University of Sheffield, UK.

Studies in global competition

A series of books edited by John Cantwell
The University of Reading, UK
and David Mowery
University of California, Berkeley, USA

Economics of the Firm

Analysis, evolution, history

Edited by
Michael Dietrich

Routledge
Taylor & Francis Group

LONDON AND NEW YORK

First published 2007
by Routledge
2 Park Square, Milton Park, Abingdon, Oxon OX14 4RN

Simultaneously published in the USA and Canada
by Routledge
270 Madison Ave, New York, NY 10016

Routledge is an imprint of the Taylor & Francis Group, an informa business

Transferred to Digital Printing 2009

Typeset in Times New Roman by
Book Now Ltd

British Library Cataloguing in Publication Data
A catalogue record for this book is available from the British Library

Library of Congress Cataloging in Publication Data
Economics of the firm: analysis, evolution, history/edited by Michael Dietrich.
    p. cm.
1. Industrial organization (Economic theory). 2. Institutional economics.
I. Dietrich, Michael.

HD2326.E2433 2006
338.5–dc22   2005035263

ISBN10: 0–415–39509–7 (hbk)
ISBN 10: 0–415–49407–9 (pbk)
ISBN10: 0–203–96639–2 (ebk)

ISBN13: 978–0–415–39509–0 (hbk)
ISBN13: 978–0–415–49407–6 (pbk)
ISBN13: 978–0–203–96639–6 (ebk)

Contents

Figures and tables

Figures

Tables

Contributors

Yuri Biondi, Conservatoire National des Arts et Métiers (CNAM), France

Sue Bowden, University of York, UK

Michael Dietrich, University of Sheffield, UK

Elizabeth Garnsey, University of Cambridge, UK

Paul Heffernan, University of Cambridge, UK

David Higgins, University of York, UK

Werner Hölzl, Austrian Institute of Economic Research (WIFO), Austria

Stavros Ioannides, Panteion University, Athens, Greece

Jackie Krafft, CNRS-GREDEG, University of Nice, France

Pavel Luksha, Higher School of Economics, Moscow, Russia; University of Hertfordshire, UK

Bart Nooteboom, Tilburg University, The Netherlands

Christopher Price, University of York, UK

Erik Stam, University of Cambridge, UK; Utrecht University, The Netherlands; Max Planck Institute of Economics, Jena, Germany

Hassan Yazdifar, University of Sheffield, UK

Preface

This volume emerged from the inaugural workshop of the European Network on the Economics of the Firm (ENEF) held at the University of Sheffield, UK, in July 2004. The guiding philosophy of this network was a perceived need to facilitate a loose coordination of academic research on the economics of the firm that was not constrained by a rigid view of the nature of economics. In particular the network was guided by the following principles:

1   To support and promote discussion, research contacts and collaborative work among primarily European university academics on the economics of the firm.
2   This research activity covers both theoretical and empirical work on the firm.
3   The primary intellectual focus of ENEF involves a research agenda that views the firm not simply as an economic entity. This implies that economics should be viewed as the base from which interdisciplinary work is undertaken.
4   This interdisciplinary work does not involve a dominant economic methodology taking over other disciplines but instead using the insights offered to develop new and richer frameworks for understanding the nature of the firm than those traditionally on offer within economics.

Anyone interested in this network might want to look at the website: www.enef.group.shef.ac.uk.

Such was the enthusiasm generated at the Sheffield workshop that it was decided to build on the work undertaken by holding an annual workshop. ENEF2 was held at Erasmus University, Rotterdam, in September 2005, and at the time of writing plans are being developed for ENEF3 to be held at the University of Nice in 2006. In addition it was felt that the work being undertaken was sufficiently interesting that a wider audience might be interested. So, the main Sheffield workshop organiser became an editor and Routledge (Taylor and Francis) were sufficiently interested in the project to offer a publication contract.

Eight of the eleven chapters in this volume are developed from papers that were originally written for the Sheffield workshop, i.e. chapters 2, 3, 6, 7, 8, 9, 10 and 11. Chapters 4 and 5 are authored by people who became interested in ENEF after the first workshop. They have been included by the editor because they complement the guiding philosophy of the volume and the content of other chapters. Chapter 1 has been specifically written for this volume to provide this guiding philosophy and context for the various essays. To some extent this introduction can also be viewed as an attempt to develop an ENEF manifesto. But this suggested status to Chapter 1 does not reflect any agreement by the various authors in this volume, let alone the academics associated with ENEF. Although the content of this first chapter has been improved by comments offered by the other contributors, the editor is solely responsible for its content. If anyone associated with ENEF disagrees with what is written here, then I will offer a weak apology but equally I would be happy because the content of this volume will have stimulated academic debate.

The editor has been reliant on the help and support of many people without which this project, and the wider ENEF initiative of which it is a part, would have been much more difficult than it turned out to be. Formal thanks are therefore due to many people. First, the authors of the various essays have responded to my comments in the positive way that was intended. In addition everyone submitted final copy by the deadline. This is a first in my experience! Also I would like to thank Abhi, Donna, and Mohamed who interrupted their PhD research to help organise the 2004 ENEF workshop and also coped with equanimity when confronted with my worries as the workshop approached and took place. Also as the main ENEF organiser I would like to thank everyone who has been remarkably enthusiastic about the network and those who attended the two workshops to date. But in particular I have to put on record my appreciation for the efforts of Erik, Albert, Jackie and Jacques for workshop organisation. Finally, I would like to thank the University of Sheffield for funding the 2004 ENEF workshop and for providing an academic environment that allows me to undertake research on the economics of the firm informed by an interdisciplinary perspective.

To all concerned I hope this volume reflects your efforts.

Michael Dietrich

1 Introduction

The firm in an interdisciplinary context

Michael Dietrich

It is now somewhat standard to recognise that the firm is one of *the* fundamental institutions in a market economy. Not, of course, the black-box firm of equilibrium price theory, but real firms that enact strategies, manage the creation and acquisition of information and knowledge, and that have internal organisational structures and processes. In terms of modern economics, these real firms, at the core of a market economy, are analysed by writers as different as, for example, Edith Penrose, Herbert Simon and Oliver Williamson. But the fundamental importance of the firm is not merely a modern observation. It can be traced back into the writing of, for example, Marx and Schumpeter.

The essays presented in this volume continue this tradition, emphasising *the* fundamental institutional significance of the firm, without which a market economy cannot function. They are all original contributions to the economics of the firm. While the various chapters cover different aspects of this overall topic they are united by two common themes: that an adequate economics of the firm can be usefully informed by an interdisciplinary perspective and that much existing writing on the firm is overly static. This introduction will set out the basis and background of these themes and, in particular, explore the ways in which they are interlinked in their application to the firm. For instance, for reasons set out below, an interdisciplinary perspective on the firm gains a comparative advantage in dynamic circumstances. Stressing the importance of an interdisciplinary perspective can, of course, mean different things to different people: perhaps even more so than emphasising the importance of non-comparative static reasoning. Hence, the discussion here will initially consider interdisciplinary economics in general before applying this to the firm. To some extent what is meant by 'interdisciplinary' depends on how we define an intellectual discipline in the first place. To identify the possibilities involved here, and also locate the background to the contributions in this volume, we can initially use Figure 1.1.

In Figure 1.1 the idea of an intellectual discipline is defined in terms of two features: an analytical focus and an analytical method. The possible combinations involved are illustrated, for economics, with a few suggestive

Analytical method

		Economics	Psychology	Sociology	Politics
	Economics	Core economics	Experimental economics, Behavioural theory	Economic sociology	Political economy
Analytical focus	Psychology		Core psychology		
	Sociology	Becker (1981)		Core sociology	
	Politics	Buchanan and Tullock (1962)			Core politics

Figure 1.1 A taxonomy of inderdisciplinary economics.

examples. In philosophical terms the focus and method of a subject can be viewed as, respectively, the ontological and epistemological bases involved, both of which are necessary for an effective consideration of any subject (Lawson, 1997). The analytical focus of a subject involves its domain of reference, for example:

> Economics: the study of the production, distribution and consumption of goods and services.
> Psychology: the study of mental processes and behaviour.
> Sociology: the study of the relationships between people living in groups.
> Politics: the study of the ways in which a country is governed.

To some extent these broad subject domains are artificial aggregates. For example, within economics it is common to distinguish between the micro and macro domains of the subject. Furthermore, either of these domains are also aggregates; so, for instance, microeconomics can be divided into consumer economics, the economics of the firm, etc. A complete depiction of the domain of any subject can involve a level of detail that is not necessary for the current discussion; not least because Figure 1.1 is only intended for illustrative purposes. More fundamentally, there would appear to be no unique taxonomy for any subject. Instead any detailed taxonomy would seem to depend on the use to which it is being put.

Turning to the analytical method, or epistemological base, of a subject, this is also an artificial aggregate as few subjects have a single or dominant method. Within economics, and also other subjects, we commonly distinguish between theoretical and empirical work with different characteristic methods involved. In addition, further disaggregation of both theoretical and empirical work can involve different traditions. For instance, we have neoclassical and Austrian economic theory. But as with a subject's domain, the level of detail shown in Figure 1.1 is useful for illustrative purposes.

At this point we can recognise two important complexities concerned with any discussion of the analytical methods of a subject. First, there is no obvious single taxonomy of analytical methods within any discipline. Take, for instance, the relevant (for this volume) case of transaction cost economics (TCE). The core analytical method involved here is based on the comparison of alternative institutional arrangements (or governance structure in transaction cost language) using a cost economising lens to assess the relevance of arrangements in particular circumstances (see, for example, Williamson, 1985). This analytical method is then used with a particular focus: for example, the study of the firm. But it is by no means obvious whether TCE is an analytical method in its own right. On the one hand, Williamson (1985) argues that TCE is complementary to neoclassical economics. The implication here is that the methods are consistent but different. On the other hand, it is common to view TCE as part of the same theoretical project as neoclassical economics (Hodgson, 1993; Lawson, 1994; Dietrich, 1994). The logic here is that both TCE and neoclassical theory have the same methodological principles involving, for example, individualism, atomism and a comparative static method. A key issue involves the same complexity as was just highlighted when discussing analytical focus: there may be no single taxonomy because the particular taxonomy involved can depend on the particular research agenda. So, for example, at a sufficient level of detail, and from a perspective that describes analytical tools, TCE is different from standard neoclassical theory because, for example, it recognises a form of bounded rationality that results in incomplete contracting. But if we move to a lower level of detail and move beyond description of tools to (often implicit) analytical methods the two approaches have the same roots.

The second complexity that we can recognise about the analytical methods adopted by a subject is a point suggested by Groenewegen and Vromen (1996): particular theories can be silent on particular issues. To give an example, the relevance of which will become clear in later discussion, a theory built on a comparative static method can make statements (at most) about the direction of change from one equilibrium to another, but it cannot make statements about the dynamics of the change process. In short, analytical frameworks are silent on particular issues. In terms of Figure 1.1, if we imagine a fully specified, and detailed, grid (rather than the illustrative aggregate grid shown) some cells will be empty. An important principle is that these empty cells should not be seen as reflecting an analytical failure. If we conjecture that 'formulating an all-embracing, all-condition theory is infeasible' (Groenewegen and Vromen, 1996: 372), it follows that empty cells are a pragmatic response to our intellectual bounded rationality. But even ignoring our bounded rationality, there is the danger that a theory that claims to be universal can degenerate into tautology. Take, for example, the view expressed by Hayek (1948: 33): 'the tautologies, of which formal equilibrium analysis in economics essentially consist [require] definite statements about how knowledge is acquired and communicated'. Alternatively we can cite the not inconsistent view expressed by Joan Robinson (1964: 48): '*Utility* is a metaphysical concept of impregnable circularity; *utility* is the quality in commodities that makes individuals want to buy them, and the fact that individuals want to buy commodities shows that they have *utility*' (emphasis in original).

Both writers, although coming from very different analytical traditions, stress the tautological or circular nature of formal equilibrium economics. The removal of such analytical tautology or circularity requires inputs from external methods or focus. From this perspective, being silent on particular issues, i.e. being explicit about what a framework cannot say, is a necessary characteristic of adequate theory. Groenewegen and Vromen (1996) link the incomplete nature of theoretical frameworks to the importance of accepting theoretical pluralism. We can stress a similar point and link empty cells in a diagram such as Figure 1.1 as a necessary condition for the relevance of an interdisciplinary perspective on a particular issue. In terms of the subject matter presented in this volume, if a narrowly defined economics of the firm, perhaps involving different analytical economic methods, results in all the relevant cells in the intellectual grid being non-empty, there is no obvious comparative advantage for using economics as the base for an interdisciplinary perspective. Hence interdisciplinary approaches to the firm are based on the presumption that empty cells exist in the relevant part of the intellectual grid.

Given these background points, we can now suggest that along the main diagonal of the grid in Figure 1.1 we define core subjects. In terms of the language presented by Lakatos (see, for example, Blaug, 1980), this main diagonal defines the hard core of different scientific research programmes. We should, of course recognise that some authors, for example Rosenberg (1986), deny that Lakatos's framework can be applied to economics as it gives the subject a sense of scientific content that it does not deserve. In addition we can recognise the complication identified by Groenewegen and Vromen (1996). The hard core of a scientific research programme is defined in terms of fundamental propositions that make up the heart of any framework. As such they are not subject to empirical falsification because they are shielded by the general framework. But how can we tell when we compare two different theoretical approaches whether they belong to the same or different scientific research programmes? This problem exists because, as was stressed above, the rows and columns in a grid such as Figure 1.1 have no natural taxonomy but instead the particular taxonomy can reflect (a) the level of aggregation and (b) the purpose for which the taxonomy is being used. The implication here is that the hard core of any discipline, i.e. the main diagonal of Figure 1.1, may be subject to different definitions and hence is likely to be the subject of debate rather than simply acceptance. In terms of interdisciplinary work, this contested nature of a subject's hard core might result in differing perceptions of its relevance and acceptability.

Ignoring the complications hinted at in the previous paragraph, we can now define two types of interdisciplinary study that correspond to connecting along rows or columns of cells off the main diagonal of Figure 1.1. Down the columns of the grid interdisciplinary work is defined in terms of applying a dominant method outside a normal subject focus. In this tradition we can identify Becker's (1981) analysis of the family and Buchanan and Tullock's (1962) public choice theory. Along the off main diagonal rows of Figure 1.1 we have a more eclectic interdisciplinary world in which the analytical focus of a subject is given priority. The necessary reasoning here is that, for example, the firm or consumer behaviour is inherently interdisciplinary and so requires different analytical methods for a complete understanding. The essays presented in this volume are based on interdisciplinary connections that involve such row linkages. Before giving an introduction to this work, the arguments presented above will be rendered more concrete by briefly considering two examples that involve the analysis of the firm: Oliver Williamson's transaction cost theory and John Dunning's OLI framework. Among other things, these two examples will allow the development of linkages between interdisciplinary approaches to the firm and non-steady-state analysis.

Example 1: Oliver Williamson's transaction cost theory

The basic principles of Williamson's transaction cost approach to the firm are set out in many places, perhaps most famously in his 1975 and 1985 volumes. For current purposes the development presented in Williamson (1996) is useful. In the latter work discussion is organised around a diagram, a slightly adapted version of which is reproduced here as Figure 1.2. The primary analytical focus are institutions of governance (e.g. inter-firm contracts, corporations, bureaus, non-profits, etc.), shown here in the centre of Figure 1.2. These are explained in terms of two general factors: the institutional environment and individual behavioural attributes. '*Secondary* effects are drawn as dashed arrows' (Williamson, 1996: 17–18, emphasis added). Changes in the institutional environment, either historically or geographically, are argued to shift the relative costs of different forms of governance and so lead to micro-institutional change. The key behavioural assumptions are bounded rationality and opportunism. Different form of governance are seen to evolve to mitigate the adverse effects of these behavioural assumptions. An important intervening variable here is the degree of human or physical asset specificity.

A moment's consideration of this transaction cost logic will reveal the now commonly recognised characteristic that the framework is a comparative static approach to institutions (for example, Dietrich, 1994). Among other things, this comparative static characteristic implies that the structure and functioning of the institutional environment is common knowledge to all actors. Note that this common knowledge is a matter of belief as well as

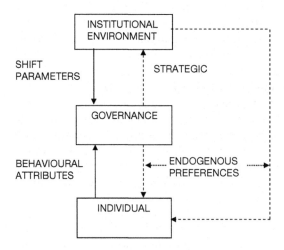

Figure 1.2 The transaction cost layer schema.

Source: Williamson (1996).

objective fact. To put the matter somewhat crudely, this common knowledge ensures that with recognised behavioural attributes and given asset specificity characteristics, economic agents will agree on the most efficient form of governance. But if one set of agents believe that, for example, legal or accounting procedures function in one way and another set of agents have differing perceptions there need be no common ground for identifying a unique set of efficient governance arrangements. This lack of common knowledge about the background institutional environment would seem to underlie corrupt firm practices (see Dietrich, 2005) and also adversarial trade union–management bargaining.

The key issue for transaction cost theory is the extent to which common knowledge of background institutional arrangements is a minor or major factor. If it is a minor issue it can be safely ignored. If it is a major factor it should be recognised as important. One obvious a priori reason why we might expect a lack of common knowledge is because of bounded rationality. This might imply that knowledge acquisition is essentially a local activity with the result that we might expect local common knowledge but global knowledge diversity (Young, 1996). This global diversity is likely to be an even more significant issue during periods of major institutional change. In general terms, this potential lack of common knowledge implies the questions of how it might be acquired and how actors could cope with it.

An upshot here is that out of equilibrium conditions must be recognised and analysed. In addition, a minimum requirement would seem to be consideration of how institutional common knowledge might evolve. Obvious building blocks here involve the consideration of cognition, learning, knowledge diffusion and institutional evolution, matters that are discussed in a number of the chapters in this volume, and also topics that have mushroomed over the last two decades (see, for example, Hodgson, 1993; Nooteboom, 1992, 1996, 2000; Witt, 1989). An additional useful building block might involve inputs from economic sociology (for example, DiMaggio and Powell, 1983, 1991; Granovetter, 1985). As considered in detail in Chapter 5 in this volume, it is characteristic in economic sociology to view institutional forms and arrangements as widespread because they are viewed as appropriate and legitimate, not because they are the most efficient. DiMaggio and Powell (1991) explicitly reject the view that efficiency leads to institutional isomorphism. Instead they argue that isomorphism leads to efficiency, since contractual relations are facilitated by being viewed as legitimate.

Using these building blocks we might suggest that in an institutional equilibrium, when common knowledge of institutions can reasonably be assumed, the major and secondary effects of environment and individual behaviour are described by, respectively, the full and dashed lines in Figure 1.2. But out of equilibrium, i.e. when common knowledge of institutions does not exist, the dominant and secondary effects are likely to be reversed. The reversal follows from the importance of cognition, learning, knowledge diffusion and institutional isomorphism. This interpretation offers a new view on the possible complementarities between economics and sociology, i.e. on the importance of interdisciplinary work. In this context we would certainly support the view expressed in Williamson (1988) that a truly dynamic process analysis is needed. But, in addition, we agree with the view expressed by Groenewegen and Vromen (1996) that transaction cost economics is not suited to carry this out. Instead we might recognise the strength that lies in the equilibrium nature of the transaction cost framework. In terms of earlier discussion we must recognise the gaps or empty cells in the theory. But also we might support the sentiment expressed in Williamson (1993) that transaction cost theory and sociological organisation theory have a lot to offer and learn from each other. The healthy tension involved might therefore be considered useful.

Example 2: John Dunning's OLI framework

The focus of the Dunning OLI framework is to explain international production and the multinational enterprise, although it will be argued below that it has wider relevance. The OLI in the title refers to the three elements upon which the framework is constructed: Ownership-specific assets, Location-specific assets and Internalisation advantages. Dunning himself refers to the resulting framework as the 'eclectic paradigm'. In this respect the relevance for the current discussion is clear. In Dunning's (1993: 91) own words: 'In the past decade, the focus of attention has been directed to more general – *and even interdisciplinary* – explanations of international production, of which the eclectic paradigm is probably the most ambitious' (emphasis added).

As with all intellectual innovations, emergence tends to evolve rather than appear over night. With respect to the OLI framework the roots can be found in Dunning's early work on the multinational enterprise (1971, 1974), through first statements of the framework from 1976 onwards (for example 1980) into what might be considered a full development (1988). The outline presented here is based on Dunning (1993), which presents a detailed survey of the development and role of the multinational enterprise using his OLI conceptual framework. Ownership-specific assets are those assets that are possessed, or can be acquired, by a firm that are only available to other firms at higher cost; as such they are firm-specific. They include tangible assets, such as labour power and capital, and intangible assets, such as technology, information, and managerial, marketing and entrepreneurial skills. In a non-spatial world, ownership-specific assets will generate firm-specific competitive advantages along the lines suggested by competence- or resource-based theorists (for example, Foss, 1993, 2005; Foss and Loasby, 1998).

Assets that are not firm-specific, but are available to all firms in a particular location, are Dunning's location-specific assets. Such assets obviously include Ricardian endowments. But in addition location advantages can arise from cultural, legal, political and institutional factors, including government legislation and policies that are spatially specific. Finally, geographically specific external economies can arise from firm activity. In a world in which only location-specific assets exist, traditional trade theory can explain the spatial distribution of output. Hence a necessary condition for the emergence of multinational enterprises is that assets are both location- and ownership-specific.

While the combination of O and L factors are a necessary condition for multinational development, sufficiency is supplied by the internalisation (i.e. the I) element of Dunning's framework. Any ownership asset can be exploited by either selling the assets, or the right of use of the assets, to other firms or by adding to internal ownership advantages. The choice here depends, in a standard transaction cost manner, on the relative organisational efficiency of hierarchies. The interesting departure with internalisation theories, as an explanation of multinational development (see, for example, Buckley and Casson, 1976, 1985; Hennart, 1982) compared to 'standard' transaction cost theory (as outlined above) is that with internalisation theory firm rather than market development is based not only on the possible organisational efficiency of hierarchies but also on effective means of exercising monopoly power over the assets under governance. This would seem to be an improvement on 'traditional' transaction cost theory (e.g. Williamson, 1985) that plays down the significance of monopoly power. Arguably this is a somewhat arbitrary dismissal in an oligopolised world.

But internalisation theory, while being subtly different from Williamsonian transaction cost theory, is still a comparative static approach to firm activity, and hence is therefore an incomplete approach to firm activity. The following critique presented by Dunning (1993: 75–6) is perfectly consistent with the criticisms of transaction cost theory presented earlier in this chapter:

> [The OLI paradigm], while accepting the logic of internalisation theory, argues that it is not, in itself, sufficient to explain the level and structure of the production of a country's own firms outside their national boundaries, or of the production of foreign-owned firms in its midst.

In addition:

> In the static model of internalisation, [ownership-specific] variables ... are taken to be exogenous ... However, viewing the growth of the firm as a dynamic process, the legitimacy of this assumption is questionable. For a firm's current core competences ... are the outcome of past decisions which, at the time they were taken, were endogenous to the firm.

Dunning's reasoning presented in these two quotations is consistent with discussion presented earlier in this chapter. In terms of Figure 1.1, the analytical focus of Dunning's framework is the multinational enterprise. The OLI framework then links analytical methods horizontally to gain an adequate explanation of this focus. His argument that internalisation theory cannot be universal is a specific application of the idea that inevitable empty cells exist in a diagram such as Figure 1.1. To this extent, it is therefore not surprising that Dunning suggests the importance of an interdisciplinary approach to firm activity, as in the quotation cited above.

One final matter can be considered in this brief presentation of Dunning's OLI framework. In principle many of the insights he offers can be applied in a non-multinational setting. Take, for example, the neo-Austrian approach to the firm presented by Langlois and Robertson (1995). They criticise traditional transaction cost economics because of its static or short-run nature. They emphasise a dynamic theory of the boundaries of the firm in which the central focus is the long-run management of idiosyncratic capabilities. This management involves dynamic or long-run transaction costs. The more fundamental the long-run change that a firm undertakes the greater the information search and management costs involved. In a static world, with no change, we are left with traditional short-run transaction costs. It is clear that the distinction being drawn here between long-run and short-run transaction costs is equivalent to Dunning's distinction between the dynamic development of ownership-specific assets and internalisation factors that determine the best way of implementing long-run strategies.

In short, we might like to claim that a neo-Austrian approach to the firm is 'Dunning without location'. While recognising the use of this essential similarity, not least for reasons set out below, we must also recognise the error in the claim. Dunning's view of ownership assets appears to be informed by, among other things, management ideas on core competences. Neo-Austrian ideas are informed by an Austrian view of subjective knowledge in which undertaking an activity reveals knowledge upon which it is based. This diffusion of knowledge implies characteristic evolutionary tendencies towards an equilibrium state that is (in theory) characterised by full knowledge. Even this theoretical possibility of full knowledge does not exist in Dunning's work because it would imply that the O element of his OLI framework is undermined to a large extent. Ignoring this theoretical difference between Dunning and neo-Austrian theory, we can explore what 'Dunning without location' might look like. We can cite Dunning's (1993: 86) view that: 'the main difference between the determinants of intra-national and international production lies in the unique economic, political and cultural characteristics of separate sovereign states'. These spatially unique institutional factors are one source of location-specific assets.

In terms of earlier discussion in this chapter, and in particular that involving Figure 1.2, Dunning appears to use 'unique economic, political and cultural characteristics' as institutional shift parameters. This essentially means that the political, cultural and institutional differences are exogenous. In earlier discussion it was claimed that this use of shift parameters was only appropriate if the (location-specific) institutional factors were essentially common knowledge to all agents. If this common knowledge does not exist it was suggested above that institutional evolution along with issues of cognition, learning and isomorphism become important.

Recognising the possibility of institutional factors not being shift parameters introduces a number of interesting possible implications for the Dunning framework. If the institutional infrastructure governing any commercial activity changes, this will offer entrepreneurial opportunities for firms involved. But, if ownership advantages are firm-specific the entrepreneurial advantages that emerge will not be common for all firms. In short, institutional evolution and O advantages are interlinked. Something of this sort seemed to occur with UK financial deregulation in the 1980s. US and Japanese firms appeared to exploit the possibilities involved more effectively than indigenous UK companies (Augar, 2001). Furthermore, any firms involved can be aware of the links of the O implications of institutional evolution. In these circumstances, a rational response may be to attempt to influence the path of institutional evolution.

While these comments have been made in the context of the Dunning framework, arguably the same analytical development is possible for a neo-Austrian view of the firm. Long-run strategies, and even the transaction costs of such strategies, will be influenced by the evolution of the institutional infrastructure. Taking a different example, other than financial deregulation, different health and safety or trade union representation regimes will influence the transaction costs of strategic change and even (possibly) the direction of such change. Once again rational firms will be aware of such linkages with obvious benefits from influencing the path of institutional evolution. This influence takes the analysis of the firm into an obvious political economy, and hence interdisciplinary, context.

Outline of the volume

The essays presented in this volume take up different aspects of the general issues raised above, and collectively stress the importance of interdisciplinary and non-comparative static reasoning. The various contributions are organised into three parts: analysis and background to the nature of the firm; how change and evolution impacts on the nature of the firm; and finally issues of history, organisation and the firm. The first part is opened with a chapter by the editor. This chapter revisits the economics of the firm with the intention of identifying the underlying principles informing different perspectives involved. It is argued that there is no single view of the firm as an institutional entity. Emphasis is placed on how the firm is defined by the legal system in practice rather than how economists traditionally assume the law defines the firm. Incorporating important legal principles allows recognition of the importance of power and authority for the firm and how such power and authority might impact on the firm as a sovereign unit. An implication of the framework developed by Dietrich is that no universal status can be claimed for any particular theoretical perspective. This implies a fundamentally empirical question as to which perspective is relevant and dominant in particular circumstances.

In Chapter 3 Bart Nooteboom examines trust, learning and the firm. It is argued that trust is full of puzzle and paradox. Trust is both rational and emotional. Trust can go beyond calculative self-interest, but has its limits. People may want to trust, while they may also feel threatened by trust. If trust is not in place prior to a relationship, on the basis of institutions, prior experience or reputation, it has to be built up, in specific relations. For that one needs to learn, in the sense of building empathy, and perhaps a certain degree of identification. In an attempt at a better understanding of the puzzles and processes of trust, this chapter applies the perspective of 'embodied cognition', and insights from mental 'framing' and decision heuristics from social psychology, as well as important principles from neuroscience and symbolic interactionism from sociology. The discussion in this chapter ends by drawing out the key implications for the theory of the firm.

Chapter 4, by Yuri Biondi, draws important linkages between the accounting, economic and legal bases of the firm. It is argued that through the accounting system the firm acquires autonomous but interdependent existence from external markets. Hence the firm is not derived from the costs of market functioning. Emphasis is placed on the manner in which the firm functions as an entity, and exists as a *managed dynamic system*. The accounting system structures the whole firm as an institution, an organisation and as a user of knowledge. The new transactional and institutional perspective opens to an interdisciplinary approach linking economics, accounting and law by the shared notion of the firm as an *entity*, which provides the 'clue' for understanding the nature of the firm as a *whole* and a *dynamic system*.

Chapter 5, by Hassan Yazdifar, provides a synthesis of new institutional sociology (NIS) and old institutional economics (OIE). The former focuses primarily on extra-(macro-)organisational-level institutions and explains how the demands of environmental factors and institutions explain system change in companies, while the latter focuses primarily on intra-(micro-) organisational-level institutions and is more suitable for studies of processes of change and resistance to change within organisations. It is argued that neither can independently fully explain organisational behaviour and the two can be complementary.

In short, all the essays in Part I of this volume create different horizontal linkages across the intellectual grid identified above, and hence create different interdisciplinary perspectives on the firm. While the first part of this volume emphasises the importance of interdisciplinarity, the second part concentrates on the second theme identified above: the shortcomings of an overly static basis to the firm. Chapter 6, by Werner Hölzl, provides a critical discussion of the evolutionary theory of the firm. The specific feature of the evolutionary approach is that it explains the adaptive behaviours of different firms through the tension between innovation and various selection mechanisms. However these mechanisms are less prominent in the evolutionary theory of firm. The evolutionary theory of the firm characterises the behaviour of a firm on the basis of technological capabilities, workers' skills and decision rules connected by organisational routines. However, the evolutionary theory of the firm is essentially a theory of why firms differ. Hölzl argues that the evolutionary theory of the firm need not be restricted to the definition of innovation possibility frontiers. However, an evolutionary theory of the firm that integrates the views of the firm as repository of knowledge and of the firm as a network of incentives and power still requires a theory of creation and change of routines in order to be based on firm theoretical grounds.

In Chapter 7, Pavel Luksha argues that the key function of an enterprise is to serve its self-maintenance and self-reproduction. Within economics, broadly defined, the resource-based approach to the firm emphasises this key function. But Luksha takes the idea further by proposing a specific model to analyse the processes involved. The model outlined in this chapter allows detailed consideration of how this reproduction is accomplished. Identification of the main elements of self-reproduction processes and major types of self-reproducing entities are emphasised as important means of understanding both a firm's routinised dynamics and evolution. The model developed here is based, in part, on modern complexity theory, and as such finds interesting groundings in a subject that has been traditionally alien to it: theoretical economics and organisation theory.

Chapter 8, by Erik Stam, Elizabeth Garnsey and Paul Heffernan provides an approach to new firm growth that views this as an unfolding developmental process. This approach is based on a Penrosean theory of the firm. It is shown that new firm growth is non-linear and prone to interruptions and setbacks to an extent overlooked in the literature. From the theory of the firm used, five propositions are drawn concerning measurable features of new firms' growth paths; these relate to patterns of survival, continuousness of growth, turning points, reversals and cumulative growth. These propositions are examined in the light of data on the growth paths of new firms in three countries, with aggregate comparisons of firms' growth paths effected by graphical representations and sequence analysis. The exploratory analysis shows that there are recurring patterns in the growth of young firms associated with typical developmental experiences. These systemic features of the growth paths of populations of new firms are consistent with theoretical explanation at the firm level, and disconfirm the assumed randomness of corporate growth.

The final essay in Part II is provided by Stavros Ionnides. Here the important links between firm change, economic organisation and entrepreneurship are explored. It is argued that the Austrian concept of entrepreneurship offers a conceptual framework in which ideas from both contracting and competence perspectives on the firm can be combined. This theme is explored using a key issue in the theory of economic organisation: namely, corporate ownership. The Austrian theory of entrepreneurship can help us understand under what circumstances a bundle of cooperating resources will remain independent – for example, in a joint venture – and under what circumstances they will be jointly owned by the legal person of the corporate firm. A bundle of resources devoted to the implementation of an entrepreneurial project may cooperate under a variety of ownership regimes. From a static point of view, it is impossible to judge which regime will be actually chosen. However, when real time is introduced into the analysis, it is shown that different ownership regimes may be linked to different visions of future entrepreneurial activity. Corporate ownership is less likely when the entrepreneurial vision is specific and unchanging over time, i.e. when new learning is minimal. In such circumstances, dispersed ownership coordinated through arm's-length contracts suffices to ensure that the organisation will have at its disposal all the assets required. By contrast, when the entrepreneurial discovery is less clear or is initially perceived as changeable over time, i.e. when the learning that will be obtained during the venture's operation is expected to be significant, ownership may be essential for the project's long-term prospects.

The final part of the volume explores issues to do with history, organisation and the firm. This combination of economics and history is the characteristic setting for interdisciplinary analysis of evolution and change. In short, Part III unites the two themes running through this volume, i.e. interdisciplinary study and non-steady-state methods. The essay by Jackie Krafft reviews the literature on the possible links between business history and the organisation of the industry. It is shown that a dominant trend considers economic models as a grid to structure historical facts, while an alternative vision leaves business history studies a larger space to refine basic economic frames on the organisation of the industry. The chapter shows that, in a context of innovation, the dominant trend is often inappropriate to deal with the question of the boundaries of firms and industries. This motivates the development of alternative approaches to business history with the aim of improved understanding of the theory of the firm and industrial dynamics.

The final chapter in the volume, by Sue Bowden, David M. Higgins and Christopher Price, considers the historical evolution of firms from a somewhat different perspective. A case study of the engineering sector in the UK economy during the interwar years is presented. This period is central to an understanding of the evolution of the modern firm. In this respect it is found that the interwar years are a transition process: important steps were taken in the evolution to the growth of equity markets, but the period was still reminiscent, in terms of shareholder characteristics, of the late nineteenth century. It is found that the interwar years were characterised by a preference for equity over debt finance in the engineering sector. This preference is explained as a rational response to the evolving environment dominated by prevailing interest rates (and in particular actual rates) and a perception that shared ownership did not constitute a real loss of control. The latter they argue was a reflection of the absence at this time of the exercise of either voice or exit by shareholders. This in turn reflected the local and personal nature of shareholding.

References

Augar, P. (2001), *The Death of Gentlemanly Capitalism: The Rise and Fall of London's Investment Banks*, Harmondsworth: Penguin.

Becker, G. S. (1981), *A Treatise on the Family*, Cambridge, MA: Harvard University Press.

Blaug, M. (1980), *The Methodology of Economics*, Cambridge: Cambridge University Press.

Buchanan, J. M. and Tullock, G. (1962), *The Calculus of Consent: Logical Foundations of Constitutional Democracy*, Ann Arbor, MI: Michigan University Press.

Buckley, P. J. and Casson, M. (1976), *The Future of the Multinational Enterprise*, London: Macmillan.

——(1985), *The Economic Theory of the Multinational Enterprise*, London: Macmillan.

Dietrich, M. (1994), *Transaction Cost Economics and Beyond: Towards a New Economics of the Firm*, London: Routledge.

——(2005), 'Firm corruption, accounting failure and anti-social entrepreneurship: an institutional perspective', presented at the European Network on the Economics of the Firm 2005 Workshop, Erasmus University.

DiMaggio, P. J. and Powell, W. W. (1983), 'The iron cage revisited: institutional isomorphism and collective rationality in organizational fields', *American Sociological Review*, 48: 147–60.

——(eds) (1991), *The New Institutionalism in Organizational Analysis*, Chicago, IL and London: University of Chicago Press.

Dunning, J. H. (1971), *The Multinational Enterprise*, London: Allen and Unwin.

——(1974), *Economic Analysis and the Multinational Enterprise*, London: Allen and Unwin.

——(1980), 'Towards an eclectic theory of international production: some empirical tests', *Journal of International Business Studies*, 11(1): 9–31.

——(1988), *Multinationals Technology and Competitiveness*, London: Allen and Unwin.

——(1993), *Multinational Enterprises and the Global Economy*, Wokingham: Addison-Wesley.

Foss, N. (1993), 'Theories of the firm: contractual and competence perspectives', *Journal of Evolutionary Economics*, 3: 126–44.

——(2005), *Strategy, Economic Organization, and the Knowledge Economy: The Coordination of Firms and Resources*, Oxford: Oxford University Press.

Foss, N. and Loasby, B. J. (eds) (1998), *Economic Organization, Capabilities and Co-ordination: Essays in Honour of GB Richardson*, London: Routledge.

Granovetter, M (1985), 'Economic action and social structure: the problem of embeddedness', *American Journal of Sociology*, 91: 481–510.

Groenewegen, J. and Vromen, J. J. (1996), 'A case for theoretical pluralism', in J. Groenewegen (ed.), *Transaction Cost Economics and Beyond*, London, Kluwer, ch. 19.

Hayek, F. A. (1948), *Individualism and Economic Order*, Chicago, IL: University of Chicago Press.

Hennart, J. F. (1982), *A Theory of Multinational Enterprise*, Ann Arbor, MI: University of Michigan Press.

Hodgson, G. M. (1993), *Economics and Evolution: Bringing Life Back into Economics*, Cambridge: Polity Press.

Langlois, R. N. and Robertson, P. L. (1995), *Firms, Markets and Economic Change: A Dynamic Theory of Business Institutions*, London: Routledge.

Lawson, T. (1994), 'Why are so many economists so opposed to methodology?', *Journal of Economic Methodology*, 1: 105–33.

——(1997), *Economics and Reality*, London: Routledge.

Nooteboom, B. (1992), 'Towards a dynamic theory of transactions', *Journal of Evolutionary Economics*, 2: 281–99.

——(1996), 'Towards a learning based model of transactions', in J. Groenewegen (ed.), *Transaction Cost Economics and Beyond*, London: Kluwer, ch. 17.

——(2000), *Learning and Innovation in Organizations and Economies*, Oxford: Oxford University Press.

Robinson, J. (1964), *Economic Philosophy*, Harmondsworth: Penguin.

Rosenberg, A. (1986), 'Lakatosian consolations', *Economics and Philosophy*, 2: 127–39.

Williamson, O. E. (1975), *Markets and Hierarchies*, New York: Free Press.

——(1985), *The Economic Institutions of Capitalism*, London: Macmillan.

——(1988), 'Economics and sociology. Promoting a dialogue', in G. Farkas and P. England (eds), *Industries, Firms and Jobs: Sociological and Economic Approaches*, New York: Plenum.

——(1993), 'Transaction cost economics and organization theory', *Industrial and Corporate Change*, 2: 107–56.

——(1996), 'Efficiency, power, authority and economic organization', in J. Groenewegen (ed.), *Transaction Cost Economics and Beyond*, London, Kluwer.

Witt, U. (1989), 'The evolution of economic institutions as a propagation process', *Public Choice*, 62: 155–72.

Young, H. P. (1996), 'The economics of convention', *Journal of Economic Perspectives*, 10(2): 105–22.

Part I
The economics of the firm
Analysis and background

2 The nature of the firm revisited

Michael Dietrich

Introduction

The overall objective of this chapter is to set out a fairly abstract discussion on the nature of the firm. Much of the literature considered here is well known, but after outlining the key issues involved a 'new' perspective is offered. The 'new' here is presented in inverted commas, as the newness is based on existing and well-known building blocks; any claim of originality is based on an attempt to integrate the presented perspectives on the economics of the firm within a unified framework.

In economics a distinction can be drawn between the firm as an institutional entity and the firm as techno-functional entity. The institutional view considers questions of basic definition, identity, internal structure and external boundaries (Hodgson, 2002). It follows that if we are to understand the economics of the firm this institutional perspective is central to our understanding. The techno-functional perspective views the firm as a black box that transforms factor inputs into outputs. According to Machlup (1967), this perspective involves how production and cost functions interact with demand on the market, i.e. the emphasis is on technical matters and how firms function in the context of the market; hence the techno-functional appellation used here. A central principle of the current discussion is that both institutional and techno-functional perspectives are useful because they allow us to answer different sets of questions. An implication therefore is agreement with Coase (1937: 386) that we require 'a definition of a firm … which is … realistic in that it corresponds to what is meant by the firm in the real world'. This realism requires both institutional and techno-functional perspectives.

A central message presented in this chapter is that the economics of the firm requires both techno-functional and institutional foundations. It follows that a basic analytical requirement is that the institutional and techno-functional perspectives are not built on inconsistent principles, i.e. the two perspectives must be isomorphic. Any inconsistencies would undermine the development of linkages between the perspectives. Such linkages need involve no more than the ability to use characteristics or predictions from one framework as conceptual inputs into the other (an example will be given in a moment). This possibility of mapping between institutional and techno-functional perspectives would allow us to switch between definitions without creating obvious conceptual problems. An inability to switch between definitions, i.e. when no linking is possible, would introduce potential shortcomings if we wished to talk about, for instance, how the boundaries of the firm are changing in the context of the interaction between cost structures and market pressures.

A specific aim of the current discussion, therefore, is to consider an institutional perspective on the firm that recognises, at least potentially, techno-functional factors. But this requirement for consistency between the perspectives does not imply a methodological or ontological equivalence between institutional and techno-functional views. A firm as a techno-functional entity implies an ability to hire, buy and organise factors of production and contract for the sale of output. This hiring, buying, organising and contracting implies a pre-existing institutional structure covering, for instance, legal and accounting systems. If we are not interested in how hiring, buying, organising and contracting is *changing* it is reasonable to ignore the institutional background to the firm, as much economics does, and concentrate only on techno-functional matters. But this does not imply that the institutional infrastructure does not exist. In short, to understand techno-functional restructuring requires a prior understanding of institutional restructuring if institutional factors are changing.

The discussion in this chapter is, therefore, guided by institutional considerations, while at the same time recognising secondary techno-functional matters. The argument is initially organised around three views on how we might conceptualise the firm as an institutional entity: (1) the firm as a legal unit; (2) the firm as a governance structure; and (3) the firm as a locus of strategic control. These three sections provide the building blocks for the final substantive section in which the basic structure of an integrated economics of the firm is presented. Finally brief conclusions are drawn.

The firm as a legal unit

A recent statement of the view that the firm should be viewed as a legal entity is provided by Hodgson (2002), although the general principle that economic activity should be understood in terms of legal structures dates back to at least the work of Commons (1924), and more recently Masten (1991). Hodgson (2002: 56) claims:

> *A firm is defined as an integrated and durable organization involving two or more people, acting openly or tacitly as a 'legal person', capable of owning assets, set up for the purpose of producing goods and services, with the capacity to sell or hire these goods or services to customers.* As a 'legal person', the firm may carry legal entitlements and liabilities in its own right. These entitlements include the right of legal ownership of the

goods as property up to the point that they are exchanged with the customer, and the legal right to obtain contracted remuneration for the produced services.

(Emphasis in original)

The basic idea behind this definition will be used in the discussion presented here, but for current purposes it is in need of development. Before indicating possible problems and developments a number of implications can be drawn out. First, this general definition can apply to many specific firm types. For instance, small service partnerships, corporations with a stock market identity, or producer cooperatives are all firms under this definition. This general applicability is considered an advantage here. Second, it is clear that from this legal perspective the idea of market processes within firms, as suggested, for example, by Coase (1991), is meaningless. If two divisions or departments within the same firm exchange a good or service there is no exchange of property rights. The people organising and undertaking the exchange do not own the goods; the firm has the legal entitlement before, during and after the exchange. Alternatively, subcontracting or a network of firms involves relations between legally separate units that have close contacts. But we can note that these contacts may be asymmetrical in terms of power (a matter considered below). A vertical chain or collection of companies with no single legal identity are separate firms no matter how close and long-term the organisational contacts. This conceptual clarity between 'firms' and 'not firms', as emphasised by Hodgson (2002), is considered a major strength of the legal perspective. Finally, this legal definition of a firm has an implied definition of markets as institutions or arrangements involving an exchange of property rights. This ability to define markets, as a direct implication of the definition of the firm, allows a mapping, at least in principle, from an institutional/legal perspective to a techno-functional perspective, as considered below.

These basic insights into the firm will be used below, but for current purposes a number of problems with the legal perspective can be identified. First, the Hodgson quotation presented above restricts the firm to 'two or more people acting as a legal person'. By implication single-person firms or sole traders are not firms, at least in an institutional sense. But clearly single-person enterprises are techno-functional firms as inputs are used to produce outputs. The important issue here is that with a sole trader the legal status of the firm and the legal status of the individual can be, not necessarily are, the same, hence the firm need not have an independent legal status of its own separate from an individual. To put the same point another way, the boundary of the firm is the boundary of the individual and issues of internal firm functioning are techno-functional rather than organisational and interpersonal.

Additional matters with a legal perspective on the firm can be approached by considering the following examples: (1) alcohol sellers in the United

Kingdom and such sellers in the United States under prohibition or in countries subject to Sharia law; (2) brothels in many, but not all, countries; (3) back-street abortionists; (4) a firm that operates in the black economy compared to a similar firm that operates openly; (5) opium sellers in nineteenth-century Britain and similar sellers today. In all these five examples economic exchanges occur and techno-functional firms exist even if they are illegal. All cases provide examples of Austrian entrepreneurship, if we define such entrepreneurship in the manner suggested by Hayek (1945) or Kirzner (1973). From this perspective entrepreneurs have (costless) subjective knowledge of demand and/or supply conditions that can be used for commercial advantage because of unexploited gains from trade. The use of such knowledge reveals its existence and equilibrates markets. But clearly in some circumstances an entrepreneur-trader may be a legal firm but in other circumstances a similar entrepreneur-trader may not be a legal firm.

We can respond to this issue in a number of ways. In principle it is possible to argue that illegal traders are not 'real' firms as they are not subject to an institutionalisation of economic activity that is socially recognised. This response to the possibility of illegal activity will not be used here because it introduces a potential divergence between institutional and techno-functional definitions of the firm. An alternative response to this issue is to view the legal firm as an ideal type. Hence a legal definition of the firm can be viewed as relevant in a modern – but abstract, not actual – market economy subject to the rule of law. It follows that in a similarly constrained situation, i.e. a modern, abstract market economy subject to the rule of law, there is no divergence between institutional and functional definitions. This response is logically coherent but is somewhat restricted in that it cannot claim to make any statement about firms that exist outside this abstract world. A third possible response, and the one developed below, is to recognise that in most cases in a modern economy firms are institutionalised by their legal status, but this need not be universal. Similar institutionalisation processes can be carried out in non-legal ways, as considered later. Non-legal and legal firms, at a sufficiently abstract level, all have common characteristics analysed below, and it is these characteristics that define a firm, not necessarily their expression as an independent legal identity; although it can be easier to use the shorthand of a firm as a legal entity.

At a general level we can recognise an important problem with the legal definition of the firm, from which the examples given above can be seen as specific instances. The legal concept of ownership is not the same as that used by economists. Kay (1997) points out that, according to legal principles, ownership is defined in terms of eleven characteristics: a right of possession; a right of use; a right to manage; a right to income from ownership; a right to the capital value; a right to security from expropriation; a power of sale or disposal; no time limit on ownership rights; a right of residual control; property can be used to obtain satisfaction of legal judgement against the owner; a duty to refrain from harmful use. The first ten principles would seem to be consistent with economic views of ownership, but the eleventh principle (a duty to refrain from harmful use) implies a generally recognised view of what constitutes harmful use. The examples given above can be viewed as specific cases of society deciding what is harmful, i.e. alcohol and drug use, payment for sex, (back-street) abortion, and non-payment of taxes. Note that harm here can be viewed as ethical or moral and possibly financial not just as physical harm. More generally a duty not to do harm need not involve the extremes of non-use and free use; instead more general intermediate cases must be recognised. This intermediate status is perhaps the case with payment for sex in the UK and current attitudes to cannabis use, hence firms involved in such activities have an equivalently ambiguous legal status. In short we must follow Kay and recognise that ownership and legal recognition are historically and culturally contingent. It follows that the legal definition of the firm is socially and culturally contingent, i.e. the way in which the law institutionalises economic activity is not universal. But arguably a techno-functional definition of a firm is universal. The complexities here are developed below.

It follows from the above discussion that the legal perspective on the firm will guide much of the discussion presented here, even if in a qualified or constrained way. But this introduces a second important issue: *why* is a non-economic factor, i.e. a 'fictional legal person' with ownership rights and responsibilities, central to the economic definition of the firm? Or to put the same issue another way: *how* is the legal status of the firm institutionalised economically? In principle this institutionalisation might be explained in individualist or non-individualist terms (Rutherford, 1996). An individualist explanation might suggest that the firm is created as an organisational unit because of the legal rights that are attached to ownership. These rights can be justified either in an antecedent or consequentialist manner (Dietrich, 2002). An antecedent explanation suggests that ownership rights are fundamental and universal and so do not require justification. Hence the firm is institutionalised because of these universal rights. This seems to be the position adopted by, for example, Hayek (1948) and the political theorist Nozick (1974). The later Hayek (1973) talks about the spontaneous nature of the common law, which is grounded in such universal rights, and allows the legal system to function and evolve in the same autonomous way as the Austrian perspective on the economic system.

But a problem here was suggested earlier, in that the economic and political-liberal notions of ownership rights are different from the legal, and hence actual, notion. In particular the legal idea of rights is always constrained by a duty not to do harm. This duty is obviously socially constructed. Recognising the socially constructed, rather than universal, nature of ownership is not, of course, an original point, even within economics. For instance Commons (1934) points out that a judge's own perceptions will shape legal judgements, a point also made by Posner (1977) and North (1981). Similarly, Sen (1987) suggests that natural disasters lead to the qualification of antecedent rights. It follows that an antecedent explanation of the firm as an institutional unit is not necessarily wrong but it is incomplete. Clearly the boundaries and internal organisation of the firm can be justified in an antecedent manner, and this justification is to some extent true. But if we wish to move from political rhetoric to economic analysis it must be recognised that this justification is (to some extent) socially constructed, i.e. it requires a non-individualist explanation.

A consequentialist legal explanation of the firm is based on effects, consequences and outcomes of particular legal structures. For instance Hart (1995) suggests that an efficient management of risk involves hierarchical governance, based around shareholder control, because this ensures an effective control over 'residual rights', i.e. ownership. In addition, all rational individuals will recognise the efficiency of this outcome and hence recognise a firm's owners as the fundamental principal in contracting and other relationships. In short, the legal right of ownership of the firm is based on individual rational choice and outcomes that follow from rational choices. There are three reasons why this explanation is inadequate. First, as Kay (1997) points out, shareholders own shares; they do not own the firm. The ownership of the firm, i.e. its legal status, is socially and historically constructed rather than being simply a response to rational decision-making. Second, as Williamson (1985) points out, any argument that links legal rights to rational decision-making must be based on complete information and costless policing of agreements. Only in this perfect world is *ex ante* rational decision-making possible. In an uncertain world with costly policing, the legal status of the firm cannot be explained simply as a response to *ex ante* rational decisions. Finally, we can recognise the experimental results of Kahneman and Tversky (2000). In an uncertain world people do not, in general, make consistent, rational decisions; rather a necessary 'framing' of decisions occurs. So, for example, a manager's decision to embezzle shareholder funds or a supplier's decision to renege on contractual agreements are not based on hyper-rational subjective utility maximisation, given a subjective probability of the truth coming to light and any punishments that result. Instead the decisions that are made are framed by the context in which they are made. For current purposes we might, therefore, suggest that the legal status of the firm is not so much a response to rational decisions but rather a context that allows decisions to be made.

This latter interpretation leads to a possible non-individualist explanation of how the legal status of the firm is institutionalised. Following Hodgson (1988) the general logic here suggests that in an uncertain and complex world institutionalisation is necessary. An institution-free world is impossible in practice because decision-making would be impossible. Institutions are necessary to structure individual mental maps and to structure expectations of behaviour. In short, legal institutions regularise expectations of behaviour. From this perspective the firm *is viewed* as having ownership and property rights, i.e. *is viewed* as being the principal in contractual and organisational relationships. Of course these perceptions are backed up by coercive legal power, but in principle the particular ownership rights constituted within the firm are somewhat arbitrary. Note that this view that the legal system regularises behaviour is not inconsistent with an antecedent justification of ownership that is viewed as evolving. An advantage here is that an evolutionary perspective can recognise the importance for owner-ship of socially constructed views of harm. Once views of harm are regular-ised and universally recognised, i.e. once harmful behaviour is generally viewed as such, property rights can be justified in an antecedent manner. But without this general acceptance of what constitutes harm an individualist antecedent justification is not possible.

In game theoretic terms we can understand the arbitrariness of legal institutions as a convention (Young 1995, 1998), i.e. an equilibrium in a game in which multiple equilibria exist. From this perspective the firm as a legal entity must exist, subject to qualifications made earlier and further devel-oped below. Without this entity, and the antecedent ownership rights it engenders, contractual and organisational relationships are not possible, i.e. the firm as a techno-functional unit is not possible. From this perspective the legal fiction of the firm can be viewed as a codified reputation that is devel-oped by consistent behaviour. Such reputations are necessary to exploit coordination advantages and hence regularise decision-making.

Two implications follow from viewing the firm in terms of codified reputation. First, the universal rights, discussed earlier, which present an antecedent justification for the firm as a legal unit, can be seen as a somewhat arbitrary convention along the lines suggested by Sugden (1986). This justifi-cation is necessary for codified reputations to develop and the coordination advantages that follow from this. But these rights are only 'locally universal' or, to use Young's terminology, there is local conformity but global diversity. Hence such rights are historically and culturally specific, i.e. are subject to change through time and space. The second implication is that the firm as a convention is not an 'optional extra' to economic activity, but is necessary to render economic activity possible. Hence even in a 'perfect' world with perfectly mobile economic agents, involving zero transaction costs and full information, an immobile system of rights and responsibilities is necessary (Dietrich, 2002). This immobility is necessary because an ability to escape from the rights and responsibilities codified by the firm undermines its coordination advantages. This is why an ideal-type firm in a law-abiding society is viewed as fundamentally a legal unit.

The firm as a governance structure

The second view of the firm identified above considers the firm as a govern-ance structure. The general idea dates, of course, from the seminal work of Coase (1937). But the specific idea of economic governance structures is a more recent development in transaction cost theory, developed, in particular, by Williamson (for example, 1975, 1985). Arguably this perspective has come to dominate analysis of the boundaries and internal structure of the firm.[1] The main focus of this approach is to view the firm as one possible means of *coordinating* resource allocation that has efficiency advantages given explicit and implicit costs of contracting. In Williamson's (1985: 22) words, 'holding the nature of the good or service constant, economising takes place ... ', whence (Williamson, 1991: 4) firms and markets are 'alternative modes for organising the very same transactions'. These statements reveal the general logic involved when the firm is viewed as a governance structure:

1   the nature of the good/service is exogenous and unchanged when governance structures are compared; and
2   decisions are motivated by economising behaviour given these exogenous conditions; hence
3   organisational characteristics are viewed as in some sense optimal given the exogenous conditions; finally
4   transaction cost and organisational characteristics will change in response to changed exogenous conditions.

In short, viewing the firm as a governance structure is a comparative static approach to institutional functioning (Dietrich, 1994). In addition we can see a mapping from a techno-functional view of the firm to an institutional view:

But this mapping is limited in two ways. First, the underlying nature of the good/service is considered exogenous. Consider the following two examples. There is no obvious attempt in transaction cost theory to examine the possibility that the detailed nature of economising behaviour, and hence the detailed nature of institutional development, might depend on the market structure that is used to produce the underlying good/service. For instance, small firms in atomistic markets might behave in different ways compared to a cohesive oligopoly.[2] Small firms, with an obvious owner/manager, may reflect the aspirations and preferences of this person. Hence transaction costs need not be simply monetary but also include issues to do with attitude to risk aversion, individual decision-making independence and the like. Large firms, on the other hand, may have a more universally monetary approach to economising behaviour. A second example might involve recognition of the importance of demand/supply elasticities. It is characteristic to link differing elasticities to the ability to shift taxes. In principle the same idea can be applied to transaction costs. Hence we might expect a difference between formal and effective incidence of such costs. If firms are able to shift uncertainty onto suppliers and/or distributors because of monopoly advantages, or competitive disadvantages to suppliers/distributors, transaction costs will be effectively shifted.

The second way in which the mapping used in transaction cost theory is limited is that it is unidirectional. There is no obvious attempt to examine the nature and extent to which institutional form can feedback onto, for instance, market structure. For example, high degrees of asset specificity are usually argued to require economic activity internalised within the firm. But the specificities and resulting administrative requirements imply the existence of sunk costs that, using standard contestability theory (Baumol, 1982), can impact on firm entry and exit decisions.

This brief discussion suggests that the two key assumptions of economising behaviour and the exogenous nature of the good/service are critical to transaction cost theory and so will be examined in turn. The assumption of economising behaviour is central to transaction cost logic. Williamson and Ouchi (1983: 33) argue for an 'unremitting emphasis on efficiency'. In principle the source for this unremitting pressure that produces economising behaviour might involve competition; hence a survival of the fittest logic is emphasised in Williamson (1985). With respect to giant firms we cannot unquestioningly use long-run conclusions derived from the theory of competitive markets based on many small firms and/or free market entry and exit. For example, there appears to be considerable turnover among the 100 largest firms in the United Kingdom and the United States over the 1980s and 1990s (Dietrich, 2003). But the firms dropping out of the top 100 and those replacing them are from very different product markets. The changes involved appear to be caused by the emergence of new markets and technologies, not competition with given markets and technologies.

In these dynamic conditions it is by no means obvious why economising behaviour should promote superior performance and survival. To indicate possible complexities here we can use the ideas presented in Langlois (1986). We can assume that in a particular market two 'types' of firms exist: 'economisers' and 'adapters'. The latter firms invest in organisational overheads involving human and other assets that allow them to promote, respond to and exploit market and technological changes. Although Langlois does not use the idea of a mapping between techno-informational and institutional views on the firm, it is clear that investment in this organisational overhead implies a feedback from the institutional to the techno-functional firm. An implication, however, is that with unchanging markets, i.e. in equilibrium conditions, the extra assets used by the adapters are unnecessary. Consequently adapters are less efficient than economisers who do not use these extra assets. We can also note that, for these two types of firms to be distinct, these assets must be sunk, which prevents switching, at least in the short run, between economising and adapting behaviour. This assumption of sunkness in the human and other assets required to manage change is not unreasonable given training requirements and asset non-transferability. In equilibrium economisers will be more profitable than adapters because of their lower costs. But out-of-equilibrium adapters will be able to manage changes more effectively and hence will generate greater profitability from new activity compared to economisers.

Equilibrium economics recognises, to some extent, this distinction between economisers and adapters. Standard oligopoly models offer a leader–follower analysis in which leaders are able to anticipate the reactions of followers and maximise profit using this capability. The result is that leaders can increase profits at the expense of follower firms. In a dynamic environment follower firms merely react to environmental changes, whereas leaders respond to such changes by incorporating the reactions of rivals. Hence a transaction cost economising firm is a follower that reacts to its environment and a Langlois adapter is able to lead adjustment processes and hence be more profitable.[3] It follows that it is by no means obvious why, in all circumstances, simple economising behaviour should promote performance and survival.[4] The relevance of this conclusion for the current era of changing technologies and markets is obvious. It follows that the firm as a governance structure may be, at most, part of a wider explanation of the nature of the firm.

This questioning of the relevance of a universal assumption of efficiency-seeking behaviour involves recognising, in non-equilibrium circumstances, the importance of 'adapter' firms that are able to promote, respond to and exploit market and technological changes. It follows that with these firms the nature of the good or service being produced is not constant and exogenous; i.e. non-equilibrium conditions lead to the questioning not only of the universal relevance of efficiency-seeking behaviour but also the constancy of non-transaction cost factors. To some extent this problem has been recognised by Demsetz (1991) and the later Coase (1991). They both claim that in viewing the firm as one possible means of coordinating resource allocation this has downplayed the basic function of the firm that involves the production of goods and services. But the issues here are more involved than correctly emphasising that firms produce as well as organise.

We can characterise the transaction costs of a firm, or more generally a governance structure, as the costs of search, negotiation and policing activities that are necessary to organise the production of the real output involved (Coase, 1960). The revenues from the sale of the real output compared to the necessary production costs involved can be called governance structure benefits (Dietrich, 1994). It follows that the rationale and nature of particular governance structures can be analysed in transaction cost terms only if the governance structure benefits are unchanged when different structures are compared. This is the reason why Williamson, in the earlier quotation, holds the nature of the good or service constant as economising occurs. If the nature of the good/service is not constant, governance structure benefits will change, and consequently the rationale for the governance structure need not depend uniquely on contracting and organisation *costs*.

The nature of real output, or governance structure benefits, can change as forms of organisation change in response to two general factors (Dietrich,

1994): changes in the ability to exploit monopoly power and changes in the ability to exploit idiosyncratic firm advantage. Marglin (1974, 1982) presents an analysis of the emergence of the firm, claiming that firms initially gained their rationale because they allowed capitalists to more effectively exploit a monopoly of knowledge compared to non-firm forms of organisation. But in the current dynamic environment of changing technologies and product markets, it is arguable that a sustained ability to exploit monopoly advantages depends on sustaining idiosyncratic firm advantages. Hence the current discussion will emphasise the latter rather than the former.

The firm as a locus of strategic control

The reasoning just presented brings us to the final perspective on the firm to be considered here: the firm as a locus of strategic control. This approach to the firm contains two strands. One strand is competence- or resource-based theory (for example, Foss, 1993, 2005; Foss and Loasby, 1998). This approach emphasises that the rationale for the firm is based on idiosyncratic characteristics. The principles of this tradition can be dated back to writers such as Penrose (1980), Richardson (1972) and more recently Nelson and Winter (1982). Penrose distinguishes between factor inputs and factor services. Inputs are tradable and as such are available for all firms. Factor services are not tradable, and are derived from the detailed use that a firm makes of factor inputs. In turn output is produced using services not (directly) inputs. There is no simple one-to-one mapping from inputs to services; rather the connections depend on idiosyncratic organisational functioning. Richardson (1972) uses similar themes in his account of the rationale of the firm. Firms group together activities based on common skills; inputs that are necessary, but outside this skills base, are provided by other firms. Finally Nelson and Winter (1982) suggest that skills depend on the development and use of tacit knowledge that can only be acquired via learning by doing rather than arm's-length acquisition. This tacit knowledge provides the basis for idiosyncratic organisational routines that are interpreted as the genetic code of a firm.

This resource-based tradition provides an explanation of why the nature of real output, or governance structure benefits, may change as forms of organisation change. A particular form of organisation may facilitate a more effective exploitation of an idiosyncratic knowledge base. This is conceptualised by Dietrich (1993) using the idea of an Alchian and Demsetz (1972) team. It is argued that modern management innovations, such as total quality techniques, have rendered an Alchian and Demsetz type of analysis of production somewhat obsolete. Instead, it is suggested, of increasing relevance to the modern firm is a non-separable knowledge base, i.e. the idea of a team applied to organisational matters rather than production.

It might be argued that, because of technological and product-market dynamics characteristic of the current era, this competence approach is more relevant to modern or new economy firms than the firm as a governance structure. But some writers (Foss, 1993, 2005; Langlois and Robertson, 1995) argue that this competence perspective is complementary to, rather than a substitute for, transaction cost approaches to the firm. The basic difference between the two approaches can be explained in game theoretic terms. Transaction cost analysis uses an implicit prisoner's dilemma framework oriented towards issues of motivation and control given the divergent incentives of the actors involved. The emphasis is, therefore, on issues of organisation rather than production. The competence perspective sees its basic nature as a coordination problem given possibly divergent capabilities. The way in which this latter coordination problem is solved influences a firm's productive capabilities.

Langlois and Robertson (1995) go further than this and argue that the central long-run focus of the firm involves the management and coordination of fundamental competences. In a dynamic environment this management involves dynamic transaction costs because of the costs of re-coordinating productive capabilities. Using an Austrian-inspired analysis, convergence to a long-run equilibrium reduces these dynamic management costs because of the diffusion of knowledge. But we are left with a static (traditional) transaction cost analysis in which the nature of the product/service is unchanged and the firm can motivate actors in the most efficient way possible.

We can see here two connections with earlier discussion. First, the linkage between the techno-functional and institutional firm is more complex. A long-run mapping operates from institutional to techno-functional matters, whereas a (traditional transaction cost) short-run mapping operates in the reverse direction. The second connection with the earlier discussion involves a possible convergence of the competence and legal perspectives on the firm. Both can be conceptualised, at an abstract level, as solutions to coordination problems. Given an equilibrium to a legal coordination problem, i.e. given a socially accepted structuring of antecedent rights, equilibria in firm-based competence games can emerge involving the specification of long-run focus and productive capabilities. A change in the equilibrium of the legal game, because of, for example, a change in socially recognised views of harm, will impact on competence games and hence long-run focus and capabilities. Both coordination problems have to be solved before a firm can effectively approach its prisoner's dilemma-type issues and hence enter the world of (static) transaction costs.

A second strand of the locus of strategic control literature is suggested by Cowling and Sugden (1998: 61). In their own words they:

> suggest that a concern with planning points to the particular relevance of strategic decision-making in today's large corporations. This leads us to define a corporation in terms of a nexus of strategic decision-making ... [This] implies different boundaries to the firm compared with those seen in the widely accepted reading of Coase. In the strategic decision-making approach what others have referred to as market exchanges

falling outside the ambit of the firm, notably subcontracting relationships, are incorporated *inside* the firm ... Our discussion emphasizes that the strategic decision-making approach focuses on the objectives and thus decisions of strategic decision-makers.

(Emphasis in original)

We can make two comments about this conceptualisation of the nature of the firm. The first concerns the linkage between the objectives of the strategic decision-makers and the boundaries of the firm. This connection can only be made if strategic decisions are explicit and rational. In this regard we can use an insight from the management literature on organisations. Mintzberg (1990) criticises views of strategy based on necessary rationality for failing to recognise the importance of individual and organisational ignorance and learning. He suggests that strategy should be viewed as *emerging* from the interaction of individuals in an organisational setting rather than being explicitly planned. This implies that firm strategies are, at least in part, not just planned and based on the objectives of senior strategists. We can only suggest that strategies are explicit and planned in the absence of ignorance, i.e. in a full information world characteristic of much economic reasoning. This criticism suggested by Mintzberg nests into the view suggested above that firm boundaries are arbitrary but a necessary means of coordination to manage informational uncertainty and complexity.

The second comment that can be made about the Cowling and Sugden conceptualisation concerns the view 'that market exchanges falling outside the ambit of the firm, notably subcontracting relationships, are incorporated *inside* the firm'. This view is clearly inconsistent with the legal perspective on the firm outlined above. To identify the source of this difference we can recognise that market relationships can involve asymmetric payoffs between contracting parties whenever differential market power exists. The only way we can ignore such asymmetries is to assume universal perfect competition. It is necessary, therefore, to separate the influence of firm strategies that are direct and internal to the firm with effects that are external and result from market power. To indicate the muddle that might emerge if internal and external effects are not separated, consider the case of a large firm that subcontracts cleaning services that were previously supplied by direct employees. Unless the 'old' employees set up their own cleaning firm, it is clear that the new supplier of cleaning services must already exist and hence supply other firms. Using the Cowling and Sugden definition this subcontractor would be part of more than one firm. To remove this possibility we would have to qualify the Cowling and Sugden perspective and suggest that subcontractors that supply one firm are part of the buying firm but subcontractors that supply more than one firm are independent firms. Apart from being arbitrary this qualification is unsatisfactory because both types of subcontractors may experience similar pressures and influence from buying firms.

For current purposes we can recognise that the Cowling and Sugden formulation is not inconsistent with the earlier perspective that the rationale for a particular organisational form might be explained in terms of governance structure benefits as well as costs. In turn, governance structure benefits can rely on monopoly advantages. These advantages lie at the heart of the Cowling and Sugden formulation. But, because of the problems just outlined, the formulation is in need of development. The extent to which strategic decision-makers are able to effectively influence and control other economic agents would seem to depend on two factors: the extent to which strategists have *power* and *authority* over other agents (Dietrich, 2002). These terms have potentially multiple meanings; hence it is important to offer specific definitions.

Within economics, power is usually defined as market power, involving in output markets the ability to raise price over marginal cost. But, at a more general level, this power relies on resource dependencies, in the sense used by Pfeffer (1981). Such dependencies produce non-contestable economic relationships, in the sense suggested by Baumol (1982). In the absence of resource dependencies any actor can exit from the control of another economic agent. It is important to recognise that even with full information, complete contracting payoff asymmetries can exist if resource dependencies and hence power are asymmetric. In short, power involves the ability to *ex ante* control the distribution of economic rents.

To define authority we can follow Tirole (1988) and distinguish between supervision and authority. The exercise of supervision is an aspect of a complete contract. It assesses the extent to which parties fulfil reciprocal obligations that are agreed upon *ex ante*. Of course, these obligations reflect power differentials. Authority only exists with incomplete contracts. In such circumstances, adaptation to contingencies is carried out *ex post*. This adaptation defines the actual rules governing the relationship and implies an unequal distribution of the potential to adapt to contingencies. Authority may be formal, as with an organisational hierarchy, or more informal, as with a charismatic leader or where one individual trusts another to make decisions perhaps linked to professional behaviour (see Dietrich and Roberts, 1999).

It is suggested in Dietrich (2002) that these twin concepts of power and authority are central to understanding the firm as a sovereign unit, i.e. an economic unit that is capable of developing and enacting independent policies. Both power and authority are necessary for the firm to have a recognised external boundary and internal coherence in its organisational processes. If there is power without authority, a firm is able to exploit a monopoly position, but the subordinate agent or unit is independent in terms of adapting to contingencies; this is the case with Cowling and Sugden subcontracting. If there is authority without power a firm may be the hub of a wider system or network and hence play a pivotal role in adjustment and adaptation but there is no asymmetric payoff, or control over distribution of rents, from this pivotal role. In terms of the earlier formulation both power and authority are necessary for effective coordination, i.e. for a firm to develop long-run focus and to coordinate fundamental competences.

Towards an integrated economics of the firm

To sum up earlier discussion it has been suggested that the economics of the firm can be understood in two distinct contexts: techno-functional and institutional. The techno-functional context involves the production of goods and services, in particular market settings. The institutional view moves beyond a black-box analysis. Ignoring for the moment the legal perspective on the firm, it has been argued that two distinct institutional views exist in economics: the firm as a governance structure and the firm as a locus of strategic control. The governance perspective is driven by issues of *efficient motivation*, the strategic approach by issues of *long-run focus*. The insights gained from these two approaches are driven by the conceptual linkages created between techno-functional and institutional matters. In schematic terms the two approaches can be summarised as follows:

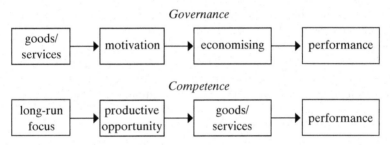

Based on earlier discussion it is clear that the conceptual linkages used here are to some extent partial or incomplete. To develop an integrated economics of the firm a more fully connected set of linkages can be recognised. In schematic terms this fully connected model of the firm is presented in Figure 2.1. The framework defined by (1) can be classed as traditional transaction cost theory; the reasoning for this was developed above and needs no further comment here. The method defined by (2) is competence- or resource-based theory, as discussed in the previous section. These first two approaches constitute what might be considered the recognised standard literature on the economics of the firm. For this reason they are perhaps less interesting than the 'alternative' frameworks defined by links (3)–(6).

The nature of link (3) can be explained in the following way. The causation operates from efficient motivation to the goods and services produced, i.e. the reverse of traditional transaction cost theory. Economising on transaction costs implies contracting or organisational productivity gains. Such gains must be based on a more effective management of search, negotiation and/or policing matters, i.e. more effective control of factors of production.

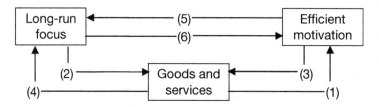

Figure 2.1 A fully connected model of the firm.

At the techno-functional level such improvement will become apparent as improved labour and/or capital productivity. Using a standard production function analysis of the firm, an increase in factor productivities will increase production-based scale economies (or reduce diseconomies) and hence influence firm size and market structure. An alternative way of conceptualising this link is to follow Morroni (1992) and suggest that organisational indivisibilities, arising from the management of transaction costs, produce economies of scale. Either way of conceptualising link (3) suggests the same conclusion: the management of transaction cost issues can impact on the techno-functional characteristics of the firm.

The characteristics of link (4) can be explained in one of two ways. First using a standard structure–conduct–performance approach, it can be suggested that different market structures can impact on firm objectives and hence performance. In the Austrian and neo-Austrian writing cited above this possible impact of market structure is marginalised. Monopoly power is viewed as a return to entrepreneurship that is a characteristic of non-equilibrium analysis. A second possible explanation is suggested by Langlois and Robertson (1995). When firms are making investment decisions, i.e. decisions involving long-run focus, the variable costs of existing ventures will be compared with the total costs of new ventures. With significant sunk costs this can produce what might be called technological path dependence, i.e. a bias towards existing ventures and technologies. This path dependence will generate inertia in the long-run focus of firms. Of course these two possible explanations of link (4) are connected. Technological path dependence is likely to be greater with a degree of monopoly power for existing firms.

Link (5), from efficient motivation to long-run focus, can be considered the organisational analogue of link (4). Given the sunk costs of setting up and managing contracting and motivation systems, a bias towards the use of existing organisational methods and processes will be introduced. If strategic re-orientation involves fundamental organisational change, such re-orientation can be rationally blocked, i.e. long-run strategies and focus will be constrained and channelled in particular directions. Mintzberg (1990) suggests that organisational rigidities – in our context, path dependence – might exist because strategies are filtered through existing learning processes. Alternatively the same result might follow from recognising that particular firm strategies reflect the orientation and interests of particular professional groups inside the firm (Dietrich, 1997). Strategic coordination is then required around the objectives of a particular professional grouping, if coordination failures are to be avoided. Firm strategic change can be understood as a change in coordination equilibrium; or, in management speak, organisational turnaround, a notoriously difficult process.

The nature of link (6) can be summarised under the shorthand of strategising or economising. Or, for reasons set out earlier, the same idea can be captured under the distinction between firms acting as leaders or followers. For firms as institutional entities leadership is not simply based on exploiting costless subjective knowledge, as traditional Austrian theory suggests. Instead if firms act as market leaders, investment in organisational assets is required to be able to develop new strategies or to manage the flexibilities required to effectively exploit market opportunities. Such assets are not necessary for follower firms. In turn the required capabilities for effective innovation and flexibility will impact on organisational motivation systems. In short organisational motivation need not be simply an efficient response to exogenous techno-functional characteristics, but in addition can depend on long-run objectives. One way of conceptualising these impacts is to distinguish between long-run and short-run economising. With short-run economising firms respond to cost and revenue potential. For long-run economising cost and revenue potential are endogenous to firm strategies, with higher costs being required for the management of faster or more fundamental change. In terms of Figure 2.1, link (5) is based on the dominance of short-run economising whereas link (6) has long-run economising as dominant.

Links (1)–(6) indicate the complexity that is potentially involved in the economics of the firm. In addition this complexity can be increased by combining the links, as is done by theorists who suggest that competence and transaction cost approaches are complements rather than substitutes, as discussed above. Arguably a full development of the complexities here would introduce significant conceptual diminishing returns. The intellectual management of such problems might involve two, non-mutually exclusive, approaches to the analysis of the firm. First, this analysis might be empirically driven. Here the emphasis would be oriented towards identifying the key linkages in particular circumstances. For instance a different conceptual framework might be appropriate for 'new' compared to 'old' economy firms. A second approach might be conceptually driven. To manage the complexities involved, particular linkages can be emphasised but the non-core linkages can be recognised and introduced as constraints. This will have similarities to the existing economics of the firm, in the emphasis on particular links, but it differs in that the non-core constraints are not apparently recognised. A general requirement here is tolerance of theoretical pluralism and diversity, as it is unlikely that any particular theoretical approach to the firm is universally applicable (Nooteboom, 2004).

This discussion, while indicating the potential complexity of the firm, ignores the earlier discussion on the firm as a legal unit. In the final part of this section the earlier discussion on the legal basis of the firm will be incorporated in the framework just suggested. The approach taken here is that the legal basis of the firm is considered an external influence on the firm in much the same way as technology is viewed in more traditional approaches. The impact of technology is felt via the techno-functional aspects of the firm, and from this to motivation and long-run focus. The legal basis of the firm is felt via long-run focus and motivation systems and from this to techno-functional characteristics. Before developing this approach a first matter must consider a few issues left unresolved in earlier discussion involving limitations of the legal perspective.

To summarise earlier discussion, in an ideal-type, law-abiding economy the legal basis of the firm can be viewed as defining 'natural rights' that are necessary for effective contractual relationships. These rights are key determinants of the power and authority that is the basis of a sovereign firm. They define the *ex ante* ability to control distribution of economic rents, i.e. power, and the status of a principal in any contractual relationship with the *ex post* authority this implies. Without both power and authority the firm as an institutional entity will not exist; instead we will have networks or sub-contracting systems, etc. But a key aspect of earlier discussion was that the specification of these rights in legal practice, rather than in economic theory, requires prior social agreement on what constitutes harm. This allowed us to identify examples of non-legal techno-functional firms.

To generalise the latter point we can recognise that, in a real economy, power and authority do not depend solely on legal factors, although perhaps in a modern economy their legal basis is paramount. A more general formulation might suggest that they depend on the credible reputations of economic actors and the behavioural regularities that therefore occur. Such reputations would seem to depend on four factors:

1   Legal recognition.
2   Personal contacts and recommendations. This factor would seem to be central to the functioning of the black economy and back-street abortionists, to use earlier examples.
3   Institutionalised, non-legal, reputations. For instance Perkin (1989) has argued that professional status and ethics have, to some extent, undermined legal rights of ownership in modern firms.
4   Violence, coercion and personal commitment. For instance, the organisation of drug trafficking, and other organised crime is based on violence and personal commitment rather than a legal right of ownership.

Arguably, in any actual economy these four factors are central to the ways in which power and authority are managed by firms, i.e. how the firm as a sovereign unit becomes institutionalised.

In short it is not the legal basis of ownership that defines the firm but rather the power and authority this buttresses. In turn this power and authority depends on accepted views of harm: for example, the extent to which trade union rights can defend health and safety inside firms, the extent to which regulation of financial institutions and corporate governance is effective, or the extent to which the mafia is tolerated. Socially accepted views of harm are not, of course, static but rather evolve and change. This evolution and change will have an impact on the institutional functioning of the firm. For example, Williamson (1985: 218–19) uses the work of March and Simon (1958) and suggests that: 'the employee stands ready to accept authority regarding work assignments provided only that the behaviour called for falls within the "zone of acceptance" of the contract'. This 'zone of acceptance' implies acceptance of the power and authority of an employer and defines the limits that are considered non-harmful. Any change in this zone will therefore impact on efficient motivation systems.

In schematic terms we can incorporate this insight into our model in the way suggested in Figure 2.2. Power and authority will impact on the long-run focus of the firm and efficient motivation, with effects depending on the extent to which firms act as leaders or followers. This impact of power and authority is equivalent to the impact of technology on techno-functional aspects of goods and services. One implication of recognising this role of power and authority allows a development of neo-Schumpeterian ideas on long-run economic evolution, a few comments on which is a useful end to the discussion in this section. Dosi (1988) argues that long-run economic evolution depends on evolving 'technological paradigms'. The impact of evolving technologies can be viewed, in Figure 2.2, as the direct impact on techno-functional firm characteristics. From this, indirect links operate via (1) the

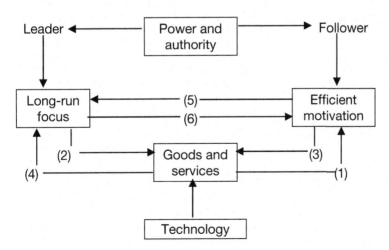

Figure 2.2 Environmental impacts on the firm.

effect on efficient motivation and (4) the effect on technological path dependence. The first effect has been recognised by, for example, Milgrom and Roberts (1990) who suggest that flexible technology is reducing asset specificity and hence leading to vertical disintegration because of transaction cost factors. Link (4) is a key aspect of the Freeman and Perez (1988) analysis of the impact of technological revolutions on institutions, with the institution in question here being the firm. While this analysis is insightful, it suffers from the problem that it is overly technologically determinist (Radosevic, 1991; McKelvey, 1991). The framework suggested here recognises that the clearly important impacts of technology on links (1)–(6) will always depend on the nature of power and authority. As the latter impacts change in space and time the impacts of technology will therefore change. In addition, technology need not be the only prime mover of institutional change, as socially accepted views on power and authority have an independent impact. For instance, Dietrich (1992) analyses this impact using a framework informed by Ponanyi's (1944) analysis of historical evolution.

Conclusion

This chapter has revisited the economics of the firm with the intention of identifying the underlying principles informing different perspectives on the firm. It was initially argued that the firm exists in two different guises in economics: as a techno-functional entity and as an institutional entity. It is argued that links between the two are central to identifying the principles involved in different perspectives on the firm. There is no single view of the firm as an institutional entity. Three different views are identified here: the firm as a legal unit, the firm as a governance structure and the firm as a locus of strategic control. The firm as legal unit identifies the firm as a distinct legal identity. In an ideal-type, law-abiding economy this is a sufficient definition of the firm. But with illegal, or more generally harmful, activity a gap develops between the firm as techno-functional entity and the firm as a legal unit. To overcome this potential problem it is argued that the firm as a legal unit is important in economics because it is the basis of the rights of ownership. In turn these rights buttress the power and authority of an independent firm. It is power and authority, rather than ownership per se, that allows an independent firm to be identified, whether this is legally recognised or not. But rights of ownership are not defined in an abstract way but as inevitably being constrained by a duty not to do harm. This duty requires a social consensus of what involves harm.

The firm as a governance structure, identified with transaction cost theory, involves linking an exogenous techno-functional firm with efficient motivation. The firm as a locus of strategic control, identified with competence theory, involves linking strategic focus with an endogenous techno-functional firm. Presenting the economics of the firm in the way suggested in this chapter allows the identification of six different perspectives on the economics of the firm, two of which are traditional transaction cost and competence theory. The effect of power and authority – for shorthand in a modern economy this can be viewed as the legal structure – then becomes an exogenous influence that determines the ways in which the six possible linkages operate, and evolve, in practice. This exogenous influence is seen to be equivalent to the impact of technology and technological change.

An implication of the framework developed here is that no universal status can be claimed for any particular theoretical perspective, i.e. a theoretical pluralism is required. In addition, a key issue here is that it is a fundamentally empirical question as to which perspective is relevant and dominant in particular circumstances. This empirically driven relevance opens up a significant, and open-ended, research agenda.

Notes

1 In the limited space available here it is not possible to present anything close to a complete survey of the voluminous literature on transaction cost economics. Instead the discussion will be restricted to those aspects of transaction cost theory that are important for understanding the general nature of the firm. For more general critiques see Dietrich (1994) and the essays in Francis *et al.* (1983), Pitelis (1993) and Groenewegen (1996).

2 The potential importance of this difference between small and large firms is informed by Galbraith (1974). He draws a distinction between the market system, inhabited by small atomistic firms, and the planning system, inhabited by large corporations. Small firms respond to exogenous demand/supply conditions, whereas corporations have the primary objective of managing market uncertainty.

3 An interesting leader–follower analysis of the firm is presented by Casson (1991). He suggests that entrepreneurs can act as strategic leaders and create business cultures to which employees react. He shows that in many circumstances this manipulation of the internal environment of the firm is a more effective means of motivating employees compared to the use of material-individual incentives. The implication is that the internal organisation of the firm cannot be explained simply in economising terms.

4 We can note an additional implication of dynamic and uncertain conditions that was alluded to in earlier discussion. Decision-making that is based on transaction cost economising requires risk-neutral economic agents. It is conventional, however, to assume that managers and workers are risk averse. With risk aversion the utility derived from using a particular governance structure depends not just on the monetary advantages derived from transaction cost savings but also on the uncertainty of returns from particular governance structures. It follows that agents may promote a particular governance structure because it promotes security rather than just efficiency. In addition, as suggested earlier, governance structures may facilitate the spreading and shifting of risk rather than just transaction cost savings.

References

Alchian, A. A. and Demsetz, H. (1972), 'Production, information costs, and economic organization', *American Economic Review*, 62: 777–95.

Baumol, W. J. (1982), 'Contestable markets: an uprising in the theory of industrial structure', *American Economic Review*, 72: 1–15.

Casson, M. (1991), *The Economics of Business Culture*, Oxford: Clarendon Press.

Coase, R. H. (1937), 'The nature of the firm', *Economica*, 4: 386–405.

—— (1960), 'The problem of social cost', *Journal of Law and Economics*, 3: 1–44.

—— (1991), 'The nature of the firm: meaning', in O. E. Williamson and S. G. Winter (eds), *The Nature of the Firm*, Oxford: Oxford University Press.

Commons, J. R. (1924), *The Legal Foundations of Capitalism*, Madison, WI: University of Wisconsin Press.

—— (1934), *Institutional Economics: Its Place in Political Economy*, Madison, WI: University of Wisconsin Press.

Cowling, K. and Sugden, R. (1998), 'The essence of the modern corporation: markets, strategic decision making and the theory of the firm', *The Manchester School*, 66: 59–86.

Demsetz, H. (1991), 'The theory of the firm revisited', in O. E. Williamson and S. G. Winter (eds), *The Nature of the Firm*, Oxford: Oxford University Press.

Dietrich, M. (1993), 'Total quality control, just-in-time management, and the economics of the firm', *Journal of Economic Studies*, 20(6): 17–31.

—— (1994), *Transaction Cost Economics and Beyond*, London: Routledge.

—— (1997), 'Strategic lock-in as a human issue: the role of professional orientation', in L. Magnusson and J. Ottoson (eds), *Evolutionary Economics and Path Dependence*, Cheltenham: Edward Elgar.

—— (2002), 'The contested sovereignty of the firm', *Review of Political Economy*, 14: 2.

—— (2003), 'Giant firms in the information economy', Department of Economics Discussion Paper, 2003006.

Dietrich, M. and Roberts, J. (1999), 'Conceptualising professionalism: why economics needs sociology', *American Journal of Economics and Sociology*, October.

Dosi, G. (1988), 'Sources, procedures and microeconomic effects of innovation', *Journal of Economic Literature*, 26: 1120–71.

Foss, N. (1993), 'Theories of the firm: contractual and competence perspectives', *Journal of Evolutionary Economics*, 3: 126–44.

—— (2005), *Strategy, Economic Organization, and the Knowledge Economy: The Coordination of Firms and Resources*, Oxford: Oxford University Press.

Foss, N. and Loasby, B. J. (eds) (1998), *Economic Organization, Capabilities and Co-ordination: Essays in Honour of GB Richardson*, London: Routledge.

Francis, A., Turk, J. and Willman, P. (eds) (1983), *Power, Efficiency and Institutions*, London: Heinemann.

Freeman, C. and Perez, C. (1988), 'Structural crises of adjustment: business cycles and investment behaviour', in G. Dosi, C. Freeman, R. Nelson, G. Silverberg and L. Soete (eds), *Technical Change and Economic Theory*, London: Pinter Publishers.

Galbraith, J. K. (1974), *The New Industrial State*, 2nd edn, Harmondsworth: Penguin.

Groenewegen, J. (ed.) (1996), *Transaction Cost Economics and Beyond*, London: Kluwer.

Hart, O. (1995), *Firms, Contracts and Financial Structure*, Oxford: Clarendon Press.

Hayek, F. A. (1945), 'The use of knowledge in society', *American Economic Review*, 35: 519–30.

—— (1948), *Individualism and Economic Order*, London: Routledge.
—— (1973), *Law, Legislation and Liberty*, vol. 1: *Rules and Order*, London: Routledge and Kegan Paul.
Hodgson, G. M. (1988), *Economics and Institutions*, Cambridge: Polity Press.
—— (2002), 'The legal nature of the firm and the myth of the firm-market hybrid', *International Journal of the Economics of Business*, 9: 37–60.
Kahneman, D. and Tversky, A. (eds) (2000), *Choices, Values and Frames*, Cambridge, Cambridge University Press.
Kay, J. (1997), 'The stakeholder corporation', in G. Kelly, D. Kelly and A. Gamble (eds), *Stakeholder Capitalism*, Basingstoke: Macmillan.
Kirzner, I. M. (1973), *Competition and Entrepreneurship*, Chicago, IL: University of Chicago Press.
Langlois, R. N. (1986), 'The new institutional economics: an introductory essay', in R. N. Langlois (ed.), *Economics as a Process*, Cambridge: Cambridge University Press.
Langlois, R. N. and Robertson, P. L. (1995), *Firms, Markets and Economic Change: A Dynamic Theory of Business Institutions*, London: Routledge.
Machlup, F. (1967), 'Theories of the firm: marginalist, managerial, behavioural', *American Economic Review*, 57: 1–33.
McKelvey, M. (1991), 'How do national systems of innovation differ?: a critical analysis of Porter, Freeman, Londvall and Nelson', in G. M. Hodgson and E. Screpanti (eds), *Rethinking Economics: Markets, Technology and Economic Evolution*, Aldershot: Edward Elgar.
March, J. G. and Simon, H. A. (1958), *Organizations*, London: John Wiley.
Marglin, S. A. (1974), 'What do bosses do? The origins and functions of hierarchy in capitalist production', Part I, *Review of Radical Political Economics*, 6: 60–112.
—— (1982), 'Knowledge is power', in F. H. Stephen (ed.), *Firms, Organization and Labour*, London: Macmillan.
Masten, S. E. (1991), 'A legal basis for the firm', in O. E. Williamson and S. G. Winter (eds), *The Nature of the Firm*, Oxford: Oxford University Press.
Milgrom, P. and Roberts, J. (1990), 'The economics of modern manufacturing technology, strategy and organization', *American Economic Review*, 80: 511–28.
Mintzberg, H. (1990), 'Strategy formation schools of thought', in J. W. Fredrickson (ed.), *Perspectives on Strategic Management*, New York: Harper and Row.
Morroni, M. (1992), *Production Process and Technical Change*, Cambridge: Cambridge University Press.
Nelson, R. R. and Winter, S. G. (1982), *An Evolutionary Theory of Economic Change*, Boston, MA: Harvard University Press.
Nooteboom, B. (2004), 'Governance and competence: how can they be combined?', *Cambridge Journal of Economics*, 28: 505–25.
North, D. C. (1981), *Structure and Change in Economic History*, New York: Norton.
Nozick, R. (1974), *Anarchy, State and Utopia*, New York: Basic Books.
Penrose, E. T. (1980), *The Theory of the Growth of the Firm*, 2nd edn. Oxford: Blackwell.
Perkin, H. (1989), *The Rise of Professional Society*, London: Routledge.
Pfeffer, J. (1981), *Power in Organizations*, London: Pitman.
Pitelis, C. (1993), *Transaction Costs, Markets and Hierarchies*, Oxford: Blackwell.
Ponanyi, K. (1944), *The Great Transformation*, New York: Rinehart.
Posner, R. A. (1977), *Economic Analysis of Law*, 2nd edn. Boston, MA: Little, Brown.

Radosevic, S. (1991), 'In Search of an alternative theory: a critique of Dosi *et al.*'s technical change and economic theory', *Review of Political Economy*, 3: 93–111.

Richardson, G. B. (1972), 'The organisation of industry', *Economic Journal*, 82: 883–96.

Rutherford, M. (1996), *Institutions in Economics*, Cambridge: Cambridge University Press.

Sen, A. (1987), *On Ethics and Economics*, Oxford: Blackwell.

Sugden, R. (1986), *The Economics of Rights, Cooperation and Welfare*, Oxford: Blackwell.

Tirole, J. (1988), 'The multicontract organization', *Canadian Journal of Economics*, XXI(3): 459–66.

Williamson, O. E. (1975), *Markets and Hierarchies*, New York: Free Press.

——(1985), *The Economic Institutions of Capitalism*, London: Macmillan.

——(1991), 'Introduction', in O. E. Williamson and S. G. Winter (eds), *The Nature of the Firm*, Oxford: Oxford University Press.

Williamson O. E. and Ouchi, W. G. (1983), 'The markets and hierarchies programme of research: origins, implications, prospects', in A. Francis, J. Turk and P. Willman (eds), *Power, Efficiency and Institutions*, London: Heinemann.

Young, H. P. (1995), 'The economics of convention', *Journal of Economic Perspectives*, 10: 105–22.

——(1998), *Individual Strategy and Social Structure*, Oxford: Princeton University Press.

3   Trust, learning and the firm

Bart Nooteboom

Introduction

Georg Simmel proposed that trust is a mixture of rationality and feeling: it is based on a certain amount of rational assessment, but also entails a leap of faith beyond that (Möllering, 2001). This seems related to the 'paradox of information' associated with trust (Pagden, 1988). On the one hand, trust requires a lack of information: if we were certain about future behaviour, we would no longer speak of trust. On the other hand, trust is based on information, in attributions of motives and competencies to people, based on observed or reported behaviour.

This chapter aims to contribute to our understanding of how this mixture of rationality and feeling, assessment and faith, information and uncertainty may 'work' in the process of the making and breaking of trust, and how a firm may provide the conditions for it. It employs the perspective of 'embedded cognition' (Merleau-Ponty, 1942, 1964), which is partly based on insights derived from recent neuroscience (Edelman, 1987, 1992; Damasio, 1995, 2003; Lakoff and Johnson, 1999). According to this perspective, cognition is rooted in brain and body, which are in turn embedded in their external environment. Here, cognition denotes a broad range of mental activity, including proprioception, perception, sense making, categorization, inference, value judgements, emotions and feelings.

One core assumption is that people perceive, interpret and evaluate the world according to mental categories that they have developed in interaction with their social and physical environment. This is consistent with the view of 'symbolic interactionism' from sociology (G. H. Mead). It is particularly relevant to trust, which builds up or breaks down in processes of interaction between people. A second assumption is that rationality and emotions, and mind and body, are intertwined (see also Simon, 1983; Nussbaum, 2001). This goes against the body–mind dualism of Descartes, and is more in sympathy with the thought of Descartes's contemporary Spinoza (Damasio, 2003). Events call forth emotions, rooted in the body, which give rise to feelings, which may lead to reflective thought, which in turn may modify emotions and yield a critical analysis of events. This is also of particular relevance to trust, where emotions play an important role in the way that trust builds up or breaks down in an emotion-laden perception and assessment of threats and risks. For a further understanding of how this works, we will employ insights from social psychology. In this chapter, trust is defined as perceived vulnerability to the actions of others, with the possibility of 'things going wrong', combined with the belief that they will not go (seriously) wrong.

The chapter proceeds as follows. First, it gives a summary of basic notions of trust on which it builds, adopted from the literature (Nooteboom, 2002). Second, it gives a further discussion of notions of knowledge and learning used, from the perspective of embodied cognition. Third, it analyses the process of trust building as a process of learning. For a closer analysis of how this works, it next employs insights derived from the theory of framing (Lindenberg, 1998, 2003) and decision heuristics from social psychology (Bazerman, 1998; Tversky and Kahneman, 1983). Finally, it considers the role of the firm in setting the conditions for trust.

Basic features of trust

According to Nooteboom (2002), trust is taken as a four-place predicate: the trustor (1) trusts a trustee (2) in one or more aspects of behaviour (3), under certain circumstances (4). Trustees can be individual people, but also collectives, such as organizations and institutions. The relation between trust in people and trust in an organization depends on the position and roles that people have in an organization (Ring and van de Ven, 1992, 1994) and on the organization's mode of coordinating behaviour. Concerning aspects of behaviour that one may trust, it is customary to distinguish trust in competence (ability to conform to expectations) and trust in intentions (to perform in good faith according to the best of competence). Competence includes technical and cognitive competence. Trust in intentions requires commitment, i.e. attention to possible mishaps and absence of opportunism. In the literature, absence of opportunism has been called 'benevolence', 'goodwill' and 'solidarity'. The dependence of trust on circumstances entails that trust should be limited: one may trust someone (in competence or intentions), under some conditions but not in others that go beyond competence or resistance to temptations of opportunism. When something goes wrong in a relationship, i.e. when expectations are disappointed, there is a problem of causal ambiguity. Broken expectations may be due to a mishap, a shortfall of competence, lack of commitment and attention, or opportunism, and it is often unclear what cause is at play. Opportunistic partners will claim accidents. When people are overly suspicious, from lack of self-confidence or adverse experience, in general or with a specific partner, they may jump to the conclusion of opportunism where in fact only a mishap occurred.

Concerning the sources of trust, there are psychological causes and rational reasons. Psychological causes include emotions and may entail reflexes or automatic response. Rational reasons entail inference, on the basis of perceived behaviour, of someone's trustworthiness. An important question is how those two sources of trust are related. Can we separate rationality from emotions and feelings? As indicated above, in this chapter the view is that they cannot be, and that emotions, rationality and feelings are intertwined. According to Damasio (2003), perceptions may trigger emotions, which in turn yield feelings, which may yield thoughts that lead to some constraint on emotions. The question is how this works in more detail. Assessment of someone's trustworthiness, on the basis of observed or reported behaviour, is limited by uncertainty and bounded rationality, and is mediated by mental heuristics in the perception and attribution of people's motives and competences. Action is based on behavioural routines and their selection, according to decision heuristics. Such heuristics of inference and decision are known from social psychology (Tversky and Kahneman, 1983; Bazerman, 1998; Smith and Mackie, 2000), and will be used in this chapter. Nevertheless, judgements of trustworthiness can be more or less rational, in efforts to avoid 'jumping to conclusions', to be reasonable, and to extend the benefit of the doubt to people when trouble occurs. How the psychology of trust may work will be discussed in more detail later in this chapter.

The next question is why people might be trustworthy. Here we focus on intentional trustworthiness, in particular why people might not act opportunistically. A distinction is made between 'micro' foundations that are specific to a relationship, and 'macro', institution-based foundations that lie in the social environment of a relationship. The distinction between macro and micro sources is also known as the distinction between 'universalistic' or 'generalized' sources versus 'particularistic' sources, made by Deutsch (1973: 55), and between impersonal and personalized sources made by Shapiro (1987), and goes back to the work of Parsons. A distinction is also made between self-interested foundations and foundations that go beyond calculative self-interest. In self-interested foundations, trustworthiness may be based on control or deterrence. The trustor may control opportunities for opportunism ('opportunity control'), or material incentives ('incentive control'). Opportunity control may be based on legal coercion ('macro') or on hierarchical 'fiat', within a relationship ('micro'). Beyond self-interest, and beyond control by the trustor, trustworthiness may be based on socially inculcated values, norms and habits ('macro'), on personal feelings of empathy or identification, or routinization of conduct in a relationship ('micro'). Empathy entails the ability to understand another's 'way of thinking', without sharing it (having mental models of other people's mental models), and identification entails that one 'thinks the same way' (having similar mental models). For trust, one needs empathy, but not necessarily identification. One needs to understand 'what makes others tick', without necessarily 'ticking in the same way'. Empathy is needed to have a sense of the limits of trustworthiness, depending on circumstances. An overview of foundations of trustworthiness is given in Table 3.1.

Table 3.1 Sources of (intentional) reliability

	Macro	*Micro*
	universalistic	particularistic, relation-specific
Self-interest		
opportunity control	contracts, legal enforcement	hierarchy, managerial 'fiat'
incentive control	reputation	dependence: unique partner value, switching costs, hostages
Altruism		
benevolence	values, social norms of proper conduct, moral obligation, sense of duty, bonds of kinship	empathy, routinization, identification, affect, friendship

Source: adapted from Nooteboom (2002).

Note that in Table 3.1 reputation is included in the self-interested foundations of trustworthiness. Here, one behaves well because bad behaviour would become known in relevant communities, whereby one would forego possibly profitable options for future relationships.

Concerning routinization (see Table 3.1), Herbert Simon a long time ago showed that routines have survival value due to bounded rationality, in the sense of bounded capacity for reflective thought. Routines allow us to reserve our scarce capacity of 'focal awareness' (Polanyi, 1962), in rational, calculative thought, for conditions that are new and demand priority. When things go well for a while in a relationship, one tends to take at least some of it for granted. One may no longer think of opportunities for opportunism open to a partner, or to oneself. On the basis of experience in relations, trustworthiness is assumed until evidence to the contrary emerges. In other words, trust is a 'default'. The possibility of opportunism is relegated to 'subsidiary awareness' (Polanyi, 1962). Generally, when something out of the ordinary occurs, our awareness shifts from subsidiary to 'focal' and we look critically at what is going on. As Simon (1983) pointed out, we need emotions of danger and excitement to catapult danger or opportunity into focal awareness. Next, in case of trouble we must control emotions to give the partner the benefit of the doubt, allowing for mishaps, rather than immediately assume the worst (opportunism). In this way, routine behaviour is not necessarily blind; or, more accurately, it is not unconditional.

According to the analysis so far, trust may be based on control (coercion, incentives). However, several authors have recognized that trust goes beyond control, in 'goodwill' or 'benevolence' (see, for example, the special issue of *Organization Studies* on 'Trust and control in organizational relations', 22/2, 2001). As noted by Maguire *et al.* (2001: 286), if we do not include the latter, we conflate trust and power. Control or deterrence is part of calculative self-interest, but benevolence is not. Many authors feel that control is foreign to the notion of trust, and that 'genuine' trust is based on other, more social and personal foundations of trustworthiness. Therefore, trust has been defined as the expectation that a partner will not engage in opportunistic behaviour, even in the face of short-term opportunities and incentives (Bradach and Eccles, 1984; Chiles and McMackin, 1996). To avoid confusion, here the term 'reliance' is used to cover all foundations of trustworthiness, and 'trust' is used for motives that go beyond self-interest.

While trust can go beyond calculative self-interest, in benevolence it does, and generally should, have its limits. Blind, unconditional trust is generally unwise. Even benevolent people need to guard their self-interest, and it is not excessively cynical to assume that resistance to temptations to opportunism or betrayal is limited. Managers may be expected to cheat to the extent that their firm is under pressure of survival in competition. An illustration is the ENRON affair. When the overriding survival criterion of a firm is short-term (quarterly) profit, and an economic slump erodes it, the firm may feel irresistible pressure to cheat on the figures. Thus, one should maintain awareness of conditions where trustworthiness may be put under too large a strain. Yet, as noted before, within limits trust can become routinized and be taken for granted. One does not continually scrutinize behaviour and conditions for opportunities for opportunism, for oneself or one's partner, until they are felt to be excessive. As noted before, in view of uncertainties concerning motives and conditions, trust can only operate as a default: one assumes trustworthiness, within boundaries, until evidence of its failure becomes manifest, and then one adjusts the limits of trust. In other words: one must trust to learn even about trustworthiness. If one only trusted under certainty one would never trust, thereby robbing oneself of the opportunity to learn about trustworthiness and its limits.

In conclusion, while trust goes beyond control, and more trust allows for less control, so that trust and control are to some extent substitutes, they also complement each other (see also Möllering, 2001) because trust has its limits. Control is needed where trust ends. Empirical evidence for this is given in a longitudinal study of trust, control and relationship development in collaboration for innovation by Klein Woolthuis *et al.* (2005). One must also learn to trust, in finding out how far trustworthiness goes, in different aspects of behaviour. How far does someone's (or a firm's) competence go? Where are the weak spots? How robust is competence under adverse conditions? How strong are pressures of competition, and how much slack in resources does a firm have under adversity before it succumbs?

After this summary of the 'basics' of trust, this chapter focuses on the 'trust process'. The question is on what heuristics of attribution and decision trust and trustworthiness are based, and how this works out in the build-up and break-down of trust.

Knowledge and learning

As indicated in the introduction, this chapter builds on the assumption that knowledge is physically embodied and socially embedded. People perceive, interpret and evaluate the world according to mental categories (or frames or mental models) that they have developed in interaction with their social and physical environment, in 'embodied realism' (Lakoff and Johnson, 1999), with the adaptive, selectionist construction of neural nets (Edelman, 1987, 1992). The term 'knowledge' here is a broad one, and denotes any mental activity, including perception and value judgements. In other words, we see cognition and emotion (such as fear, suspicion) and body and mind as closely linked (Merleau-Ponty, 1964; Simon, 1983; Damasio, 1995; Nussbaum, 2001).

The notion that cognition is embedded, arising from interaction with the environment, goes back to Vygotsky (1962) and Piaget (1970, 1974), with their idea that 'intelligence is internalized action'. In sociology, the idea that cognition arises from the interaction of people with their (especially social) environment arises, in particular, in the 'symbolic interactionism' proposed by G. H. Mead (1934, 1982). As a result of differences in physical and cultural environments and individual paths of life that are embodied in cognition, perception, interpretation and evaluation are path-dependent and idiosyncratic to a greater or lesser extent. Different people see and experience the world differently, to the extent that they have developed in different physical, social and personal surroundings and have not interacted with each other. In other words, past experience determines absorptive capacity, and there is greater or lesser 'cognitive distance' between people (Nooteboom, 1999). This yields both an opportunity and a problem. Because one cannot 'climb down from one's mind' to assess whether one's knowledge is properly 'hooked on to the world', the variety of perception and understanding offered by other people, on the basis of a variety of experience, is the only source one has for correcting one's errors. Greater distance yields greater novelty value. However, greater distance also makes it more difficult to understand each other and to agree on aims and procedures. If effectiveness of learning by interaction depends on the mathematical product of increasing novelty and decreasing understandability, it has an inverted U-shaped relationship with cognitive distance. This entails a difference between crossing cognitive distance (in understanding people who think differently) and reducing it (thinking more alike). This is the same as the difference between empathy and identification, discussed before. As relationships last longer, cognitive distance is reduced, and identification takes place, especially if the relationship is exclusive, i.e. there are no outside relationships. That is good for trust building but bad for learning. As a result, there is also an inverted U-shaped relation between learning and the duration of a relationship. First, learning increases due to increased understanding, but then declines for lack of cognitive distance in the process of identification. For empirical tests of the hypothesis of optimal cognitive distance, see Wuyts *et al.* (2003). According to Damasio (2003), events, appraised in perception and interpretation, trigger emotions, seen as bodily responses, which may yield automatic response, but also yield feelings that may lead on to critical reflection on the perceived event, its interpretation, consequences and possible response.

How to begin, to adapt and to end a relationship?

Let us turn to a more detailed analysis of the process of trust development. First, I turn to rational analysis, and psychological processes will be elaborated later. As a transaction relation unfolds in time, one can accumulate more or less reliable information about trustworthiness. And such experience can be communicated in reputation mechanisms. The sociological literature gives extensive instructions on how to infer intentional trustworthiness from observed behaviour (Deutsch, 1973). Did the partner act not only according to the letter but also to the spirit of the agreement? Did he give timely warnings about unforeseen changes or problems? Was he open about relevant contingencies, and truthful about his dealings with others who might constitute a threat? Did he defect to more attractive alternatives at the earliest opportunity? Or, to use Hirschman's (1970) notions of 'voice' and 'exit', how much voice rather than exit did he exhibit?

In interaction, partners may get to understand each other better, which enables a better judgement of trustworthiness, in 'knowledge based trust'. In ongoing interaction they may first develop insight into each other's cognitive frames, in empathy. This does not entail that they always agree. There may be sharp disagreements, but those are combined with a willingness to express and discuss them more or less openly, in 'voice', extending mutual benefit of the doubt. As a result, conflicts may deepen the relationship rather than breaking it. Next, partners may develop shared cognitive frames, by which they may identify with each other's goals, in 'identification based trust', with understanding or even sympathy for weaknesses and mistakes (McAllister, 1995; Lewicki and Bunker, 1996).

How, then, does trust develop if there was none before, when there is no basis for *ex ante* trust based on earlier experience? The assumption here is that vulnerability cannot be avoided: to achieve its purpose the relationship entails risks of dependence. As indicated earlier (in Table 3.1), one solution might be to rely on reputation mechanisms. Zucker (1986) suggested that one may infer trustworthiness on the basis of social characteristics, such as upbringing and membership of social groups (such as families, clubs, associations of trade or profession; see also Putnam, 2000). Let us suppose, then, that neither reputation nor reliable characteristics are available.

One view is that under those conditions one can only start with control (Lewicki and Bunker, 1996), on the basis of contracts, for example, and then shift to trust as knowledge and empathy grow. One problem with that is that in learning and innovation there is likely to be too much uncertainty to specify the conditions of an extended contract, and limited opportunities for monitoring contract execution. Another possibility is to develop the relation in a careful balance of mutual dependence, so that there is a threat of retaliation when temptation towards opportunism arises. Another possibility would be to start with small steps, with limited risk, and expand vulnerability as trust grows. One problem with that is that it may take too long. Under present market conditions there is often a need for speed. To reduce risk and to speed up relationship development, one may also profit from the service of specialized intermediaries. There are a host of different types of intermediaries or go-betweens whose task it is to help judge performance and to provide intermediation or arbitration in conflicts. Shapiro (1987) called these intermediaries 'guardians of trust', Zucker (1986) saw them as part of 'institutions based trust', and Fukuyama (1995) used the term 'intermediate communities'. Many of these serve to develop and police technical or professional standards with certification systems. There are also roles for go-betweens as consultants in the management of inter-organizational relationships (Nooteboom, 2002) in offering arbitration or mediation in conflict, assessing the value of information before it is traded, creating mutual understanding (helping to cross cognitive distance), monitoring information flow as a guard against the spillover of sensitive information, guarding hostages, and supporting a reputation system. A further, and perhaps most crucial, role is to act as an intermediary in the building of trust. Trust relations are often entered into with partners who are trusted partners of someone you trust. If X trusts Y and Y trusts Z, then X may rationally give trust in Z a chance. X needs to feel that Y is able to judge well and has no intention to lie about his judgement. This can speed up the building of trust between strangers, which might otherwise take too long. Intermediation in the first small and cautious steps of cooperation, to ensure that they are successful, can be very important in the building of a trust relation. The intermediary can perform valuable services in protecting trust when it is still fragile: to eliminate misunderstanding and allay suspicions when errors or mishaps are mistaken for signals of opportunism. S/he may also help in the timely and least destructive disentanglement of relations. To eliminate misunderstanding, to prevent acrimonious and mutually damaging battles of divorce, a go-between can offer valuable services, to help in 'a voice type of exit'.

Framing and relational signalling

For a deeper analysis, we need to know more about how, in the building and breakdown of trust, people make inferences from observed behaviour, and how they act on them. In particular, we want to know how rationality and emotions are combined, and how people go beyond calculative self-interest and yet refrain from blind, unconditional trust. Here we employ insights from the theory of framing and from social psychology. The basic assumptions of framing are the following. People act on the basis of cognitive frames with different motives or goals. At any moment one frame tends to be salient or 'in focus' (Polanyi) while others are in 'subsidiary' awareness. Mental frames are connected with repertoires of action, such as threat, attack, retaliation, defence, surrender, withdrawal, avoidance, approach, offer, receipt, negotiation, etc. In human relations, two basic repertoires of action may be those of 'voice' or 'exit', proposed by Hirschman (1970). Frames, together with situational conditions, trigger behavioural routines that enact the frame. Selection and switches of frames are typically based on emotions, triggered by events in specific contexts of action. Emotions may yield automated, reflexive behaviour, or may lead on to feelings that give rise to rational considerations by which emotions may to some degree be held in check or modified. The importance of emotions here is that they form the trigger of frame switching.

Lindenberg (2003) proposed the following frames:

- 'guarding one's resources', i.e. focusing on survival or self-preservation;
- 'acting appropriately', i.e. according to norms of behaviour (in a community) or shared values (in a specific relationship), gaining social legitimation;
- 'acting as a friend';
- 'hedonics', i.e. giving in to urges of gratification.

In social psychology, Smith and Mackie (2000) recognized three basic motives of human behaviour: striving for mastery, seeking connections with others, valuing yourself and connected others. Damasio (2003) refers to Spinoza's thought in terms of two basic human drives: towards self-perpetuation, which seems similar to Lindenberg's 'guarding one's resources', and towards perfection, which seems similar to what Smith and Mackie recognized as a 'striving for mastery'. Damasio proposed a hierarchy of bodily and mental regulation, as illustrated in Figure 3.1. Here, the 'drives', which Spinoza called 'appetites', of hunger, thirst, sex, etc., seem similar to Lindenberg's 'hedonics'.

Here, for maximum simplicity, but in broad agreement with the typologies indicated above, I assume two basic sets or families of frames: self-directed (including concern for survival, resources, gratification) and other-directed (acting appropriately, as a friend, connections with others, social legitimation). Note that this brings us close to the classification of sources of (intentional) reliability in Table 3.1.

Stability of relations depends on frame stability, which depends on how salient a frame is, which depends on how strongly it is held, on what frames are subsidiary and on the extent to which they are complements or substitutes to the salient frame (Lindenberg, 2003). If, for example, the salient frame is to act in regard for others, and the frame of self-interest is subsidiary, they complement each other when self-interest is served by collaboration with others. When self-interest is threatened, beyond some tolerance level,

Feelings	
Emotions:	social emotions: sympathy, embarrassment, shame, guilt, pride, jealousy, envy, gratitude, admiration, indignation, contempt
	primary emotions: fear, anger, disgust, surprise, sadness, happiness
	background emotions (state of being): enthusiasm, edginess, excitement, tranquillity
Drives (appetites):	hunger, thirst, curiosity and exploration, play, sex
Pain and pleasure:	yielding reflexes of withdrawal, attraction, protection, expression of alarm
Immune response	
Basic reflexes:	startle reflex
Metabolic regulation:	endocrine/hormonal secretions, muscular contraction (heart, digestion), heart rate, breathing, blood pressure, storage and deployment of proteins and carbohydrates

Figure 3.1 Hierarchy of bodily and mental regulation.

Source: adapted from Damasio (2003).

the stability of an other-directed frame is precarious. This is how I reconstruct the limits of trust in psychological terms. The analysis leads on to the notion of 'relational signalling': perceived actions operate as signals that indicate in what frame of mind the other person is, and how stable that frame is. This, in turn, leads to an analysis of what effects one's own actions may have on triggering or maintaining an other-directed frame on the part of the other person.

Decision heuristics

The question now is what heuristics are used in these processes of the formation, selection and enactment of frames. Here I turn to decision heuristics proposed in social psychology by Bazerman (1998):

- Representativeness heuristic: the likelihood of an event is assessed by its similarity to stereotypes of similar occurrences.
- Availability heuristic: people assess the probability and likely causes of an event by the degree to which instances of it are 'readily available' in memory, i.e. are vivid, laden with emotion, familiar, recent and recognizable. Less available events and causes are neglected.
- Anchoring and adjustment. Judgement is based on some initial or base value ('anchor') from previous experience or social comparison, plus incremental adjustment from that value. People have been shown to stay close even to random anchors that bear no systematic relation to the issue

at hand. First impressions can influence the development of a relation for a long time.

These heuristics serve to give more substance to the notion of absorptive capacity, i.e. the ability to perceive and interpret phenomena, and to the claim, made in embodied cognition, that rationality and emotions are inter-twined. The heuristics are not rational in a calculative sense (*calculative rationality*). Indeed, they serve to show how bounded rationality works. However, they are 'adaptively rational' in the sense of contributing to survival under uncertainty and bounded rationality, and the need, in many situations, to decide and act quickly (*adaptive rationality*). Nevertheless, they can lead to error, as will be discussed. In the elaboration of these heuristics I present what I make of them, from the perspective of embodied cognition and framing theory, and this may deviate from established practice in social psychology.

Prospect theory (Tversky and Kahneman, 1983) has demonstrated that people are not risk-neutral, and tend to be risk-taking when a decision is framed in terms of loss, and risk-averse when it is framed in terms of gain. This entails people accepting a greater risk of conflict when they stand to incur a loss than when they stand to make a gain. As a result, the frame of guarding resources, or going for material self-interest, splits up into a frame of loss and a frame of gain. Related to this effect is the *endowment effect*: people often demand more money to sell what they have than they would be prepared to pay to get it. In the first case one wants to cover for loss.

Yet another psychological mechanism is that in violation of rational behaviour sunk costs, such as sacrifices made in a relationship, are not seen as bygones that should be ignored in an assessment of future costs and benefits. They are seen as sacrifices that would be seen as in vain if one pulled out after incurring them. This yields what is known as *non-rational escalation of commitment*. It is associated with *cognitive dissonance*: cutting one's losses and pulling out would entail an admission of failure, of having made a bad decision in the past. Deutsch (1973) gave the example of the United States finding it increasingly difficult to pull out of Vietnam as the number of casualties accumulated. The phenomenon is confirmed in empirical research, which shows that when the decision is to be made by someone not involved in the initial commitment, or when the threat of an admission of failure is removed, the rational decision to pull out is made. Again, one cannot say that this mechanism is always bad, because it also demonstrates perseverance in the face of setbacks, which can be a good thing, and is in fact a trait of many a successful innovating entrepreneur. This phenomenon can be connected with the effect of a loss frame versus a gain frame. The person, or group, that made the initial decision experiences a loss frame, with the inclination to accept further risk in order to prevent acceptance of the loss. The decision maker who enters fresh experiences a gain frame, to make a decision that will offer profit or prevent further loss in the future, regardless of past sunk costs.

Evolutionary psychologists claim that certain psychological features or mechanisms are 'in our genes' as a result of evolution (Barkow *et al.*, 1992). They emerged as features that gave selective or reproductive advantage, over the millions of years that the human species evolved in hunter–gatherer societies. For example, survival required the basic ability to identify objects and movement, to categorize natural kinds (plants, animals), distinguish the animate from the inanimate, and natural kinds from artefacts (Tooby and Cosmides, 1992: 71). On top of that, it requires the ability to recognize objects, judge speed and distance, to avoid predators and to catch prey (Tooby and Cosmides, 1992: 110). Survival also requires mother–infant emotion communication signals (Tooby and Cosmides, 1992: 39). Such instincts contribute to the heuristics of availability and representatives in our framing of the world.

These heuristics and principles from social and evolutionary psychology are consistent with the perspective of embodied cognition, and indeed serve to elucidate and extend it, in their integration with emotions, their pragmatic role in survival under conditions of radical uncertainty, and their embedding in processes of practical action.

Application to trust

In my interpretation, the *representativeness heuristic* constitutes our repertoire for categorization, i.e. what we *can* attend to, in our absorptive capacity. There is a connection with the role of 'prototypes' or 'exemplars' in language and categorization (Rosch, 1978; Nooteboom, 2000). Since definitions can seldom offer necessary and sufficient conditions for categorization, and meaning is context-dependent and open-ended, allowing for variation and change, we need prototypes. Prototypes are salient exemplars of a class that guides categorization by assessing similarity to the prototype. We try to fit or assimilate observed behaviour into prototypes in our cognitive repertoire, and when we recognize some features as fitting, we tend to attribute remaining, unobserved attributes that belong to the prototype. The mechanism of attributing unobserved characteristics upon recognition of observed ones enables fast pattern recognition, which is conducive to survival. The downside of the representativeness heuristic is that it also yields prejudice, in the premature, erroneous application of stereotypes, and in mistaken attributions. In the present framework, the representativeness heuristic regulates the *cognitive content* of frames in terms of the categories that they employ. In the context of trust, I see the representativeness heuristic as providing benchmarks, in the form of prototypes, for efficient, fast identification of trustworthy and untrustworthy behaviour, and guidelines or exemplars for trustworthy behaviour. In organizations such prototypes for trust are often part of organizational culture. The *availability heuristic*, in my interpretation, regulates what we *actually* attend to, by filtering impressions, in emotions that contribute to the selection of frames. If we did not apply such filters, our consciousness would likely be overloaded. We cannot afford to pay attention to everything that is presented to our senses, and we need to select what appears to be salient and urging attention. Much of our conduct is based on routines that are relegated to subsidiary awareness. Then, as discussed earlier, we need emotions to catapult attention back into focal awareness when a threat or new opportunity emerges. Emotions tend to be stronger when personal desires or interests are at stake than in more abstract, impersonal motives. Thus, frames of hedonism and 'guarding resources' tend to acquire salience more easily than a normative frame (Lindenberg, 2003). However, when the desire to 'act appropriately' is based on emotions of friendship or kinship, it will have greater 'availability'.

As noted before, trust may become routinized, when a relationship has been going well for a while. Trustworthiness is taken for granted, until something exceptional arises, in observed behaviour or conditions that might yield a temptation or pressure that a partner may not be able to resist. This evokes feelings of fear, suspicion or indignation that break routinized trust open to critical scrutiny. Earlier, we noted the role of identification in trust, on the basis of shared categories concerning motives and conditions of behaviour. Here, availability is based on familiarity. It affects both one's own trustworthiness, in the willingness to make sacrifices for others, and one's trust, in the tolerance of behaviour that deviates from expectations. One will more easily help someone when one can identify with his need. One can more easily forgive someone's breach of trust or reliance when one can identify with the lack of competence or the motive that caused it. One can more easily accept the blame for oneself. Since one can identify with him, one may sympathize with his action, seeing, perhaps, that it was in fact a just response to one's own previous actions. One might have reacted in the same fashion as he did.

While it is adaptively rational, the availability heuristic yields several problems. One is that anger may overshoot its function of calling attention and propels impulsive defensive or retaliatory conduct. Another problem is that attention is called only by extreme emotional appeals, so that more subdued, nuanced appeals and weak signals tend to be ignored. The availability heuristic yields useful emotional triggers to create focal awareness of possible risk in relations, but next one should be careful not to jump to conclusions, and to exercise the benefit of the doubt wherever possible. This is the case, in particular, because when 'things go wrong' in a relationship, there may be a multitude of possible causes: an accident, lack of resources, lack of competence and opportunism. One may jump to assuming the worst, opportunism, while that conclusion is not justified.

Anchoring and adjustment indicates that once we select a frame, with corresponding behavioural routines, we do not easily drop it. Deutsch (1973) also argued that beginnings are important and may be difficult to turn around. He suggested that there is circular causation between characteristics of participants and the results of interaction in his 'crude law of social relations': 'The characteristic processes and effects elicited by a given type of social relationship (cooperative or competitive) tend also to elicit that type of social relationship.' Under uncertainty cognition does need such an anchor. Studies of learning and adjustment have shown that hasty and large departures from existing practices can yield chaotic behaviour (March, 1991; Lounamaa and March, 1987). It is adaptively rational to experiment with small, proximate change and to accumulate motivation for more radical change, as well as insights into directions and elements of change that are likely to be viable and worth the upheaval (Nooteboom, 2000). However, this heuristic also entails risk of inertia: the inability to make needed drastic change in the face of a crisis.

This heuristic is related to the notion of trust as a default, and routinized trust. The notions of default and routine entail that one sticks to an established form of behaviour until new evidence compels its change. As already noted, the heuristic of anchoring and adjustment entails that beginnings are often difficult to turn around. This relates back to the discussion of how to start a relationship when at the beginning there is no basis for trust. If one takes the advice from Lewicki and Bunker to start on the basis of control, this may be seen as a sign of distrust, which is not only likely to evoke a similar response, with the risk of a vicious circle of control upon control that constrains the scope for flexibility, improvisation and innovation in the relationship, but may also be difficult to turn into trust as the relationship develops.

These heuristics appear to complement each other. Representativeness determines how one can interpret behaviour, availability determines which interpretation is triggered, and anchoring stabilizes chosen behavioural routines. Of the three, availability is the most laden with emotion, and representativeness is the most concerned with learning. Availability causes frame switches, and anchoring and adjustment serve to constrain such switches. The first is needed for guarding survival, the latter is needed to make framing less unstable and precarious.

The notion of a *loss versus a gain frame*, from prospect theory, has important implications for the stability of relationships (Nooteboom, 2004). It was noted earlier that one way to start a relationship without prior trust is to develop it in a careful balance of mutual dependence. Then, however, the problem often is that the balance is broken by a change of conditions, such as a change of technology or market whereby existing competences lose relevance, in different degrees for different partners, or the emergence in the arena of a new player who yields a more attractive alternative for one of the partners. This partner may then want to exit while the other partner wants to hold on to him. Then, the first partner is in a gain frame (getting more out of an alternative relationship), while the other is in a loss frame (losing a valuable partner). According to the theory, the latter would go to greater extremes, in emotional and even self-destructive actions (slander, hopeless litigation), to retain the partner, than the other partner would engage in to realize his exit.

The phenomenon of *escalation of commitment* also contributes to the stability of a relationship. After a relationship has cost an accumulation of sacrifice, it may become increasingly difficult to exit from it, since that would suggest that past sacrifices were wasted. Such partnership may quickly unravel under new management that is not compromised by past sacrifices.

In sum, there appear to be three mechanisms for the stabilization of relationships: anchoring, loss versus gain, and escalation of commitment. Evolutionary psychology claims that in the hunter–gatherer societies in which man evolved, the variance of yields, in gathering edible plants, roots, nuts, etc., and even more in hunting, with the impossibility of instantly consuming large game, together with problems of durable storage, entails an evolutionary advantage of *reciprocity*, in the willingness to surrender part of one's yield to others in need, in the expectation of receiving from them when they are successful (Cosmides and Tooby, 1992: 212).[1] This is enhanced by the supposed ability to assess such willingness among others, in a 'cheater detection mechanism', and to signal a credible, often emotion-laden threat to sanction lack of reciprocity (Frank, 1988). This purported natural inclination towards reciprocity would contribute to a solution of the problem, discussed before, of how to start a relationship without trust based on prior experience, while allowing trust to develop. Presumably, the principle works only under conditions of stability of communities, where recipients of goodwill will 'stay around' to engage in reciprocity. A similar condition was discussed for a reputation mechanism. Reciprocity and reputation are mutually reinforcing.

The heuristics have implications not only for starting and adapting a relationship, but also for ending one. The ending of relationships is at least as important as the issue of starting one, in view of the fact that relationships may last too long, yielding too much identification, resulting in lack of cognitive variety for further innovation. Nooteboom (1999, 2004) proposed that there is a hostile and a collaborative mode of exit from a relationship. In the hostile mode, one would try to prepare one's exit, no longer engaging in relation-specific investments, retrieving hostages, and building up investments in a new relationship, as surreptitiously as one can, and then spring a surprise exit on the partner, who is left with the unforeseen damage of worthless specific investments and a discontinuity in production. In the collaborative mode, in a 'voice mode of exit', one would announce one's intentions towards exit ahead of time, help the partner to disentangle the relationship with minimum damage, and help to find a replacement. The advantage of the latter mode would be that the partner is less in a loss frame, and hence less likely to take radical actions of binding and retaliation. There is a risk, however, that the partner would have more time and opportunity to take such actions. Here, the anchoring and adjustment heuristic also kicks in. If the relationship had been collaborative, based on benevolence, that would set the norm, and a hostile mode of exit would constitute a greater shock than in a more calculative relationship, with greater risks of extreme retaliatory behaviour.

In sum, the decision heuristics and other phenomena from social and evolutionary psychology are highly relevant to the development of trust, because they affect attribution of characteristics, expectations of trustworthiness, and choice of action.

Theory of the firm

For firms to function, I propose and will argue here that they must offer conditions for trust to develop and be maintained. Indeed, one of the reasons for firms to exist is that they can offer such conditions that go beyond the wider institutional conditions for trust that are part of an ordered society, in conditions that are more specialized and tailored to the activities of the firm. This view is part of a wider view of the firm as a 'focusing device' (Nooteboom, 1992, 2000). The argument for that view of the firm is based on the theory of knowledge summarized in an earlier section. If there is cognitive distance between people as the result of differences in life paths, along which cognitive categories are developed, then to achieve efficiency in collaboration cognitive distance must be limited, to some extent, in a shared cognitive 'focus' of what the purpose of the firm is, what knowledge is to be taken for granted, and what values and norms apply for the coordination of activities and conflict resolution. Such focus constitutes the cultural identity of the firm that forms a distinctive style of operations. Without such focus, too much time would be lost in the explication of meanings and the elimination of misunderstandings, the setting of priorities, the design of procedures, and the prevention and resolution of conflicts. Such focus has a substantive cognitive dimension, related to competence, and a moral dimension, related to governance. The first affects competence trust and the latter affects intentional trust. This view is similar to transaction cost economics (TCE) in that it explains the firm, in part, as a means of governance, but it is different in that it also assigns a cognitive function to the firm and in that governance is a matter also of culture, not only of monitoring and control.

The moral dimension of organizational focus can now be further specified on the basis of the determinants of trust set out above. To set the conditions for reliability we can use Table 3.1. A firm can choose what sources of reliability it wants to employ, and when it has no deliberate policy, conditions that have emerged unintentionally will affect the conditions of reliability. Concerning the self-interested motives, for opportunity control a firm can institute generalized rules of conduct ('macro'), or leave it up to direct hierarchical control in specific relationships (micro). The first entails the monitoring of compliance, which may not always be feasible, and the latter raises the question of what codes of conduct managers should employ, and what competences they have, in their monitoring and control of opportunistic conduct. For incentive control the firm could employ an internal reputation mechanism. This may work when people have the freedom to decline cooperation with people with a bad reputation. Reputation mechanisms are not automatic, and one must avoid false, unfounded gossip and ostracism. For sources of trust more properly speaking, i.e. benevolence, one needs a set of moral values and norms, on the macro side, or one goes for more personal, 'thick trust' between people on the basis of empathy, identification, routinization and personal affect. Here the notion of 'communities of practice' comes to mind. One problem with values and norms is that they tend to be fairly general and abstract, and may not give specific guidance in specific conditions. In view of that one may, and firms often do, resort to exemplars or prototypes of proper conduct, in organizational stories or myths, supported by symbols, that are set as examples to be emulated. A possible danger of the latter type of source, in personal relations, is that groups close themselves off to outsiders and become too inward looking. In the choice of sources of reliability, there is no single best design.

Often, organizational focus and culture bear an imprint from the founder of the firm, whose conduct and preferences set the values, norms and practices of a firm, which are subsequently perpetuated by the selection and self-selection of staff joining the firm, and processes of socialization into the firm. Especially the use of exemplary behaviour, discussed before, perpetuates styles of conduct. The heuristic of anchoring and adjustment, discussed above, contributes to the perpetuation of practices.

What works for a firm depends on contingencies related to the kind of work involved, related to products and markets, and corresponding types of technology and knowledge. Those have implications, in particular, for opportunities for monitoring and programming conduct, which are relevant for the more control-oriented sources. In view of the limits of trust, discussed before, one should be aware that trust depends, in this case, on internal competition for jobs and positions, and on guarantees or threats of employment as a function of economic and market conditions. What works under favourable conditions may break down in crisis, and vice versa. That is why under a shift of conditions a replacement of top management may be needed, to shift to a different style of governance, in an attempt to turn around the culture.

Using the mental framing and relational signalling approach, Six (2005) analysed 'trust and trouble' in two contrasting firms, investigating what actions engender the emergence and stability of the other-directed frame of 'acting appropriately', to support trust, and how this differed between the two organizations, depending on organizational culture. A core question was when trouble yields a breakdown of trust, when suspicion accompanied by the benefit of the doubt in a wary continuation of a relationship, and when a deepening of trust due to the resolution of conflict. As an example of organizational prototypes of behaviour, Six found in one of the two firms, but not the other, the precept that in case of trouble, 'people should not complain *about* people but *to* them'. Here, the organizational ethic is one of voice: when trouble arises, be open about it and try to work it out together. Another precept in that organization, but not the other, was to give public compliments to staff whenever that was justified.

The decision heuristics, discussed above, help to identify and understand actions that are likely to trigger or maintain other-directed mental frames, and to prevent a switch to self-interested frames that yield undue suspicion and fear. Six (2005) identified 21 potential trust building actions. Such actions can be classified according to their effects. For example, according to the *loss vs. gain frame*, it is important to prevent a mistaken sense of loss, which may yield an emotion-laden response of fear, suspicion and defence. One way of doing this is to bolster the self-confidence of a partner by demonstrating his strength and contributions to the relationship. This is one way of interpreting the effect of giving public compliments. It was noted earlier that trust suffers from causal ambiguity: when something goes wrong it may be due to a mishap, a shortfall of competence, or a shortfall of intentions. For this reason, openness is important for trust and the willingness to accept influence from a partner (Zand, 1972), to give insight into what is happening for what reasons and causes, and to accept correction. It is also important to prevent undue disappointments, which requires clarity about what can and cannot be expected.

On the basis of a questionnaire survey among a thousand managers in Europe that were clients of a firm supplying management and sales training, Six and Nooteboom (2005) found that 19 out of 21 hypothesized trust building actions were indeed significantly correlated with trust. Using factor analysis, they found that five hypothesized classes of actions were indeed confirmed (explained variance better than the null hypothesis of only one or fewer factors). These classes were the following: enact solidarity (demonstrate care and help), accept influence, prevent misunderstandings (about expectations and about events), and bolster self-confidence. Such classes of action provide repertoires that firms can employ or not, and can be supported by means of organizational procedures, rules or values, as part of organizational culture.

Conclusions

A central claim of this chapter is that for an understanding of how trust is built up and broken down, and how trust can go beyond calculative self-interest without becoming blind or unconditional, we may profit from the application of the theory of framing, relational signalling and decision heuristics derived from social psychology. They are consistent with the perspective of embodied cognition, and yield an elaboration of it. In particular, they elaborate the idea that rationality and emotions are intertwined, and that psychological mechanisms arise from conduct that is selected for survival. A frame is an intentional stance, guiding perception and action, which focuses on a limited range of possible other-directed or self-interested goals or motives. At any moment one frame tends to be salient while others are subsidiary, and perceptions of events may cause switches. This helps to understand the limits of trust. Decision heuristics help to explain how this happens. The following heuristics are discussed:

- the representativeness heuristic;
- the availability heuristic;
- the anchoring and adjustment heuristic;
- the phenomenon of escalation of commitment;
- the phenomenon of cognitive dissonance;
- the notion of a loss frame versus a gain frame;
- the notion of an instinct for reciprocity, combined with a cheater detection mechanism.

The representativeness heuristic was interpreted as yielding a repertoire of possible frames and behavioural routines, constituting a cognitive repertoire, in the form of prototypes, in terms of which judgements of (un)trustworthiness are made and translated into action. The availability heuristic was interpreted as determining which frames are salient and which are subsidiary, and how switching between them occurs. This is governed by emotions and by familiarity. Emotions serve to break behavioural routines open for scrutiny. On the other hand, the heuristic of anchoring and adjustment, escalation of commitment, and the notion of a loss versus a gain frame serve to stabilize behaviour. Anchoring and adjustment clarify why it may be difficult to turn suspicion around into trust and why it is risky to take a hostile, abrupt approach to exit if the relationship was based on benevolence and voice. The notion of an instinct towards reciprocity helps to start a relationship in which there is no prior trust based on experience.

Here also we find paradoxes. These heuristics and phenomena are adaptively rational, given bounded rationality and the pressure to survive under conditions of radical uncertainty and the need for speedy response. However, they can yield irrational actions, in prejudice, blindness, injustice, inertia, lack of adaptiveness under crises, and impulsive behaviour. They help to enable and support the building of trust, but may also prevent it, and may cause unjustified breakdowns of trust.

A recurrent theme in the process of trust is openness, in a voice-based approach. The importance of that was argued earlier by Zand (1972). Since there may be many causes of disappointed expectations, it is important to be open about problems that one may cause to a partner. Silence until the problem becomes manifest is likely to be interpreted as a sign of the worst possibility of opportunistic behaviour. An imposition of control and requisite monitoring has adverse effects, indicated before, of a vicious circle of control that blocks scope for learning and innovation, and starts a relation on a footing of mistrust that may be difficult to turn around. If, on the other hand, one voluntarily accepts or even invites some control by the partner, and opens up to monitoring, this greatly facilitates trust building. This indicates the importance of voluntary transparency for trust relationships. A timely announcement of intentions to exit may greatly help to disentangle relationships without too much damage. If one shies away from exhibiting one's fears of relational risk, one thereby robs the partner of the opportunity to reduce that risk.

The analysis of trust has implications for the theory of the firm. In a cognitive theory of the firm, the firm serves as a focusing device, for people to share basic views of the world and of how people (should) interact, in order to efficiently achieve shared goals. Such organizational focus is reflected in and based on organizational culture. The analysis of framing and relational signalling yields a taxonomy of trust building actions that help to trigger and maintain other-directed mental frames and to prevent switching to self-interested frames that destroy trust. Firms are characterized by actions employed in the building or destruction of trust, and by cultural features that enhance such actions.

Note

1 The argument requires that group selection is viable. In spite of earlier arguments that group selection is dominated by individual selection, according to later arguments it can be viable. That is the case if opportunistic intruders into a reciprocity-based society are pre-empted before they get a chance to develop reproductive advantage (Ridley, 1997).

References

Barkow, J., Cosmides, L. and Tooby, J. (1992), *The Adapted Mind: Evolutionary Psychology and the Generation of Culture*, Oxford: Oxford University Press.

Bazerman, M. (1998), *Judgment in Managerial Decision Making*, New York: Wiley.

Bradach, J. L. and Eccles, R. G. (1984), 'Markets versus hierarchies: from ideal types to plural forms', in W. R. Scott (ed.), *Annual Review of Sociology*, 15: 97–118.

Chiles, T. H. and McMackin, J. F. (1996), 'Integrating variable risk preferences, trust and transaction cost economics', *Academy of Management Review*, 21(7): 73–99.

Cosmides, L. and Tooby, J. (1992), 'Cognitive adaptations for social exchange', in H. Barkow, L. Cosmides and J. Tooby, *The Adapted Mind*, Oxford: Oxford University Press, pp. 163–228.

Damasio, A. R. (1995), *Descartes' Error: Emotion, Reason and the Human Brain*, London: Picador.

——(2003), *Looking for Spinoza*, Orlando, FL: Harcourt.

Deutsch, M. (1973), *The Resolution of Conflict: Constructive and Destructive Processes*, New Haven, CT: Yale University Press.

Edelman, G. M. (1987), *Neural Darwinism: The Theory of Neuronal Group Selection*, New York: Basic Books.

——(1992), *Bright Air, Brilliant Fire; On the Matter of Mind*, Harmondsworth: Penguin.

Frank, R. H. (1988), *Emotions Within Reason: The Strategic Role of the Emotions*, New York: W.W. Norton.

Fukuyama, F. (1995), *Trust, the Social Virtues and the Creation of Prosperity*, New York: Free Press.

Hirschman, A. O. (1970), *Exit, Voice and Loyalty: Responses to Decline in Firms, Organisations and States*, Cambridge, MA: Harvard University Press.

Klein Woolthuis, R., Hillebrand, B. and Nooteboom, B. (2005), 'Trust, Contract and relationship development', *Organization Studies*, 26(6): 813–40.

Lakoff, G. and Johnson, M. (1999), *Philosophy in the Flesh*, New York: Basic Books.

Lewicki, R. J. and Bunker, B. B. (1996), 'Developing and Maintaining trust in work relationships', in R. M. Kramer and T. R. Tyler (eds), *Trust in Organizations: Frontiers of Theory Research*, Thousand Oaks, CA: Sage Publications, pp. 114–39.

Lindenberg, S. (1998), 'Solidarity: its microfoundations and macro-dependence: a framing approach', in P. Doreian and T. J. Farro (eds), *The Problem of Solidarity: Theories and Models*, Amsterdam: Gordon and Breach, pp. 61–112.

—— (2003), 'Governance from a framing point of view: the employment relationship and relational signalling', in B. Nooteboom and F. Six, *The Trust Process in Organizations*, Cheltenham, UK: Edward Elgar, pp. 37–57.

Lounamaa, P. H. and March, J. G. (1987), 'Adaptive coordination of a learning team', *Management Science*, 33: 107–23.

McAllister, D. J. (1995), 'Affect- and cognition based trust as foundations for interpersonal cooperation in organizations', *Academy of Management Journal*, 38(1): 24–59.

Maguire, S., Philips, N. and Hardy, C. (2001), 'When "silence = death", keep talking: trust, control and the discursive construction of identity in the Canadian HIV/AIDS treatment domain', *Organization Studies*, 22(2): 285–310.

March, J. (1991), 'Exploration and exploitation in organizational learning', *Organization Science*, 2(1): 101–23.

Mead, G. H. (1934), *Mind, Self and Society; From the Standpoint of a Social Behaviorist*, Chicago, IL: Chicago University Press.

—— (1982), *The Individual and the Social Self*, unpublished work of G. H. Mead, ed. D. L. Miller, Chicago, IL: University of Chicago Press.

Merleau-Ponty, M. (1942), *La structure du comportement*, Paris: Presses Universitaires de France.

—— (1964), *Le visible et l'invisible*, Paris: Gallimard.

Möllering, G. (2001), 'The nature of trust: from Georg Simmel to a theory of expectation, interpretation and suspension', *Sociology* 35(2): 403–20.

Nooteboom, B. (1992), 'Towards a dynamic theory of transactions', *Journal of Evolutionary Economics* 2: 281–99.

—— (1999), *Inter-Firm Alliances: Analysis and Design*, London: Routledge.

—— (2000), *Learning and Innovation in Organizations and Economies*, Oxford: Oxford University Press.

—— (2002), *Trust: Forms, Foundations, Functions, Failures and Figures*, Cheltenham, UK: Edward Elgar.

—— (2004), *Inter-Firm Collaboration, Learning and Networks: An Integrated Approach*, London: Routledge.

Nussbaum, M. C. (2001), *Upheavals of Thought: The Intelligence of Emotions*, Cambridge: Cambridge University Press.

Pagden, A. (1988), 'The destruction of trust and its economic consequences in the case of eighteenth-century Naples', in D. Gambetta (ed.), *Trust, the Making and Breaking of Cooperative Relations*, Oxford: Blackwell, pp. 127–41.

Piaget, J. (1970), *Psychologie et epistémologie*, Paris: Denoël.

—— (1974), *Introduction à l'épistémologie génétique*, I and II, Paris: Presses Universitaires de France.

Polanyi, M. (1962), *Personal Knowledge*, London: Routledge.

Putnam, R. D. (2000), *Bowling Alone; The Collapse and Revival of American Community*, New York: Simon and Schuster.

Ridley, M. (1997), *The Origins of Virtue*, London: Viking Press.

Ring, P. Smith and van de Ven, A. (1992), 'Structuring cooperative relationships between organizations', *Strategic Management Journal*, 13: 483–98.

——(1994), 'Developmental processes of cooperative interorganizational relationships', *Academy of Management Review*, 19(1): 90–118.

Rosch, E. (1978), 'Principles of categorization', in E. Rosch and B. B. Lloyd (eds), *Cognition and Categorization*, Hillsdale, NJ: Erlbaum, pp. 27–48.

Shapiro, S. P. (1987), 'The social control of impersonal trust', *American Journal of Sociology*, 93: 623–58.

Simon, H. A. (1983), *Reason in Human Affairs,* Oxford: Basil Blackwell.

Simon, H. A. and Nooteboom, B. (2005), 'Trust building actions: a relational signalling approach', paper in review.

Six, F. (2005), *The Trouble about Trust: The Dynamics of Interpersonal Trust Building*, Cheltenham, UK: Edward Elgar

Smith, E. R. and Mackie, D. M. (2000), *Social Psychology*, Philadelphia, PA: Taylor and Francis.

Tooby, J. and Cosmides, L. (1992), 'The psychological foundations of culture', in J. H. Barkow, L. Cosmides and J. Tooby, *The Adapted Mind*, Oxford: Oxford University Press, pp. 19–136.

Tversky, A. and Kahneman, D. (1983), 'Probability, representativeness, and the conjunction fallacy', *Psychological Review*, 90(4): 293–315.

Vygotsky, L. (1962), *Thought and Language*, ed. and trans. E. Hanfmann and G. Varkar, Cambridge, MA: MIT Press.

Wuyts, S., Colombo, M. G., Dutta, S. and Nooteboom, B. (2003), *Empirical Tests of Optimal Cognitive Distance*, Research Report, Erasmus Institute for Research in Management, Erasmus University, Rotterdam.

Zand, D. E. (1972), 'Trust and managerial problem solving', *Administrative Science Quarterly*, 17(2): 229–39.

Zucker, L. G. (1986), 'Production of trust: institutional sources of economic structure', in B. M. Staw and L. L. Cummings, *Research in Organizational Behaviour* 8: 53–111.

4 Accounting and the economic analysis of the firm as an entity

Yuri Biondi[1]

Introduction

The box that neo-classical theory designs for the firm appears neither black nor empty. The skeletal machinery built on marginal cost pricing ought to grasp the economic and monetary process inside the firm, at least in its fundamental elements and results. Together with some 'principle of maximisation' and with perfect competition on efficient markets for all factors or products, this machinery aims to explain selling price, cost, quantity and the resultant (no) profit for each product separately. This bundle of instruments allows *the price system alone to dominate the firm*, at least from an economic viewpoint, when creation and allocation of resources are concerned.

Following Coase, Shubik and Simon, instead, the inner working of organisation and of the accounting system is called into question for understanding how the special economy of the firm supersedes the price system. This chapter aims to develop this issue, exploring the accounting system, its nature and role in the special economy of the firm concerned with real dynamics and complexity.

In this context, the accounting system copes with the economic and monetary process generated by the whole firm and tries to jointly represent business capital and income related to the firm seen as an entity. By the working of an accounting system, then, the special process of the firm acquires autonomous but interdependent existence from external markets (both factor and product markets). The accounting system constitutes the 'veil' that allows this special process to exist. A further glance at the entity view provided by dynamic accounting also enhances the economic understanding of the separation between ownership, control *and management* (as discussed some years ago by Berle and Littleton), not only between ownership and control alone. *Even to protect shareholders*, this kind of control and *accountability* is required, far away from the irrevocably lost proprietary sovereignty.

From this perspective, the firm as an entity functions and exists as a *managed dynamic system* characterised by different structures of production: institutional, organisational or epistemic (related to the nature and role of institutions, internal organisation and knowledge in the firm). The accounting system becomes a constituent of these structures and of the whole firm. The new transactional and institutional perspective opens up to an interdisciplinary approach linking economics, accounting and law, by the shared, synthetic notion of the firm as an *entity*, which provides the 'clue' for understanding the nature of the firm as a *whole* and a *dynamic system*.

The following discussion is organised into three sections. The first section discusses some recent suggestions by Coase and Shubik calling for an exploration of the relationship between accounting and the economic nature of the firm. The second section explains how and why accounting provides a special view of the firm that economics should integrate. This view is especially concerned with the economic and monetary process generated by the whole firm. The third section will finally demonstrate how this accounting view offers further implications for a new theory of the firm based on the synthetic, interdisciplinary notion of the firm as an entity.

Accounting and the economic nature of the firm: the missing connection

Why delve into accounting to understand the nature of the firm? Under *price system* economics, institutions are relegated to an exogenous framework that plays a very limited and passive role in the economic and monetary process.[2] Business entities are neutral (so-called 'black boxes') and institutions simply do not matter. Notwithstanding, the box that neo-classical theory designs for the firm appears neither black nor empty. The skeletal machinery built on marginal cost pricing ought to grasp the economic and monetary process inside the firm, at least in its fundamental elements and results. Together with some 'principle of maximisation' and with perfect competition on efficient markets for all factors or products, this machinery therefore aims to explain selling price, cost, quantity and the resultant (no) profit for each product separately. This bundle of instruments allows the price system alone to dominate the firm, at least from the economic viewpoint, when creation and allocation of resources are concerned.

When we turn to this equilibrium economics with increasing degrees of abstraction and sophistication, not only institutions, but also real dynamics and complexity vanish. All problems involving the complexity of one business entity having its own accounting, organisation and management, dealing with its inner working rules and norms, coping with bounded knowledge, accountable for its business capital and income streams, are abstracted away in the broad framework provided by the price system.

> Time and uncertainty have essentially disappeared from this apotheosis of the price system. But it is time and uncertainty which are the concerns of everyday economic life and the problems of how to account for the influence of time and uncertainty in the ongoing economic process are central to the development of accounting.
>
> (Shubik, 1993: 228)[3]

Just like all the other institutions, accounting also (in all its manifestations) has been neglected for a long while and relegated to the margins of analysis, although such leading economists as Walras, Menger, Pantaleoni, Schumpeter and Hicks paid special attention to its role. For all intents and purposes, the views, principles and working norms embedded into accounting did not matter.

In such a way, the economic analysis of the firm framed by equilibrium economics has dealt essentially with statics. Microeconomic theory shows the virtues of a firm fundamentally framed by the price system, but abstracts from price formation, overheads allocation and all the problems raised by microeconomic accounting, which appear in real dynamics and complexity. Such a theory represents, at best, an *ex ante* mode of functioning based on atomistic elements or individuals alone, and indeed neglects the genuine implications of the actual dynamics for the whole firm confronted with real hazard and complexity.

First and foremost, accounting grapples with the dynamics (and the complexity) of the firm, trying to cope with ongoing, enduring problems of day-by-day and year-by-year managing, organising and knowing. A reconciliation between accounting and economic theory is hence required if we want to understand the key cognitive and economic processes of a modern society.

Looking for a reconciled framework, the 'new institutional revolution' fostered by Coase appears to be encouraging. This perspective deals with the opposite insight from usual neo-classical economics: institutions matter and the firm must have its special economics, alternative and complementary to the price system. Concerned with the process of creation and allocation of resources, Coase has especially stressed: (a) the economic distinction between firm and market, i.e. how the firm *supersedes* the price system; (b) the *active* role of legal institutions in the special economic process thus generated by the firm; (c) the inner working of organisation and of accounting systems as key tools for this special economics of the firm.

In his 'classic' on the nature of the firm, Coase (1937) characterises this nature as direction of resources (provided either by employees or shareholders). He distinguishes the market transaction, characterised by 'marketing costs', or 'costs of using the price mechanism', and the firm, characterised by some 'decreasing returns to the entrepreneur function' already advocated by Kaldor (1934). In more recent papers (Coase, 1988), the firm is further understood as management (running a business),[4] dealing with 'the range of goods and services supplied, the pricing practices, the contractual arrangements, the forms of economic organization' (Coase, 1988: 63). The old-fashioned link[5] with such a mythic personage as the proprietary entrepreneur is to some extent dismissed,[6] and the firm is especially characterised by its own accounting system (Coase, 1990) as a feature distinct from the price system provided by the market.

In this planned society, the firm costs do not, in the main, arise directly out of the operations of the market but are computed and provided by the accounting system. While outside the firm prices and therefore costs are explicit (because of the demands of others for resources) and are determined by the operations of the market, within the firm there are explicit costs *for exactly the same reason* but they are provided by the accounting system. This internal system takes the place of the pricing system of the market.

(Coase, 1990: 11, italics added)

The danger with such a dualism between the firm and the market is to misunderstand the effective interaction and the nature of both, for example by *personifying* the firm or the market. This approach understands every economic interaction as *make or buy, own or hire* decisions. Its geometrical metaphor is simply a continuum – a straight line between two merely contrasting terms.

Firm	Market
Accounting system	*Price system*

From the economic viewpoint, the market is not a person and, in particular, cannot act as a person; nor can the firm. More properly, the market is a *price system* which, new theories suggest, interacts with the firm as alternative but complementary modes of the functioning of economic activity. The firm as a whole does not act, but constitutes the *managed economic system* that creates and maintains the favourable conditions allowing the business activity to become and fulfil needs if possible. In this context, Coase (1990) neglects to link the accounting system to the 'institutional structure of production' (Coase, 1992), which was and still is understood only in an ownership perspective based on property rights alone.

In the spirit of Coase and Shubik, therefore, a new transactional and institutional perspective should delve into accounting as a mode of looking inside the firm to grasp its special economic process. In fact, these scholars give us the idea but they do not develop it far enough. This chapter aims to develop this accounting and economics issue, exploring the accounting system and its nature and role in the special economics of the firm.

The accounting contribution to the economics of the firm

In spite of the above insights of Coase himself, its early promoter, incomplete contracts economics (either transaction costs theory, positive agency theory or property rights theory) does not deal very well with important legal and accounting features of the 'structure of production' generated by the firm:

- Its notion of 'property rights' is not what the law and legal principles

frame and what judges have been applying in the context of corporations.
* Its notions of assets, liabilities, costs and revenues do not fit the
accounting views, principles and norms as currently applied by firms and
economic organisations.

Its view of the institutional structure of production and the related notion of
property rights do not fit the law (Kirat and Bazzoli, 1998; Hodgson, 2002),
economics (Hölmstrom, 1999; Demsetz, 1998), and accounting (Scott, 1979)
for assets or claims into the firm. For example, that notion neglects the
collective nature of property within the firm, which allows the entity to own
and possess the assets.[7] Furthermore, the legal structure of the firm is thus
reduced to individualistic property rights (however defined) and completely
neglects other varieties of legally enforceable norms, dealing with, for
example, accounting-based constraints. In fact, the world of business laws is
not a claim for unlimited laissez-faire advocated by contemporary 'contract-
arians' in the current governance debate. Neither judicially enforceable
norms nor allowances for autonomous regulation are promoting the 'far
west' in the field of the firm. In the firm's legal world, legally relevant
interactions are always ultimately framed and shaped by laws, at first settled
by inner arbitrating managerial processes and eventually enforced by courts.
Many regulating devices, different in kind and nature, establish and enhance
the inner working of institutions, including accounting regulation and
disclosure.[8] At the same time, ownership always involves complementary
duties not to do harm or employ *guile*, and the property rights and duties thus
established sometimes fit property laws, sometimes corporate laws having
different frameworks and rules.

Important law and accounting features tell us about the functional distinction between the firm as an entity and its 'owners': the entity as a whole owns
or possesses the assets, is able to assume its own obligations, and has priority
rights in collecting economic and monetary streams and results. Law and
regulation first protect actors other than owners. Ownership consists of
certain subordinated rights to the ultimate liquidation of prior investments
and of subordinate interim rights to share in enterprise earnings at the
discretion of shareholder-elected 'boards of directors', which allow for
retained earnings too. Individual shareholders have to ultimately commit
equities, as dynamic financing sources, with a lack of individual power on
such fundamental matters as investment and dividends pay-out policies, or
management remuneration and tenure, and without the legal right of with-
drawing the equity committed.[9]

Furthermore, accounting regulation does not allow dividends until earnings actually emerge, and prevents repaying equity to owners. At the same
time, making an immediate expenditure under an accounting convention
which treats it as an investment (capitalised as an accounting asset) may
completely transform a tax bill (relevant for shareholders' value and

dividends' distribution). Until liquidation, the firm-entity must not repay equity shares to their value, in terms of either market or book values. Not only are ownership and control separate, but so are ownership, control and *management*, as early recognised by Berle[10] and Littleton,[11] and only management can organise business activity and dispose of assets and streams.

Under this accounting framework, the business incomes are essentially related to the special economic and monetary process generated by the whole firm as an entity, such that an accounting system, with limitations, helps to know, organise and regulate. To be sure, incomplete contracts economics also deals with the special field provided by the firm and with the related income, but this (specific or residual) income is essentially linked to the ownership of the firm and to the related investments by proprietors, often of their own assets. Incomplete contracts economics stresses here the governance arrangements that encourage firm-specific owners' investments and thereby enhance ownership's value. Firms efficiently exist because of incomplete contracting that requires a frame of property rights. Thus the firm and its special income exist (and are justified) because of the firm's ownership. But the dynamic accounting view distinguishes the alleged ownership and the economic dynamics of the firm. In the field of the firm, incomes factually relate to the firm's revenues at first (i.e. to the interaction between the business entity and ultimate consumers), as well as to other kinds of entity investment financing, especially longer-term credits. Furthermore, linking business income to ownership makes it difficult to understand why taxes on streams other than dividends and capital gains exist. Finally, as income to ownership justifies the firm's economic process, what about losses? What about the constraints of dividends? What about the double taxation of dividends and of net income to the firm?

Filling the gap between accounting, law and the economics of the firm implies the severance of some ties to classical economics (which partly survived the further evolution of neo-classical economics), with which the old nineteenth-century business, law and accounting shared certain basic assumptions. Under that earlier framework, the leading personage was the *lonely entrepreneur*, proprietor and equity provider, managing his own business.[12] This capitalistic hero takes and bears the risks and endorses the management (supervision, co-ordination, decision-making, control) of his own economic activity. In this context, the firm is relegated to a legal and economic device for entrepreneurial action. Decision-making and control relate essentially to the *ownership* of the firm, and the role and function of the firm as a whole disappears.[13]

In such a context, first and foremost, the economic theorist aiming to become an accounting friend needs a charming journey to Mars, as previously advocated by Herbert Simon:

> It occurred to me also that any creature floating down to our Earth from
> Mars would perceive the developed regions to be covered mostly by

firms, these firms connected by a network of communications and trans-actions that we know as markets. But the firms would be much more salient than the markets, sometimes growing, sometimes shrinking, sometimes dividing or even swallowing one another. *Surely they would appear to be the active elements in the scene.* How curious, in the light of this predominance of firms, that in economics we describe the firms as small skeletal structures embedded in the network of markets, rather than describing markets as threads that link robust firms.

(Simon, 1997: 35, italics added)[14]

Starting from the emerging notion of the firm as an *entity*, Simon further discusses the production process and the related web of product selling transactions. Here the emphasis is on the notion of a *dynamic system*, with its key feature of *feedback* effects, far away from the equilibrium mechanism advocated by neo-classical economics:

The common and understandable practice of pricing by *marking up* costs assures liquidity, at least in the short run, if only there is at least a modest base of fixed costs.[15] The *adjustment of production rates* to sales holds price margins within a moderate range without excessive absorption of cash by inventories. *All of this has little or nothing to do with the usual theorems of optimal pricing and production rates.* A simple *feedback* of price, inventory and sales information adjusts production and prices and maintains a *tolerable steady state* over considerable intervals of time without any close calculation of margins or optima.

(Simon, 1997: 37, italics added)

In this way, Simon shakes the very foundations of the neo-classical theory and analysis of the firm, i.e. the profit maximisation approach and its under-lying equilibrium framework. Instead, he rediscovers a steady view of the economy flowing, nevertheless enhanced with a decisive dynamic glamour. The firm as an entity is hence understood as a *dynamic system of interactions, interdependencies and complementarities*, not only contractual or bargain-ing, located in time and space, and different in nature from any equilibrium nexus of prices, contracts or property rights. 'Firms' surely are growing, shrinking, dividing or even swallowing one another, but what is staying there and becoming? The firm is not so much the corporation, nor the partnership, nor some other special legal arrangement, as the overarching business entity over and above such a networking of corporations (and of other arrange-ments) that currently constitute its legal bundling.[16]

In understanding this entity system, the accounting system may provide the next theoretical step. In a dynamic context, accounting can provide an original view of the special economics of the firm. It may further constitute the 'veil' allowing the firm to *supersede* the price system, since:

- Accounting deals with the firm as an entity: business activity is seen as a dynamic concern and the accounting system has to report on it.
- This reporting is especially concerned with the representation of the business income to the firm (so-called earnings). It is for this income that the entity is accounted for (accountability).
- The accounting system, therefore, becomes a mode of knowing, organising and regulating the economic and monetary process belonging to the firm as an entity.

In this context, accounting may provide an alternative frame of analysis to grasp the special economics of the whole firm as an entity, and to overcome indeed the alleged dualism between the firm and the market. Accounting, in fact, stands on general principles[17] that we can summarise in the following way:

1   the *entity* principle: the business firm is an entity and a going concern, autonomous from whichever stakeholders (including shareholders);
2   the *matching* principle: a special method to link economic and monetary entity's streams to the reference period;
3   the *historical or invested cost* principle: a special method to recognise and estimate actual business activities as assets and liabilities, costs and revenues.

These principles were and still are in question, but they are, at present, the principles generally accepted to represent the firm by accounting. They constitute the accounting view we are looking for.[18]

Disagreements about them relate also to the special view of the firm these principles imply. As recognised by leading accounting theorists (Zappa, Schmalenbach, Littleton, Ijiri, Anthony),[19] the accounting view deals with the firm as an entity and with its events, resources and transactions in real dynamics and complexity. According to Shubik (1993), time and uncertainties have essentially disappeared from the apotheosis of a *price system* driven by an equilibrium framework, but they remain the concerns of everyday business activity. The problems of how to account for their influence in the ongoing economic *process* are central to the development of accounting, and lead to the original accounting view of the special economy of the firm seen as an entity.

The entity's real dynamics implies uncertainties, bounded knowledge, potential and actual mistakes and mis-organisation. Dynamics inscribes one business activity into its special economic *process* of becoming, and accounting has to cope with this entity's process. The accounting view represents the economic and monetary process of the whole firm in a very different way from the equilibrium framework, as indicated in Table 4.1.

Be it instantaneous or stationary, an equilibrium framework seeks for synchronicity of costs and revenues, which are conceived as simultaneous

Table 4.1 Equilibrium and accounting frames

	Assets	*Liabilities*
Equilibrium frame of analysis	Future monetary *entries* discounted	Claims on future monetary *exits*
Accounting frame of analysis	Actual monetary *exit* (expenditure) capitalised	Advances on future monetary *entries* (concerned with real dynamics)

cash flows imputed to each product separately. Every transaction is thus closed by a monetary flow that is a market price.[20] A limiting identity is assumed between contractual transaction, market exchange and market price, allowing the independence of periods.[21] No economic system of anything exists but prices in equilibrium.

The accounting system is grounded on events, resources, transactions and combinations as they actually happen and are engaged or committed by one firm. It represents the special economics of the firm starting from the dynamic connection between two autonomous and interdependent patterns of economic streams. They relate either to the cost side or to the revenue side of the business activity of investing, producing and selling. Such a system deals with the whole firm as an entity, mingles real and monetary matters, and makes periods interdependent. Starting from actual monetary transactions between the entity and its world,[22] the accounting system fills in the inner and inter-temporal allocations of price-related and income-related *accounting values*.

The accounting system provides a representation of the economic and monetary process of the firm-entity in real dynamics, focalised on the resources' application for which the entity is accounted (*accountability*). The dynamic connection between streams of costs and revenues constitutes a traceable and reliable aggregation that allows the estimation of the actual performance generated by the whole firm as an entity during the reference period. Thus, the accounting notions for costs, assets and selling prices represent the economic and monetary process of the firm in an original way:

- Accounting costs *match* either the actual products sold or the reference period (costs of being in business) for income representation.[23]
- In most cases, accounting values for capitalised costs (i.e. assets) do not discount future entries (i.e. results) from related business activity, since obviously the actual determination of these emerging results (if any) is the primary purpose for which that entity is accounted for.
- Selling prices do not constitute merely informative signals to actors engaged in equilibrium adjustments, but payment inflows necessary to recover costs incurred, repay debts for investment and working capital and meet other obligations and claims in real time.[24]

In this context, most accounting assets relate to specific financial exits (called expenditures) that accounting rules capitalise, instead of entries discounted. These assets bring the whole firm as an entity in a potentially irreversible path, since expenditures might never be recovered by future selling revenues.[25] At the same time, contrary to the myth of the lonely entrepreneur, shareholders' equity does not appear here as a claim on asset *values*, but as an advancing of revenues for *costs* invested. Shareholders' equity is such a *source of financial flows* that is waiting for eventual dividends. But accounting *earnings*, as ultimate outcome of the working of an accounting system, provide a legal upper constraint on those dividends, and indeed participate in the active role of institutions in business income allocation.[26]

Not only does the real dynamics ask for the entity view on the firm advocated by dynamic accounting, but so does the separation between ownership, management and control previously recognised by Berle and Littleton. This view recognises the old-fashioned proprietary view to be irrevocably lost, especially in such networking of corporations (and of other legal arrangements) that currently constitute the legal bundling for business entities. *Even to protect shareholders*, we need a new kind of control, different from the irrevocably lost ownership sovereignty.

As shown in Table 4.2, under the real dynamics and this separation, the accounting representation of the firm does not fit together rents, properties and claims on them based on (well-defined) property rights, but copes with actual revenues, invested costs and funds incurred for these economics streams. An accounting system cannot and may not establish expected results for whichever stakeholder, but the actual entity's performance represented in a reliable and traceable way, able to settle divergent interests.[27] In summary, by means of its dynamic entity view, the accounting system defines business income to the firm-entity, as previously recognised by Zappa,[28] and plays an active role on its allocation,[29] allowing the special economics of the firm as an entity to supersede the price system.

According to Baker, Gibbons and Murphy, business income stemming from the entity's co-ordination essentially relates to such an entity's ability to go on and perform.[30] As long as the actual co-ordination goes on, it involves a relational and informal component beyond the contract for every provider of resources committed to. This commitment implies, for example, bearing some business risks involved in the business activity, i.e. the risks taken

Table 4.2 Proprietary and entity views

	Incomes	Assets	Liabilities
Proprietary view	Rents or quasi-rents	Properties	Claims and rights on properties
Entity view	Business income to the firm (based on actual revenues and costs)	Costs invested	Revenues advanced (concerned with real dynamics)

by management and implemented by actual organisation in real dynamics. This commitment modifies income allocation, attaching a relational, specific income to every provider, subject to different arrangements. Furthermore, the institutional structure shaping the business activity asks for *prior* recovery of invested costs for the entity as a whole, costs which ought to include a fair equity interest for providers of equity finances (holders of equity shares), based on actual funds committed in the past.

The enduring existence and financial viability of the firm-entity is fundamental for effective economic production – much more fundamental than the so-called 'owners' of the firm (especially shareholders) and their 'property'. The notion of *organisational capital*, therefore, as suggested by Rajan and Zingales, may be reformulated within the *flow* basis of dynamic accounting, subject to the distinction between *intended* results (the old-fashioned financial goodwill based on discounting), and *actual*, emerging incomes as represented by the accounting system.[31]

In an accounting-friendly perspective, management is *accountable for* making the costs invested productive and effective for both stakeholders and society (*accountability*). Managerial intent may be incomplete, vague, and tentative, since it tries to link the past and the future with the present. *Intended and actual results* may and will surely differ, but the firm-entity has to be managed in some manner to effectively produce in real dynamics and complexity. In this process, all the stakeholders are both framing purposes (related to intended results) and providing resources (committed to the internal organisation and involved in the entity's process of becoming). Even though stakeholders have purposive *expectations* on an entity's results, whether promised or residual, *actual* fulfilment of them depends on the stakeholder involvement in the inner working of the organisation co-ordinated by management by reason of its fiduciary authority.

In this economic and monetary process, sources of funds incurred (equities and liabilities), as well as invested costs (assets), imply a dynamic commitment subject to real hazard and complexity, which allows the firm-entity to endure and develop as a whole financial and economic *core*. The firm-entity is then active and productive – but is so because it is managed and organised, not because it is 'owned'. Its value depends, not on wealth of resources passively held, but on the managed system dealing with the *flow of relationships* involved: that is, on dynamics and process. Stop the dynamics, and its value as an entity disappears.

An accounting system therefore stands for the epistemic, organisational, institutional mode helping management and disclosure to cope with the economic and monetary process of the whole firm. Thus assets and liabilities, as resources (means) allowed by stakeholders, are in intention and in effect an advancing of costs and an investment for the future. And revenues are, in part, a way of recovering these costs that have been advanced. They are both a fruition of a future that is becoming the present, and some accomplishments that have been secured.

In this context, the ultimate message of an accounting system is not merely the final, net figure of the income statement. The real story lies in the kinds and relative amount of costs invested and revenues advanced (resources engaged in making the working process), and in the kinds and relative amounts of revenues actually generated. This flow basis (and method) is the accounting way of saying that the firm's economic and monetary process transforms the capital invested, rather than it simply accruing to the total stock of capital. No such thing as permanent capital exists according to this accounting view, but instead cost invested and revenues advanced confronted with actual costs and recovering revenues (the first couple being especially represented by the balance sheet, the latter one by the income statement).[32]

In conclusion, the accounting system becomes a constituent part of the 'structure of production', institutional, organisational or epistemic, which we cannot reduce to property rights alone. In particular, the firm as an entity and its accounting system plays an active role in the economic process of creating and allocating resources. Indeed, such an accounting-friendly approach, based on the notion of the firm as an entity, can explain in an original way the economic nature of the firm.

The firm as an entity: further implications

In summary, the following three points distinguish the accounting system from the price system:[33]

- An accounting system is accruals- and not cash-based, and it is grounded on financial transfers not only on cash (so a 'veil' is provided between every monetary price and the inner economic process).
- Accounting's special logic of regulating, organising and representing the firm's activity (related to overheads, accruals and other income-related accounting values) further modifies the economic and monetary process of the firm as an entity under real dynamics and complexity.
- Consequently, an accounting system provides relevant figures to *active* legal rules:[34] (1) constraining dividends if they might damage the firm as an entity, and (2) revealing the tax base on the special income generated by the entity itself.

An accounting system, then, with limitations, copes with knowing, organising and regulating the special process of becoming as it emerges into the whole firm.[35] This dynamic understanding of the role of the accounting system in the special economics of the firm has further implications for the economic theory of the firm as an entity.

In the black box, no system of anything exists but prices in equilibrium (the firm as a nexus of prices), framed by some 'principle of maximisation' and by efficient markets (i.e. a price system). In order to overcome this bias, understanding the firm as a *nexus of contracts*, even though incomplete contracts, is not enough. In fact, the firm is not a legal fiction which serves as a nexus for a set of contracts among individuals or proprietors, devoted to the quick pursuit of immediate shareholders' wealth: neither legal nor accounting logics and principles currently share this view on the firm and on its role in economy and society. Furthermore, this framing links business income to ownership and maintains some 'principle of maximisation',[36] since the firm is nothing other than an owners' device. The distinction between *expected* and *actual* results is thus mingled, and the role of such matters as bounded knowledge and uncertainties is reduced. Concerning internal organisation, this framing forces a rigid design, critically based on such hypotheses as incomplete contracts, opportunism and complete external unverifiability (*ex ante* and *ex post*) that are the sole justifications for the design itself.[37] The special economic *activity* of the firm, therefore, seems to disappear, as well as its *active* role in creating and allocating resources.

Disagreeing with Coase, Arrow (1986) questions that *property rights* alone suffice for social welfare under bounded rationality. In spite of them, he calls for the *price system* as a frame of competitive interactions. Under incomplete and imperfect markets, nevertheless, only firms as *active* entities provide sustainable conditions the for effective business activity of investing, producing and selling. In fact, the 'contractarian firm' does not appear to emerge so much in the making of reality,[38] as in the day-dreaming field of the price system. Under real dynamics and complexity, instead, the leading personages on the socio-economic scene are the entities-firms.[39] Neither property rights nor markets (i.e. the price system and competitive conditions) alone ever assure economic effective production.

Therefore, emphasis is placed here on the need for a new perspective that understands the firm as a managed and organised *system of relationships*, not only contractual or bargaining. The firm provides the special field (the entity) in which individuals and structures mutually interact. In the special economic environment that is the firm-entity, both order and disorder, efficiency and waste, honesty and guile, development or distress have much to do with the structures of such relations – more than existing theories have already recognised. The entity's process is thus 'structured' in the sense that it arises as much from the working structures of the parts' relationships as from the individual attributes (or behaviour) of the parts actually involved.

Here accounting system jointly relates to the basic learning, diffusion and information processes (the *epistemic* structure of production), to the closeness of products, technologies, resources and internal organisation (*organisational* structure), and to the role of working rules and norms, related or not to financial matters and regulation (*institutional* structure). Under real dynamics and complexity, the accounting system functions as:

- a mode of knowing (and representing) the going process and its *actual*, emerging results (epistemic role);
- a mode of regulating the entity's activity and shaping its special process

of becoming for the stakeholders and the law, especially concerned with the structured allocation of *intended* results (institutional role);

- a mode of organising the economic activity in accordance with the ongoing economic and monetary process of the whole firm-entity (organisational role).

The accounting system, therefore, constitutes one of the modes of functioning (constituents) of the activity of the firm-entity, either as a *cognitive tool*, as an *organisational instrument* for management, and as a *working norm* (and *rule*) related to the institutional structure of production.[40]

The accounting system deals with the effect on each entity of events, resources, transactions and combinations which take place in the entity's special process of becoming. Under real dynamics and complexity, however, the accounting system may never *determine* this process that it helps to represent, organise and regulate. Instead, the accounting system and the ongoing process have to be distinguished. For example, the accounting system – as one of the entity's modes of functioning – involves the use of money as a symbol, whilst transactions between one entity and its world involve the use of money as a medium of exchange.[41]

Since the accounting system may never determine the related economic and monetary process,[42] its *epistemic* role does not fit any 'principle of value maximisation'. Instead, according to Anthony (1983), the accounting framework begs for concepts and norms making the *history* and *evolution* of the firm-entity understandable in *synthesis* under bounded rationality. Accounting is concerned here with the capacity of the firm-entity to go on, become and fulfil in a situated, changing context.[43] This capacity relates to the *recovery of invested costs* in real dynamics, as well as to the satisfying creation and allocation of business incomes for all the stakeholders, including satisfying *equity interest* for shareholders as providers of equity finance.[44] As a reasonably aggregated, *reliable* mode of knowledge, an accounting system is suitable indeed for settling conflicting interests, helping the proper formation of prices on the stock market in time, and evaluating the entity's and managerial performance.

From this perspective, a new interdisciplinary approach is required, linking economics, accounting and law by means of a unique synthetic notion: the firm as an entity, still common to the three fields and understood here as a whole (according to old institutional economics) and a dynamic system (according to accounting and continental business economics, in turn related also to old institutionalism).[45] The need for such an integrated approach is not isolated. For example, resource-based theories are delving into management studies (and issues) to enhance the economic theory of the firm,[46] but other scholars have also called for such an approach, for example:

- Baker, Gibbons and Murphy argue for the management of relational, enduring, and informal interactions to understand the special economic environment called the firm.

- Both Rajan and Zingales and Blair argue for the economic integrity of the firm as such against the 'dark side of ownership' (they say).
- Yet another approach relates to the Carnegie School, since incomplete contracts economics has neglected, at least in part, the actual renewing force of such ideas as bounded rationality and of the critique of the equilibrium firm Simon developed. Simon quotes Commons and old institutionalism as one key thought-provoking precedent to his own theorising, stressing the need for a new theory grounded on *active firms* instead of efficient markets.

Looking for this new transactional and institutional perspective, the dualism[47] between the 'price system' and the 'firm as economic organisation', however sophisticated, can never suffice to understand their mutual interaction and the nature of the firm. In spite of this alleged dualism, we suggest viewing the firm as a *five*-terms system. The three *inner* constituents are: (a) management, (b) organisation, and (c) its special process.[48] The two *outer* constituents are: (d) the incomes and results emerging from this process, and (e) all the stakeholders concerned with the firm, related, more generally speaking, to the institutional environment and to the entity's world.

This five-terms system (Biondi, 2005a), depicted in Figure 4.1, would be better suited to understanding the economic nature of the firm than the now-prevailing two-terms system between the market and the firm. The inner relationship refers to the business entity as *actual economic co-ordination*, where management direction co-ordinates and focuses the inner working of organisation into the ongoing economic and monetary process. This dynamic *managed system* defines the entity's economic nature and generates the *economic activity* of the whole firm. This activity is outlined by the *outer* relationships, which consider the business entity from an external viewpoint. Here emphasis is on the mutual link between the functional entity seeking for realisations of its activity (incomes and results) and the stakeholders

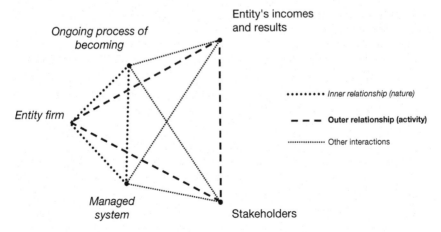

Figure 4.1 The firm-entity as economic organisation and institution.

looking for them. Management co-ordinates the business activity with the fiduciary authority conferred by all the stakeholders (by will or habit) and according to institutional arrangements.

In this context the accounting view provides a viable alternative to *marginal cost pricing* in understanding the economic and monetary process as it actually emerges and becomes into the firm-entity *as a whole*. Under real complexity (and moreover if together with real dynamics), the 'black box' – i.e. the straightforward logical chain linking such atomistic elements as selling price, quantity and cost for each product separately – is disregarded as a fundamental frame of analysis for the entity's economic *process*.[49] Instead, some degree of stabilising aggregation is required, from whole operational processes to the whole entity, to allow relevant and reliable representation of all the business figures that the accounting system has to offer to the modern economy of a business firm.

In this way, the accounting view of the firm as an entity finally provides valuable insights to better understand (1) the economic nature of the firm, (2) the way in which the firm *supersedes* the price system, and (3) the separation between ownership, control and management.

Notes

1 A version of this chapter was presented to the Seventeenth Meeting of SASE, 'What Counts? Calculation, Representation, Association', in Budapest, 1 July 2005.
2 Also called the process of 'creation and allocation of resources' or 'of production and distribution'.
3 Cf. also Kirman (1987).
4 Cf. Coase (1988: 65).
5 Coase (1937: 240–1) and note 10.
6 Coase (1988: 58–9).
7 The Incorporation Act also establishes this ability by law, cf. especially Blair (2003). An interesting legal-economic view is further provided by Dibadj (2005). The chief reference here is still the work of A. A. Berle Jr. See note 10.
8 These institutions could not be legal or judicial in nature and action.
9 Furthermore, in the world of Enron, many shareholders were and still are second-hand buyers of shares that derived from a pool formed by some financial institutions and whose value is partially influenced by gatekeepers (financial analysts, rating agencies and leading accountants' firms sometimes involved in trying to please their big clients) and also by the 'open market' operations of the firm's management itself. Cf. also Aglietta and Rebérioux (2005), especially chapter V.
10 Adolf Augustus Berle Jr (1895–1971). Scholar of law and economics, lawyer and public official, he served in World War I and was a member of the American delegation to the Paris Peace Conference. Resigning in protest against the terms of the Versailles Treaty, Berle returned to practise law in New York City and later (1927) became professor of corporate law at Columbia, where he developed a impressive research programme on law, economics and finance that generated his classic study *The Modern Corporation and Private Property* (with G. C. Means, 1933; rev. edn 1968). As a specialist in corporation law and finance, he became a member of Franklin Delano Roosevelt's Brains Trust and helped shape much of

the banking and securities legislation of the New Deal. As Assistant Secretary of State for Latin American Affairs (1938–44), Berle attended many inter-American conferences and acted as spokesman for Roosevelt's 'Good Neighbour Policy'. After serving as ambassador to Brazil (1945–6), he resumed his professorship at Columbia and was a founder and chairman (1952–5) of the Liberal Party. In 1961, Berle headed a task force for President John F. Kennedy that recommended the 'Alliance for Progress'. Other writings include *The 20th Century Capitalist Revolution* (1954), *Power without Property* (1959), and *The American Economic Republic* (1963).

11 Charles A. (A. C.) Littleton (1886–1974), (B.Sc. 1912, M.Sc. 1918, Ph.D. 1932, University of Illinois). Professor of Accountancy (1915–52) at the University of Illinois and strongly engaged in academic and research work, he drew up the first graduate courses in accountancy at the University of Illinois, and the first Ph.D. programme in accountancy in the United States. With William A. Paton, he played a key role in developing and enforcing the American corporate accounting standards in the 1930s and 1940s. With his leading research work exploring some fundamental issues in accounting theory and principles, and the interaction between accounting, economics and law in a theoretical and historical perspective, he was a pioneer in the accounting and economics field. His classic writings include *Accounting Evolution to 1900* (1933), *An Introduction to Corporate Accounting Standards* (with William A. Paton, 1940), *Structure of Accounting Theory* (1953), *Studies in the History of Accounting* (with B. S. Yamey, 1956), *Essays on Accountancy* (1961).

12 Cf. Stauss (1944), but also the valuable critique of Berle (1965) of classical economics. In accounting, this personage influenced the old-fashioned *proprietary view* on the firm; cf. Gynther (1967) and Sprouse (1957). The notion of a 'going concern', as it emerged in accounting theory and principles (and in the American framework for corporate law), appeared to be the first way of overcoming that ownership view of the firm. In economic theory, it was early developed by the institutional economics of Commons and others (see Gruchy (1947) for a meaningful synthesis of institutional theorists on this point). Some differences nevertheless remain between the dynamic entity view and the 'going concern', the main one being precisely the role played by ownership and property rights. In the going concern field, the entity can still be seen as an *association* of *independent* proprietors that have committed their efforts to the joint concern. Stauss (1944) and Biondi (2005b) discuss this point with reference to Commons' institutional economics. Biondi (2005a) further speaks of a 'becoming concern'.

13 From this perspective, all the French traditions of equilibrium theory, especially Walras and Pareto, make a difference by distinguishing (1) profit from rent; (2) entrepreneurial from capitalist role; (3) firm's income from shareholders' equity interest; and finally (4) value from selling price from full cost.

14 Cf. also Simon (1991: 27). François Perroux also speaks about *active units* in understanding the role and functions of firms in the economic system.

15 Here Simon applies the following assumptions: (a) fixed costs are completely sunk, i.e. already paid out as actual past expenditures capitalised into accounting assets; (b) production is accomplished under the maximal level of utilisation for that bundle of fixed/invested costs.

16 In this context, the entity question for accounting regulation is not so much in the valuation of single assets, as in recognising the actual firm's economic system (and associated risks and implications) over and above the very thin corporate frontiers. The so-called *off-balance sheet* items are not *off* the flow of relationships constituting the firm as an entity.

17 Cf. Boussard (1997) for a careful representation and Anthony (1983) for further developments. Cf. also Biondi (2003: 33–50).

18 Accounting notions, therefore, stand here for the usual notions and rules framed by the GAAP (General Accepted Accounting Principles) and by the historical cost approach. In this context, especially *accruals* generate such an original view and frame of analysis that accounting provides for the economic process of the firm-entity as a whole. Littleton (1953: 24) adds on a fourth principle of enterprise service: 'Business enterprises are accepted and used because they perform effective economic function in supplying goods (for living) and employment (for earning).' Even though recent developments enhance the role of discounting-based values for some special cases, the genuine originality of the accounting view still remains. In fact, under real dynamics and the separation between ownership, management and control, the accounting system frames and modifies the economic and monetary process of the firm *whichever accounting approach is retained*.

19 Cf. also Swanson and Miller (1989).

20 'Money talks' in Williamson's terms; cf. Williamson (1991).

21 A 'limiting identity' is an alleged identity link between some notion that actually *limits* our understanding of the related phenomena and their interaction. In this case, any connection between actors within the firm is considered as a contract. This connecting contract is considered as (framed by) a market exchange, and, as such, it is (concluded by) a market price. So we could understand any connection within the firm as a market price, i.e. *contract = market exchange = market price*. Also, the 'independence of periods' is another logical joke that prevents us from grasping economic processes under real dynamics and complexity. As Hicks (1965: 32) explains: 'in static theory, [economic analysis] treat[s] the single period as a closed system, the working of which can be examined without reference to anything that goes on outside it (in the temporal sense)'. In this context, as Shubik (1993: 229) adds, 'one may make a simple *pro forma* change of notation which treats goods in different time periods as different goods'.

22 As a method of recognition and measurement, business accounting is not grounded on cash receipts and disbursements (cash-basis accounting). In short, either cash transfers or occurrences of credits/debts suffice to record transactions into accounts. In such a way, as well as by accruals and overheads allocation, the accounting method makes periods inter-dependent. See also note 49.

23 Cf. Anthony (1983), chapter 5, especially pp. 124 ff.

24 Furthermore, selling prices relate to the interaction between the firm-entity and the final consumers, including discriminatory and multiple price policies.

25 Thus, *income to the firm-entity* does not essentially relate to stockholders' sub-ordinated claims, but first to the selling revenues from consumers. It further relates to satisfying actual results for all stakeholders involved in the business activity.

26 The accounting role in business taxation is another fundamental matter.

27 According to Zingales and Novaes (2004), this role is performed by bureaucracy. On this role as performed by accounting, cf. also Ijiri (1975). This role is an *active* one, concerned with real dynamics and complexity, not only an *ex post* measurement. See also note 31.

28 Gino Zappa (1879–1960). Professor of accounting and business economics (1906–50), Zappa was a student and the youngest assistant of Fabio Besta, the leading accounting theorist in the early 1900s in Italy. With his masterpiece *Il reddito d'impresa* ('The Income to the Enterprise', published firstly in 1920–9 and revised, with a few modifications, in 1937), Zappa dramatically changed the framework provided by Besta, and developed it in a forward-looking manner. Zappa's original accounting system, based on the notion of business income to the firm, stresses the need for bridging accounting and economics, especially on such fundamental issues as income, capital, wealth, value, price and cost. Zappa drove

the development of the Italian accounting and business economics tradition thereafter, grounded on a special theory of the firm as actual economic coordination and going concern. For many years (1906–50), he was in charge of graduate and research work at some leading Italian universities (L. Bocconi in Milan, Venice and Genoa). Other writings include *Le produzioni nell'economia delle imprese* ('Productions in the economy of firms', 1956–7) and *L'economia delle aziende di consumo* ('The economics of non-business entities', 1962).

29 In this context, market equilibrium cannot provide a comprehensive framework to cope with the business income to the firm. The (static) *equilibrium* notion is disregarded and replaced with the (dynamic) *system* notion. The so-called 'business profit' may not be understood as a vague premium on equilibrium rewards, but as the result of the flow of relationships that the firm-entity generates. All the rewards ultimately flow from the common source of the business income to the whole firm, as entity defines. Historically speaking, the *originalities* of C. Menger marked the emergence of continental European accounting and business economics traditions dealing with the business income dynamics involving the firm, especially in Italy (Zappa) and Germany (Nicklisch, Schmalenbach). But W. Rathenau, the leader of the European institutionalist school, also influenced them. In fact, this dynamic view of business income seems to be more radical than the disequilibrium profit advocated by later Austrian approaches. See Biondi (2002) for further developments.

30 Cf. also Crémer (1986).

31 This distinction between *intended* and *actual* context is not exactly the same as the distinction between *ex ante* and *ex post* previously developed by Hicks; cf. Biondi (2003), especially pp. 21–5. In particular, the actual accounting figures – stated period by period – do need to consider the future, as do the intended purposes that management may figure out in a more or less quanitified way. The latter are factually grounded on the past and start from actual conditions, expecially epistemic ones. There the frameworks and methods fundamentally differ.

32 The usual metaphor of business capital (assets, investments) accumulation applied to all firm-specialised and firm-specific resources and processes, as well as all the stuff of 'intangibles', are thus misleading. It especially prevents us grasping resource commitment *and* actual resulting losses at the same time. See also note 16.

33 Even though the *fair value* approach includes special values based on discounting and market-to-models, these values cannot and may not make the accounting system become a price system; see also note 18.

34 And to other legally enforceable constraints.

35 At this level of generalisation, an accounting system stands for (1) operational costs and managerial accounting (especially related to the organisational structure); (2) financial accounting and tax accounting (especially related to the institutional structure); (3) disclosed accounting information (related to managerial and financial accounting and integrated into the epistemic structure).

36 Or 'economizing', in Williamson's terms.

37 Cf. also Favereau (1997).

38 In spite of the methodological realism Coase (1988: 52–4) advocates.

39 We are neglecting the mystery of other 'black boxes' such as the state, families, non-business entities, and the monetary and financial system.

40 Following Anthony (1983: 208, note 6), the usual barrier between financial and management accounting is left out and further developed as inner and outer accountability.

41 Cf. Zappa (1937), Raby (1959) and the chapter entitled 'Symbols of Reality' in Littleton (1961: 226–7). In the price system, which makes money and credit neutral, 'each individual at the start of the trade has available implicitly a credit

line equal to his net worth "at market" – i.e. at the worth of his initial assets *at the final market price'* (Shubik 1993: 230, italics added). The dynamic accounting view of money and financial devices is very different, and allows the presence of money (as credit money) to play an active role in the economic and monetary process.

42 Even though the accounting system may somewhat shape and modify this process.

43 Anthony directly refers to Simon's approach. Cf. Anthony (1960 and 1983).

44 This interest may constitute an accounting way to bridge the *intended* and the *actual* results in real dynamics. A sort of equity interest is calculated also by the *Economic Value Added* (EVA) approach to residual income, even though it usually starts from capital invested (capitalised as accounting assets). Our approach, instead, suggests taking *actual funds committed* (recognised as accounting liabilities or equities) as the basis, as Schumpeter (1912) early justified.

45 Cf., respectively, Gruchy (1947) and Biondi (2005a), providing further references.

46 An economic theorist aiming to explore the resources of the firm would pay attention both to the asset side and to the liability side of the entity's accounting system, since resources can be represented as assets as well as liabilities. Furthermore, monetary inflows (or other results) related to interactions with the ultimate consumers are also resources, but recognised as revenues, as well as work time and commitment provided by employees, thus recognised as expenses. Finally, resources alone, however recognised, are not enough. Still involved in the ongoing process, they need to be integrated into the whole *activity* by effective management and organisation. They need dynamic capabilities belonging to this activity level of the business entity (Biondi, 2005a). At this level, such *collective* dynamic resources as trust and *core* competencies emerge.

47 Dualism here means a two-term system, or dialectics.

48 The special process is (a) the entity-related management process, (b) the inner working of the managed system, and (c) the special process of becoming generated by the whole firm as an entity.

49 Ijiri (1967: 58–64; 1975: 183–6) provides a deep analysis of the different *imputation* logic underlying accounting and economics. He explains how even simple production processes blur the straightforward logical chain of cost, quantity and selling price for each product separately required by the *black box* firm. In such cases, the black box asks for some further conditions (epistemic or organisational) external to the accounting system and provided by the price system. The dynamic accounting approach, instead, based on historical or invested costs, does not requires the *separability, stability and uniqueness* of that logical chain (cf. also Biondi 2003: 19–21). Its approach is more aggregating than individualistic; its figures are more actual amounts recognised than market or discounted values; it prefers traceable and reliable discretionary methods (accruals) to optimising or market-to-models methods. On the dynamic accounting approach under real dynamics and complexity, cf. also Lim and Sunder (1991).

Kirman (1997) enhances the economic viewpoint by dealing with the evolving network of agents involved. His conclusions are thus very different from the usual approaches grounded on isolated or representative actors. His analysis treats in particular the monetary profit, actual and *cumulated*, generated by each transaction separately.

References

Aglietta, M, and Rebérioux, A. (2005), *Corporate Governance Adrift. A Critique of Shareholder Value*, Cheltenham, UK: Edward Elgar.

Anthony, N. R. (1960), 'The trouble with profit maximization', *Harvard Business Review*, 38(6), November–December: 127–34.

—— (1983), *Tell It Like It Was: A Conceptual Framework for Financial Accounting*, Homewood, IL: Richard D. Irwin Inc.

Arrow, J. K. (1986), 'Rationality of self and others in an economic system, Part 2: The behavioral foundations of economic theory', *Journal of Business*, 59(4): S385–99; reprinted as 'Economic theory and the hypothesis of rationality', in J. Eatwell, M. Milgate and P. Newman (eds) (1987) *The New Palgrave Dictionary of Economics*, London: Macmillan, pp. 69–75.

Baker, G., Gibbons, R. and Murphy, J. K. (2001), 'Bringing the market inside the firm?', *American Economic Review*, 91(2): 212–18.

—— (2002), 'Relational contracts and the theory of the firm', *Quarterly Journal of Economics*, 117(1): 39–84.

Berle, A. A. Jr (1947), 'The theory of enterprise entity', *Columbia Law Review*, 47(3): 343–58.

—— (1965), 'The impact of the corporation on classical economic theory', *Quarterly Journal of Economics*, 79(1): 25–40.

Biondi, Y. (2002), *Gino Zappa e la rivoluzione del reddito. Azienda, moneta e contabilità nella nascente Economia aziendale* ['Gino Zappa and the business income to the firm. Firm, money and accounting in the Italian business economics revolution'], Padua: CEDAM.

—— (2003), 'La nature économique de l'entreprise au croisement des théories économiques et de la comptabilité' ['Economic organisation between economic theories and accounting'], Ph.D. dissertation, co-supervised by the Université Lumière Lyon 2 and the Università degli Studi di Brescia.

—— (2005a), 'The firm as an entity: management, organisation, accounting', Department of Business Economics, paper no. 46, University of Brescia, available at http://ssrn.com/abstract=774764.

—— (2005b), 'G. Zappa, T. Veblen, J. R. Commons e l'impresa come istituzione economica' [Zappa, Veblen, Commons on the firm as an economic institution], *Storia del Pensiero Economico*, 2005(1): 93–120.

Blair, M. (2003), 'Locking in capital: what corporate law achieved for business organizers in the nineteenth century', *UCLA Law Review*, 51(2): 387–455. http://ssrn.com/abstract=495984.

Blair, M. and Stout, A. L. (1999), 'A team production theory of corporate law', *Virginia Law Review*, 85(2): 247–328.

Boussard, D. (1997), *La modélisation comptable en question(s)*, Paris: Economica.

Coase, R. H. (1937), 'The nature of the firm', *Economica*, new series, 4, November: 386–405.

—— (1960), 'The problem of social cost', *Journal of Law and Economics*, 3(1): 1–44.

—— (1988), 'The nature of the firm: origin, meaning, influence', *Journal of Law, Economics, and Organization*, 4 (Spring): 3–47. Also in Williamson and Winter (1991).

—— (1990), 'Accounting and the theory of the firm', *Journal of Accounting and Economics*, 12: 3–13.

—— (1992), 'The institutional structure of production', *American Economic Review*, 88(4): 713–19.

Colasse, B. (2000) (ed.), *Encyclopédie de comptabilité, contrôle de gestion et audit*, Paris: Economica.

Commons, J. R. (1934), *Institutional Economics. Its Place in Political Economy*, London: Macmillan; reprinted New Brunswick, NJ: Transaction Books, 1990.

Crémer, J. (1986), 'Cooperation in ongoing organizations', *Quarterly Journal of Economics*, CI(1), February: 33–50.

Demsetz, H. (1998), Review of O. Hart's *Firms, Contracts, and Financial Structure: Clarendon Lectures in Economics* (Oxford University Press, 1995), *Journal of Political Economy*, 106(2): 446–52.

Dibadj, R. (2005), 'Reconceiving the firm', *Cardozo Law Review*, 26(4), March: 1459–1534.

Favereau, O. (1997), 'L'incomplétude n'est pas le problème, c'est la solution', in B. Reynaud (ed.), *Les limites de la rationalité*, vol. 2: *Les figures du collectif*, Paris: La Découverte, pp. 219–304.

Grossmann, S. and Hart, O. (1986), 'The costs and benefits of ownership: a theory of vertical and lateral integration', *Journal of Political Economy*, 94: 691–719.

Gruchy, A. (1947), *Modern Economic Thought*, New York: Prentice-Hall.

Gynther, R. (1967), 'Accounting concepts and behavioral hypotheses', *Accounting Review*, XLII(2), April: 274–90.

Hart, O. (1989), 'An economist's perspective on the theory of the firm', *Columbia Law Review*, 89(7): 1757–74. Reprinted in O. E. Williamson (1990) (ed.), *Organization and Theory from C. Barnard to the Present and Beyond*, Oxford: Oxford University Press.

Hicks, J. (1965), *Capital and Growth*, New York: Oxford University Press.

Hodgson, G. M. (2002), 'The legal nature of the firm and the myth of the firm-market hybrid', *International Journal of the Economics of Business*, 9(1): 37–60.

Hölmstrom, B. (1999), 'The firm as a sub-economy', *Journal of Law, Economics and Organization*, 15: 74–102.

Ijiri, Y. (1967), *The Foundations of Accounting Measurement: A Mathematical, Economic and Behavioral Inquiry*, Englewood Cliffs, NJ: Prentice-Hall.

—— (1975), *Theory of Accounting Measurement*, Studies in Accounting Research, no. 10, Sarasota, FL: American Accounting Association.

Kaldor, N. (1934), 'The equilibrium of the firm', *Economic Journal*, 44: 60–76. Reprinted in N. Kaldor (1969), *Essays on Value and Distribution*, London: Duckworth.

Kirat, T. and Bazzoli, L. (1998), 'L'entreprise et les règles juridiques: une perspective d'économie institutionnaliste', *Revue interdisciplinaire d'études juridiques* (RIEJ), 40: 47–78.

Kirman, A. (1987), 'The intrinsic limits of modern economic theory. The emperor has no clothes', EUI working paper 87/323, Florence: Department of Economics, European University Institute.

—— (1997), 'The economy as an evolving network', *Journal of Evolutionary Economics*, 7: 339–53.

Lim, S. and Sunder, S. (1991), 'Efficiency of asset valuation rules under price movement and measurement errors', *Accounting Review*, 66(4), October: 669–93.

Littleton, C. (1928), 'What is profit?', *Accounting Review*, III(3), June: 278–88.

—— (1937), 'Concepts of income underlying accounting', *Accounting Review*, XII, March: 13–22.

—— (1938), 'A substitute for stated capital', *Harvard Business Review*, 17(1), Autumn: 75–84.

—— (1953), *Structure of Accounting Theory*, Sarasota, FL: American Accounting Association.

—— (1961), *Essays on Accountancy*, ed. C. A. Moyer, Urbana, IL: University of Illinois Press, especially: Part One, On Accounting History; Part Two, On Accounting Theory.

Pareto, V. (1974 [1906]), *Manuale di economia politica*, with Proemio: 'Introduzione alla scienza sociale', Padua: CEDAM. First French edn, Lausanne 1909. Also in V. Pareto (1981) *Œuvres complètes*, vol. VII, Geneva: Droz.

Raby, W. (1959), 'The two faces of accounting', *Accounting Review*, 34(3), July: 452–61.

Rajan, R. G. and Zingales, L. (1998), 'Power in a theory of the firm', *Quarterly Journal of Economics*, 113(2): 387–432.

—— (2001), 'The firm as a dedicated hierarchy: a theory of the origin and growth of firms', *Quarterly Journal of Economics*, 116(3): 805–51.

Richard, J, (2000), 'Plans comptables', in B. Colasse (ed.), *Encyclopédie de comptabilité, contrôle de gestion et audit*, Paris: Economica, article 71, pp. 943–59.

Rutherford, M. (1994), *Institutions in Economics: The Old and the New Institutionalism*, Cambridge: Cambridge University Press.

Schumpeter, A. J. (1912), *Theorie der wirtschaftlichen Entwicklung*, Leipzig: Duncker und Humblot; 2nd edn, 1926.

Scott, R. A. (1979), 'Owners' equity, the anachronistic element', *Accounting Review*, 54(4), October: 750–63.

Shubik, M. (1993), 'Accounting and its relationship to general equilibrium theory', *Economic Notes*, 22(2): 226–34; also in M. Shubik (ed.), *Accounting and Economics*, New York and London: Garland Publishing, 1995.

Simon, H. A. (1991), 'Organisations and markets', *Journal of Economic Perspectives*, 5(2), Spring: 25–44.

—— (1997), *An Empirically Based Microeconomics*, Cambridge: Cambridge University Press.

Sprouse, R. T. (1957), 'The significance of the concept of the corporation in accounting analyses', *Accounting Review*, XXXII(3), July: 369–78.

Stauss, J. H. (1944), 'The entrepreneur: the firm', *Journal of Political Economy*, 52(2), June: 112–27.

Swanson, G. A. and Miller, J. G. (1989), *Measurement and Interpretation in Accounting*, New York: Quorum Books.

Veblen, T. (1904), *The Theory of Business Enterprise*, New York: Scribner's; reprinted New Brunswick, NJ: Transaction Books, 1978.

—— (1923), *Absentee Ownership*, New York: B. W. Huebsch; reprinted 1954.

Williamson, O. E. (1975), *Markets and Hierarchies. Analysis and Antitrust Implications*, New York: Free Press.

—— (1991), 'Comparative economic organization: the analysis of discrete structural alternatives', *Administrative Sciences Quarterly*, 36, June: 269–96.

Williamson, O. E. and Winter, S. G. (1991) (eds), *The Nature of the Firm. Origins, Evolution, and Development*, Oxford: Oxford University Press.

Zappa, G. (1937), *Il reddito d'impresa*, Milan: Giuffré; first complete edn, Rome: ALI, 1929.

Zingales, L. (2000), 'In search of new foundations', *Journal of Finance*, 55(4): 1623–53.

Zingales, L. and Novaes, W. (2004), 'Bureaucracy as a mechanism to generate information', *Rand Journal of Economics*, 35(2): 245–59.

5   The value of integration

Old institutional economics and new institutional sociology

Hassan Yazdifar

Introduction

During the last two decades organizational researchers have paid significant attention to the study of organizational action from several perspectives (Martinez and Dacin, 1999). The dominant perspectives include contingency theory (Child, 1972; Miller and Friesen, 1984; Mintzberg, 1979, 1981), population ecology (Hannan and Freeman, 1977, 1984), resource dependence (Pfeffer and Salancik, 1978), and various institutional theories such as transaction cost economics (Williamson, 1975, 1981, 1985), new institutional sociology (DiMaggio and Powell, 1983; Meyer and Rowan, 1977; Scott, 1995; Zucker, 1987) and old institutional economics (Veblen, 1898, 1909, 1919; Hodgson, 1993; Mayhew, 1987).

The organizations literature continues to see increasing convergence and integrative efforts among these theoretical approaches (for example, see Amburgey and Dacin, 1994; Baum, 1996; Gupta, Dirsmith and Fogarty, 1994; Madhok, 1997; Tolbert, 1985; and Martinez and Dacin, 1999). These integrations, or eclecticism as Romslad (1996) calls it, have enabled us to better understand such phenomena as organizational change, vital rates (founding and failure), adoption of innovations, organizational coordination and control, as well as the development of organizational capabilities (Martinez and Dacin, 1999). However, there have been lesser signs of convergence between new institutional sociology (NIS) and old institutional economics (OIE) (e.g. Yazdifar, 2004). In this paper, it is argued that an institutional perspective incorporating both NIS and OIE expands the levels of analysis encompassing both extra-(macro) and intra-(micro) organizational factors and consequently enhances our conceptualization of organizational actions and practices.

It is argued that the two can be complementary and that neither can independently fully explain organizational behaviour. For instance, NIS cannot account for intra-organizational processes of change (or lack of change) while OIE does not accommodate extra-organizational (environmental) factors in its analysis. In this chapter a conceptual merger of the two is described in terms of how environmental pressures impinge on the intra-organization, and become accepted and taken for granted or resisted and rejected. It reviews each of these approaches and provides a brief on how these perspectives might be broadened via this synthesis.

The remainder of the chapter is structured as follows. The next section provides an overview of NIS and outlines its criticisms. Then, attempts to complement some of the NIS limitations are presented. The following section provides an overview of OIE and an explanation of the processes of institutionalization. Then a major limitation and criticism made of OIE will be argued. The final main section explains the need for fusing NIS and OIE to extend our scope of analysis and enhance our understanding of organizational practices. The chapter ends with concluding remarks.

NIS and its criticisms

During the last two decades, in particular, researchers have increasingly adopted institutional theory to assist them in conceptualizing and explaining organizational actions and practices (see, for example, Covaleski and Dirsmith, 1988; Mezias, 1990; Carpenter and Feroz, 1992). This has been stimulated by the growing number of organizational researchers adopting NIS because of its challenge to conventional wisdom and the prevailing research beliefs that assert that organizations are bounded, relatively autonomous and made up of rational actors (Abernethy and Chua, 1996: 571; see also Baxter and Chua, 2003).

NIS theory views organizations as embedded within larger inter-organizational networks and cultural systems. This institutional environment not only influences the organization's input and output markets but also its beliefs, norms and historical traditions. Furthermore, the institutional environment is characterized by the elaboration of rules, practices, symbols, beliefs and normative requirements to which individual organizations must conform to receive support and legitimacy (Abernethy and Chua, 1996: 571–74). The success of an organization from an NIS perspective is defined by the extent to which it embodies societal 'ideals' (myths) regarding norms of rational behaviour. Carruthers (1995: 315) states:

> [NIS] believes that people live in a socially constructed world that is filled with taken-for-granted meanings and rules. Much of their action is neither intentional nor conscious, for it is undertaken unconsciously and as a matter of routine.

NIS maintains that an organization's internal and formal structures and processes – that is, all the procedures, rules and routines defining how the organization's activities need to be done in order to achieve its goals – are formed by its (external) wider social environment/societal, institutionalized rules (Meyer and Rowan, 1991; Scott, 1991; Scott and Meyer, 1983), rather than, say, overriding (internal) aims for cost-minimization or internal technical requirements (as is the basic assumption in neo-classical economics and new institutional economics). DiMaggio and Powell (1991a: 8), as two of its better-known writers in recent years, explain this form of institutionalism as NIS comprising:

> a rejection of rational-actor models, an interest in institutions as independent variables, a turn toward cognitive and cultural explanations, and an interest in properties of supraindividual units of analysis that cannot be reduced to aggregations of direct consequences of individuals' attributes or motives.

Defining an institution according to NIS theory, Scott (1995: 33–4) states that:

> Institutions consist of cognitive, normative and regulative structures and activities that provide stability and meaning to social behaviour. Institutions are transported by various carriers – cultures, structures, and routines – and they operate at multiple levels of jurisdiction. In this conceptualization, institutions are multifaceted systems incorporating symbolic systems – cognitive constructions and normative rules – and regulative processes carried out through and shaping social behaviour. Meaning systems, monitoring processes, and actions are interwoven. Although constructed and maintained by individual actors, institutions assume the guise of an impersonal and objective reality. Institutions ride on various conveyances and operate at multiple levels – from the world system to subunits of organizations.

According to this theory, an organization's formal structure: 'dramatically reflect[s] the myths of their institutional environments instead of the demands of their work activities' (Meyer and Rowan, 1977: 341). Such myths are: 'highly institutionalised, rationalised and impersonal prescriptions', which specify in a rule-like manner ways of pursuing social goals that can then be identified as 'technical' goals rationally (Meyer and Rowan, 1977: 343–4). Scott (1995: 136) says:

> All organizations are institutionalized organizations. This is true both in the narrower sense that all organizations are subject to important regulative processes and operate under the control of both local and more general governance structures, as well as in the broader sense that all organizations are socially constituted and are the subject of institutional processes that define what forms they can assume and how they may operate legitimately.

Organizations which operate in similar environments are said to experience comparable demands over what is generally regarded as being 'acceptable' behaviour – and, consequently, will have similar structures and processes (DiMaggio and Powell, 1991b). An organization that conforms to societal rules obtains external legitimacy and increases its chance for survival, irrespective of whether new rules or procedures would make the organization more effective (Carpenter and Feroz, 2001: 569). Thus, being efficient is not the only way that organizations can survive. Legitimacy in the external environment, that is from the state, the government, the parent companies and other external bodies, is another means of ensuring survival (Carruthers, 1995). Such congruence in organization structures and processes, grounded in the 'pressures' of environmental expectations and beliefs, is said to have emerged through a 'process' of *isomorphism* (DiMaggio and Powell, 1991b).

The central tenet of NIS is that organizations are pressured to become isomorphic with, or conform to, a set of institutionalized beliefs (Abernethy and Chua, 1996). Isomorphism here means 'the concept that best captures the process of homogenization' (DiMaggio and Powell, 1991b: 66). There are two main components of isomorphism (DiMaggio and Powell, 1983), namely: (1) competitive isomorphism and (2) institutional isomorphism. The former defines how competitive forces drive firms towards adopting the least-cost, efficient structures and practices. However, most NIS theorists de-emphasize isomorphism which is said to be grounded in such rationalistic, 'technical' criteria, and instead stress institutional isomorphism which portrays the permeation from environment to firm as a predominantly cultural and political process (Burns, 2001: 16–17).

DiMaggio and Powell (1991b) identify three mechanisms through which institutional isomorphic change occurs, each with its own antecedents. The first is *coercive* isomorphism, which stems from political influence and the problem of legitimacy. It is the response to 'both formal and informal pressures exerted on organizations by other organizations [and impinging external factors e.g. government policy, regulation, supplier relationship] upon which they are dependent and by cultural expectations in the society within which organizations function' (DiMaggio and Powell, 1991b: 66). The second mechanism is *mimetic* isomorphism which 'occurs when organizations face uncertainty and model themselves on other organizations'. Organizations will tend to copy those organizations in their organizational field that are perceived to be more legitimate (e.g. parent company) or successful or those outside their organizational field that are similar to themselves in complexity (see DiMaggio and Powell, 1991b; Tolbert and Zucker, 1983). The third mechanism is *normative* isomorphism which is 'associated with professionalization' (DiMaggio and Powell, 1991: 66) and 'arises when professionals operating in organizations are subject to pressures to conform to a set of norms and rules developed by occupational/professional groups' (Abernethy and Chua, 1996: 574). In the latter form of isomorphism, firms feel obliged to adopt structures and processes that have been advocated by dominant professions and professional bodies (Burns, 2000b: 15).

Figure 5.1 portrays the mechanisms and the drivers of homogeneity in organizational forms and practices from NIS view. In summary, NIS focuses on change at an extra-organizational (or *macro*) level and *primarily* focuses on the 'legitimation' of organizational structures, forms and processes in society. The success of an organization from an NIS perspective is defined by the extent to which an organization embodies society 'ideals' (myths) concerning norms of rational behaviour. Furthermore, from this perspective, more societal legitimacy is said to be achieved through conforming to society norms. Such legitimacy affects an organization's structure, defines an organization's domain of activity, and is the main factor for survival and growth (Meyer *et al.*, 1993).

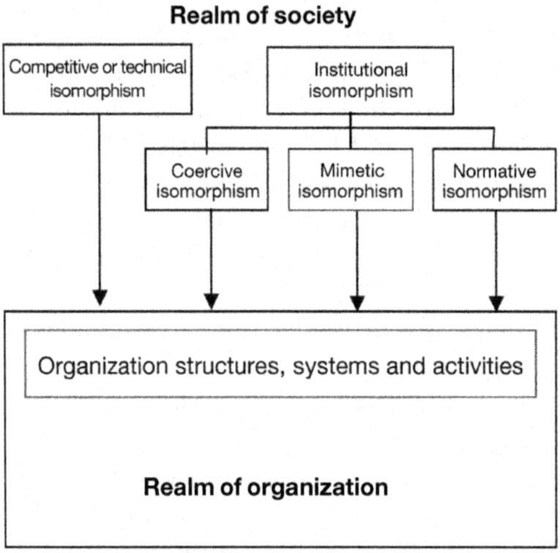

Realm of society

Figure 5.1 Mechanisms and drivers of homogeneity in organizational forms and practices – an NIS view.

Nevertheless, despite its current vogue in organizational analysis, NIS is not without problems. Perrow (1991) depicts it as a theory full of contradictions and Scott (1987) concedes that it is still in its 'adolescence' (see also Major and Hopper, 2002). Amongst other things, there are three interrelated concerns.

First, *neglect of power issues and actors' interest-based behaviour.*

> NIS is frequently criticized for its deterministic nature and its neglect of the role of active agencies and issues of power and interest at intra-organizational (micro) level (Carmona *et al.*, 1998). The concern expressed by Powell (1991: 194) is that NIS 'portrays organizations too passively and depicts environments as overly constraining' (see also Collier, 2001: 466; Oliver, 1992). According to Zucker, NIS researchers

risk treating institutionalization as a 'black box at the organizational level' without solid cognitive micro-level foundations (Zucker, 1991: 105) (see also DiMaggio and Powell, 1991a; Covaleski and Dirsmith, 1995; Dirsmith *et al.*, 1997; Covaleski *et al.*, 1993; Perrow, 1986; Oliver, 1991, 1992; Carruthers, 1995; Greenwood and Hinings, 1996; DiMaggio, 1988; Carmona *et al.*, 1998; Powell, 1991). Carruthers (1995: 325) also adds that NIS 'is too concerned with culture and taken-for-granted meanings to be able to discern the conflicts that abound in organizational life, and that to focus on myth and ceremony is to overlook power and control'.

Second, *incapacity to explain processes of organizational change.*

Critics of NIS argue that it precludes inquiry into what causes organizations to challenge, discard or abandon institutionalized procedures (Oliver, 1992). The focus of NIS is on the study of persistence rather than understanding organizational change. Hence, NIS is pointless for the study of the processes of organizational change (Genschel, 1997), and offers not 'much guidance regarding change' (Ledford *et al.*, 1989). Similarly, Greenwood and Hinings argue that the theory 'is weak in analysing the internal dynamics of organizational change. As a consequence, the theory is silent on why some organizations adopt radical change whereas others do not, despite experiencing the same institutional pressures' (1996: 1023). The same authors add 'institutional theory is not usually regarded as a theory of organizational change, but usually as an explanation of the similarity ("isomorphism") and stability of organizational arrangements in a given population or field of organizations' (1996: 1023). Likewise, Buckho comments that institutional pressures are 'a powerful force' against transformational change (1994: 90) (see also Carmona *et al.*, 1998; Greenwood and Hinings, 1996; Oliver, 1992; DiMaggio and Powell, 1991a; Genschel, 1997). Collier (2001: 469) also criticizes NIS due to its inability, at an organizational level of analysis, to provide a theory as to how these competing interests can be accommodated or reconciled by management.

Third, *lack of consideration of internal generation of institutionalized forms.*

The theory does not consider the path of change in the organizational realm (micro level); rather it focuses on change at an extra-organizational (or *macro*) level (Abernethy and Chua, 1996: 572). Scott argues that the focus of the theory is on 'examining the effects of institutional environments on organizational structures rather than with examining the internal generation of institutionalized forms within organizations' (1991: 165). He, for example, criticizes Selznick's (1949) work as 'largely definitional rather than explanatory: he defined and described the process but did not explicitly account for it. His treatment of institutionalization informs us that values are instilled; not *how* this occurs' (Scott, 1987: 495). Abernethy and Chua (1996: 572) echo that view, stating that the theory provides only limited insight into 'institutionalization in the making' (as opposed to institutionalization as an achieved state) and de-institutionalization processes (DiMaggio, 1988). 'That is, it does not provide an adequate answer to the question, how do new values and beliefs take root and supplant earlier norms?'

These criticisms indicate that the theory suffers from 'inadequate consideration of the relationship between environment/institutional determinism and cultural and political factors within organizations' (see Child, 1972; Abernethy and Chua, 1996). Therefore, for NIS theory to fulfil its promise for organizational studies, researchers must develop dynamic models of institutions (see Whittington, 1992) and devise methodologies for investigating how organizational actions and environmental institutions are recursively related (Barley and Tolbert, 1997). In so doing, Scott (1987) has pointed out that NIS needs to be complemented by other perspectives.

Attempts at complementing the NIS limitations

Some researchers have attempted to address the criticisms above by integrating NIS into the 'resource dependency' framework proposed by Pfeffer and Salancik (1978) and developed by Oliver (1991) to study the relationship between institutional pressure and strategic choice (Modell, 2001). These studies recognize that while institutional forces can act as a constraint, organizations do not necessarily change their structures, systems and practices in the face of institutional pressures. Oliver (1991), for example, blended NIS and resource dependence theory (and also strategic choice theory) to develop a conceptual framework allowing us to examine organizational responses to institutional processes (see also Modell, 2001). In her model, Oliver (1991) identified a number of possible responses (along a continuum of resistance) to institutional pressures (see Table 5.1). At one end of the continuum is a high degree of conformity where the focal organization will acquiesce, through to the opposite end of the continuum where the organization will avoid and defy institutional pressures (Abernethy and Chua, 1996: 575). The framework thus provides a synthesis of the insights of the early NIS literature while accommodating some major criticisms levelled at this body of knowledge. However, as Abernethy and Chua (1996: 572) argue, the framework still suffers from inability to provide insight into the processes of 'de-institutionalization' and 're-institutionalization' of new values and beliefs. Again, it does not provide an adequate answer to the question, 'How do new values and beliefs take root and supplant earlier norms?'

Table 5.1 A continuum of managerial responses to institutional pressures

	Strategies	Tactics	Examples
	Acquiesce	Habit	Following invisible, taken-for-granted norms/rules
		Imitate	Mimicking institutional models
Low		Comply	Obeying rules and accepting norms
	Compromise	Balance	Balancing the expectations of multiple constituents
		Pacify	Placating and accommodating institutional elements
Level of active resistance to institutional pressures		Bargain	Negotiating with institutional stakeholders
	Avoid	Conceal	Disguising nonconformity
		Buffer	Loosening institutional attachments
		Escape	Changing goals, activities or domains
	Defy	Dismiss	Ignoring explicit norms and values
		Challenge	Contesting rules and requirements
High		Attach	Assaulting the sources of institutional pressure
	Manipulate	Co-opt	Importing influential constituents
		Influence	Shaping values and criteria
		Control	Dominating institutional constituents and processes

Source: Oliver (1991: 152).

This draws attentions to the need for alternative theories to integrate with NIS to embrace the effect of internal organizational dynamics in order to satisfactorily explain organizational actions and change (Major and Hopper, 2002). One theory that could enhance NIS's capacity to tease out the complex dynamics of change at intra-organizational level and explain how particular systems, practices and values emerge, sustain and/or change over time – i.e. the dynamics of the change process rather than the outcomes of a change event – and also explain conflict and actors' struggle for power could be 'old institutional economics' (OIE). In this paper, we point out that it may be more useful to think of NIS and OIE as complementary approaches and believe that the overall scope of our organizational theorizing can be enhanced by applying both theories to explain organizations actions. Thus, in order to adopt a holistic framework, we propose a 'hybrid' framework (Burns, 2001) blending NIS and OIE. This allows us to examine organizational responses to the institutional environment while relaxing the assumption that these primarily follow a pattern of passive acquiescence, in the search for conformity and legitimacy (Modell, 2001), and the model also has the capacity to explain the processes of change at intra-organizational level.

The concept of OIE theory: an overview

OIE's roots are grounded in the American institutionalist tradition, mainly the work of Thorstein Veblen (1898, 1909, 1919), and emerged *as opposition to* the 'static' rational-actor *economic* theorizing that was prevalent at the turn of the nineteenth century. The theory explicitly rejects the assumptions of given (rational-optimizing) individuals, and thus there is a clear overlap between OIE and NIS, although until very recently this was hardly a well-appreciated fact within either founder discipline (Burns, 2001).

Typically, this theory criticizes the two core assumptions of neoclassical economics (rationality and equilibrium) and believes that individuals' behaviour is significantly influenced by the institutional context. The OIE intends basically to understand and explain organizational behaviours/ changes in 'processual' terms, and describe *why* and *how* these phenomena become what they are (or are not) through time (Burns, 2000b: 19).

OIE supposes that individual and organizational actions are determined by the socially learned and acceptable pattern of behaviours (Hodgson, 1998; Nelson, 1994; Abdul Khalid, 2000). However, being influenced by the institutional context does not mean that individuals are passive. Rather, both individual behaviour and societal norms are mutually reinforcing; they both influence and are influenced by each other (Hodgson, 1993: 7; see also Dugger and Sherman, 1994). In addition, individual behaviour is seen to be driven by habit. When habits become part of group action, they can evolve into routines and customs (Hodgson, 1998). Hodgson (1998) links the concept of habits with the notion of institutions. Therefore, from the OIE viewpoint, institutions embrace settled ways of thinking and doing, which are common to a specific community/group (Burns, 2000b). Khalil (1999) states that an OIE theorist regards institutions as substantial, ingrained modes which define the contours of behaviour. Thus OIE views institutions as '"paradigms" which define the nature of the actor' (Khalil, 1999: 61).

Although, there are many definitions given to the concept, the term of *institutions* has been used by this theory as a conveyer of the idea. Describing this, Neal (1987: 1202) says that the term 'institutions' is being used 'to convey the idea that peoples' actions are shaped by and reflect culturally inherited but socially evolving social rules or relationships'. Hence, it could be said that institutions are the rules that govern individual behaviour, and therefore represent constraints on the options that individuals and collectives are likely to exercise, albeit constraints that are open to modification over time (Barley and Tolbert, 1997). OIE theorists, like NIS theorists, acknowledge that cultural constraints do not completely determine human action (DiMaggio 1988; Oliver, 1991; Strang and Sine, 2002). Rather, institutions set bounds on rationality by restricting the opportunities and alternatives we perceive, and thereby increase the probability of certain types of behaviour, although, through choice and action, individuals and organizations can deliberately modify, and even eliminate, institutions (Barley and Tolbert, 1997).

For OIE researchers, the adoption of new structures, systems and behaviour in organizations would be seen to be strongly influenced by politics, society and the cultural environment. OIE theorists argue that the adoption or rejection of changes should be studied in relation to historical, cultural, social and political issues that are relevant to comprehend organizational change in its full complexity (Scapens, 1991). Such institutionalists contend that the adoption of change might be a potential source of conflict and resistance. The implementation of new systems will succeed to the extent that there is broad congruence between the new systems (rules) and existing routines and institutions (or taken-for-granted assumptions) in companies. That is, the adoption and successful implementation or rejection and resistance to change to a new system and practice are dependent on whether the norms and values underpinning their adoption and implementation are in accordance with the norms and values of actors in organizations: those who are going to adopt, implement and use them.

The OIE perspective is more about *why* and *how* particular systems and practices emerge, sustain and/or change over time – i.e. the dynamics of the change process rather than the outcomes of a change event (Burns, 2001). As Scapens (1994) argues, it is more fruitful to use the OIE framework to understand the processes of change, change facilitators and resistance to change. OIE highlights institutions (with habits and routines as their building blocks) at individual, group, firm and/or society levels of analysis and focuses on both formal (rules-based) and informal (tacit/cognitive-level) aspects of institutions (Burns, 2001). So, and in summary, whereas an NIS approach would focus primarily on the impacts of societal or macro-level institutions on organizations' internal structures, systems and practices, an OIE approach would more directly consider why and how such organizations' activities emerged, were sustained and/or changed over time.

Drawing on the OIE framework sketched by Barley and Tolbert (1997) and further developed by Burns and Scapens (2000), the following presents the OIE framework (see Figure 5.2) that conceptualizes change (to new systems, practices and values) and resistance to change and explains how the new systems, practices and rules introduced to an organization may become institutionalized.[1] The introduction of the change may be due to several internal and external factors, including government rules, a suggestion by a new parent company, agency or consultant or propagators of a new technique at a conference.[2] However, and before embarking on presenting the framework, it should be noted that the framework is concerned with the processes of change in organizations, i.e. with organization-specific institutions, or 'intra-organizational', rather than with macro or 'extra-organizational' processes of change.

To explain the framework of the institutionalization of new systems and practices, we should first explain that, from an OIE perspective, there are institutional and action realms. 'Whereas institutions constrain and shape action *synchronically* (i.e. at a specific point in time), actions produce and

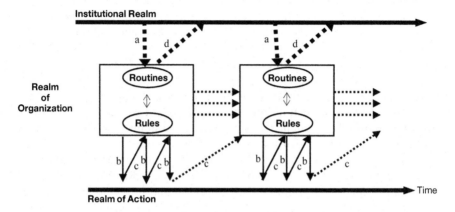

Figure 5.2 The process of institutionalization.

Source: adapted from Burns and Scapens (2000: 9).

reproduce institutions *diachronically* (i.e., through their cumulative influence over time)' (Burns and Scapens, 2000: 10). So synchronic and diachronic elements are combined in Figure 5.2. However, change processes in the institutional realm occur over longer periods of time than change in the realm of action. The top of the figure represents the institutional realm, whereas the bottom represents the realm of action. Both realms are ongoing in a cumulative process of change through time, as represented by the solid lines at the top and bottom of the figure.

The central part of Figure 5.2 illustrates the way in which rules and routines act as the modalities which link the institutional realm and the realm of action. Rules and routines are also in a cumulative process of change, as will be described below. However, from time to time new rules and new routines may be introduced or emerge in a more discrete way. The four arrows (labelled a–d) represent the synchronic (a and b) and diachronic processes (c and d).

To explain the process of institutionalization as a way of thinking in the model, we begin with arrow a. This step shows the *encoding* of the existing institution and taken-for-granted assumptions and meanings into the new rules, routines and procedures which embody organizational values. This means that new rules or procedures are usually interpreted in terms of the current norms and values of the group who use the system.

Arrow b is related to individuals' behaviour when enacting these new rules, routines and procedures which embody deep values. These rules are enacted when organizational members use them in their daily ongoing activities. The way these rules are enacted depends on existing institutions. Burns and Scapens (2000) argue that the successful enactment of the new rules depends on whether the norms and values underpinning them are in line or compatible with the norms and values of those who will enact or implement them. However, the process of *enactment*, especially if the rules and routines challenge existing meanings and values, and actors or individuals have sufficient resources of power to intervene in this process, can be *subject to resistance*. In other words, there could be resistance if the new rules require a different way of thinking and doing things in the organization. The new system might not be considered as legitimate, and organizational conflict could arise due to the implementation of the new procedures.

The third step (arrow c) 'takes place as repeated behaviour leads to a *reproduction* of the routines'. This constitutes part of the continuous process of 'social validation' that *for some specific values* embedded in rules and routines will lead to a further transformation in *shared* taken-for-granted assumptions. Such a transformation (arrow d) involves the *institutionalization* of the values (embodied and embedded in rules and routines) which have been reproduced through the behaviour of the individual actors. Such institutionalized rules and routines become 'taken-for-granted ways of behaving ... They become the unquestioned (and unquestionable) way of doing things' (Burns and Scapens, 2000: 11). Therewith, these underlying shared assumptions will be encoded into the ongoing behavioural rituals, and so on, within the continuous process of social reproduction and validation characterizing the evaluation of organizational culture (hence the progressively denser background signifies the change of culture's contents over time).

Drawing on the framework, the shared basic assumptions may be conceptualized as 'the structural properties, which comprise the taken-for-granted assumptions about the way of doing things, which shape and constrain the rules and routines, and determine the meanings, values, and also powers of the individual actors'. Furthermore, as they are disassociated from the particular historical circumstances, they exist only in the understandings and stocks of knowledge of the individuals and groups (Macintosh and Scapens, 1990). Therefore, such underlying assumptions are obviously more abstract than the rules and routines they affect – hence the dotted lines used for arrows a and d (see Schein, 1992) – and they bind time by shaping social interaction period by period (hence the several b and c arrows for each pair of a and d arrows). Moreover, the phases of encoding and institutionalization are 'ongoing processes, rather than distinct identifiable movements' – hence, the broad lines used for arrows a and d (Burns and Scapens, 2000: 11).

The above was a review of the process of institutionalization and the interaction of existing routines and institutions within organizations or at an intra-(micro-) organizational level. However, an organization's survival requires it as much to conform to societal norms of acceptable practice as to achieve high levels of production efficiency and effectiveness (Covaleski *et al.*, 1993).

From the NIS perspective, the success of an organization is defined to the extent to which the organization embodies societal ideals (myths) concerning norms of rational behaviour. From this view, more societal legitimacy can be achieved by more conformity to societal norms. This legitimacy, which affects the organizational structure defining its domain of activity, is the main factor in the survival and growth of an organization (Meyer *et al.*, 1993). In the previous section, the 'realm of societal interaction' or 'macro' level and its influence on the micro level or 'organization' was explored.

With regard to the effectiveness of OIE theory in the conceptualization of organizational actions and change, OIE is not without problems. The concern expressed regarding the limitation of OIE is its 'neglect of how agents [and organizations] absorb their paradigms' from the environment (Khalil, 1999: 62). OIE is criticized as its focus is primarily on the micro (individuals, groups and organizations) rather than the macro-level institutions. Burns (2000a, 2000b, 2001) argues that OIE is more suitable for studies of processes of change and resistance to change within organizations. In particular the theory is effective in investigating the role of power, politics and vested interests in change at micro (organizational) level.

Therefore, a more capable/suitable theory to conceptualize organizational behaviour is the one that accommodates both extra- and intra-organizational factors in its analysis. The merger of the two institutional theories, NIS and OIE, represents how in order to improve their legitimacy to external onlookers, firms adopt society-level rules, expectations, myths, procedures, fashions, and so on which over time may become institutionalized in the day-to-day life of firms.

Fusing OIE and NIS

An NIS-informed perspective of organizational studies is one which emphasizes the importance of external (usually society-level) rules, expectations, norms, etc. (i.e. sources of change) for driving such change, through isomorphism. In this respect, there is certainly overlap with an OIE perspective, which also emphasizes the importance of 'settled patterns of thinking and doing' for driving the pace and direction of change within firms (Burns, 2001: 27). NIS and OIE theories provide complementary insights. Both share the premise that action is largely organized by institutions, and widely held definitions of the behaviour and relationships appropriate for a set of actors.

Therefore, to extend the scope and enhance our understanding of organizational behaviour and action, there appears to be a need for a shift towards more pluralistic dialogue and multi-institutional theoretical outlooks. Consequently, this (hybrid) theoretical framework provides a different and broader view in explaining organizational change (or lack of change) and, in adopting this viewpoint, it is hoped that the analysis may provide a more holistic picture in the study of various organizational phenomena, such as change in organizational systems and practices.

The multi-institutional framework (see Figure 5.3) exhibits how, following the establishment of new systems and practices, which are forced or advocated by extra-organizational factors and adopted by firms through

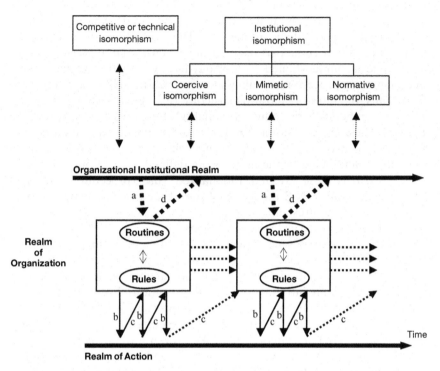

Figure 5.3 Multi-institutional framework incorporating both NIS and OIE.

isomorphism processes, in time the new systems and rules become 'taken-for-granted' activities such that their re-enactment is performed without conscious recourse to the initial rules. The new practices and emerging routines are said to be 'institutionalized' at firm level when they become widely accepted in a firm to the extent that they are an unquestionable form of the organization's systems. In which case, they have become an inherent feature of the organizational systems and processes, represent 'expected' patterns of behaviour, and define the relations between a firm's groups and/or individuals on one hand, and extra-organizational factors/institutions on the other (Burns, 2000b).

For example, when a new system and practice, such as an accounting system, has become generally perceived as a 'rational' and 'efficient' means to control activities (Meyer, 1986), the firms are coerced to adopt the new system through mechanisms of isomorphism i.e. the 'process' through which environmental factors permeate firm-level structures and processes (Burns, 2000b: 14). Following the adoption of the new system and practice by a firm, certain individuals have the regular task of providing and/or collating information, as well as numerous other regular tasks associated with the new accounting system. The re-enactment of such tasks underpins, and is under-pinned by, individuals' habits and routines. Furthermore, at group level, senior managers 'routinely' analyse the reports prepared by the new account-ing system at the monthly board meeting. Then, over time, the new system and practice may become part of the firm's taken-for-granted assumption, i.e. become an unquestioned part of day-to-day activities, underpinning decision making processes, meanings and organizational language (Preston, 1995). Thus, the intra-organization structure (e.g. the accounting one) and processes symbolically reproduce 'rationality' at society level (see Meyer *et al.*, 1983). These external rationalized rules and myths (e.g. the new account-ing system) can over time begin to underpin a firm's taken-for-granted assumptions and beliefs – the latter being defined as intra-organizational institutions. It is these external 'rationalized' rules, procedures, etc. that define 'institution' in NIS theory. And once they become integral to the firm's internal structures and processes, such factors can also be said to be institutions at the micro level (Burns, 2000b).

However, in some cases, new 'mechanical' routines may emerge over time from the new systems and practices without these new ways of thinking becoming institutionalized because they are unable to 'replace' or live alongside the existing intra-organizational institutions. Furthermore, if the assumptions underlying the change are inconsistent with the taken-for-granted assumptions in the firm, we can expect conflict and resistance (Burns *et al.*, 2003). For example, if the taken-for-granted assumptions in the firm are production/sales-oriented, a major accounting change (grounded in accounting-oriented rules, routines and taken-for-granted ways of thinking) can give rise to resistance, as many organizations experience. Thus the framework does not profess that all adopted/implemented systems and practices become routinized and/or institutionalized; but rather that there is potential for routinization and institutionalization to occur (Burns, 2000b).

Therefore, the framework contributes to our understanding of how rationalized myths are applied in particular situations and are also subject to the influence of intra-organization factors. The framework highlights that 'organizations are not passive actors being imprinted by cultural templates' (Scott, 1991: 170). Scott points out that organizational environments are differentiated, as are the sources of formal structures. Culture is not homo-geneous, and its plurality provides the basis for a more active and discretionary appropriation of formal structure by organizations. As he puts it: 'most types of organizations confront multiple sources and types of symbolic or cultural systems and … they exercise some choice in selecting the systems with which to connect' (1991: 181). Multiple, and even contradictory, cultural systems allow organizations to play them off against one another, rather than repro-duce internally a monolithic and unitary culture. The multiplicity of cultural sources grants organizations a measure of cultural autonomy. Carruthers (1995: 323–4) states that firms can choose from among a set of legitimating cultural 'scripts' or 'templates'. The same author explains the situation of the Progressive Era women's political organization as an example. He states that they could model their formal structure on business organizations (thus emphasizing their efficiency and rationality), political parties, unions, clubs or fraternal organizations, or combine elements from several of the alternatives. There was no single model with which women's organizations were compelled to comply. Their legitimacy was more creatively constructed than externally imposed (Carruthers, 1995).

The framework also conveys the message of a two-way interaction between environment and organizations. This is in line with the stress by some contributors that a firm's internal structure, systems and practices might shape external rules, etc. rather than merely represent such firm-level structures and processes as passive reactors to external stimuli (Burns, 2000b; Carruthers, 1995). This may lead to the question that how intra-firm factors can actively shape their own institutionalized environment. As Carruthers (1995: 324) states:

> Frequently, organizations play an active role in constructing rationalized myths, playing them off against each other, or shaping how they are applied in particular instances. Organizations are not only granted legitimacy; sometimes they go out and get it.

In summary, the hybrid institutional framework stresses that the causal flow between environment and firms is two-way (see Yazdifar, 2004). The framework reveals mechanisms through which society-level rules and myths through time impinge on intra-organizational activities and come to underpin a firm's specific 'know-how' or 'memory', and how an organization's systems and practices, whose origins lie outside the organization, may come to be embedded within the company and create a reality (Scott, 1987: 505) in which the extra-organizational expectations of appropriate organizational forms, systems and behaviour come to take on rule-like status in thought and action (Covaleski and Dirsmith, 1988: 562). The multi-institutional framework conceptualizes how the external 'rationalized and legitimized' policies that define 'institutions' at extra- (macro-) organizational level, become integral to an organization's internal structures and processes, which can be said to be institutions at intra- (or micro-) organizational level (Soin *et al.*, 2002). Furthermore, the framework highlights the role of intra-organizational factors in the adoption, implementation or possible resistance and rejection of the new systems. Being able to accommodate both extra- and intra-organizational factors in analysing organizational behaviours and actions, the framework is suitable to conceptualize how organizational and environmental factors interact.

Conclusion

The integration of the two institutional theories, NIS and OIE, serves to narrow the gaps in organizational theorizing, contributes to the compensation of the limitations of the two theories discussed above, and expands the level of analyses. Therefore, the framework can be adopted as a theoretical model to explain how institutions (at macro and micro levels) shape and constrain the behaviour and actions of individuals and organizations and to analyse how individuals themselves in turn modify and transform institutions and organizations. Hence, this theory provides a different and broader view of organizational change. Therefore, by taking the perspective outlined above, the analysis may provide a more holistic picture of various organizational phenomena, such as change in structures, systems and practices. The multi-institutional framework appeared to be more suitable and appropriate than applying a single institutional theory for exploring organizational interaction with the environment and the dynamics of change implementation in organizations, and provides a more comprehensive conceptual framework for understanding organizational behaviour. While a more detailed overview/analysis of such work would have been possible, the intention here was to highlight how the two theories can compensate for each other's weaknesses and flaws and act as complementary theories, thereby enhancing our understanding of organizational behaviour and actions.

Notes

1 Nelson and Winter (1982) proposed that to understand the processes of change and institutionalisation, it is necessary to conceptualise how new practices appear and emerge to become an institutionalised activity in an organization.
2 Dawson (1994) suggests that the initial need to change might be due to both external and internal pressures facing the organization by stating that:

> The increased complexity and uncertainty of international business markets has led some organizations to base change on imitation (which organizations are successful and what changes they have introduced), rather than on any conception of a need to adopt untried technologies or techniques [. . .] What is important is how the conception of a need to change can be influenced by factors residing within the organisation such as organisational inefficiencies, industrial relations disputes or those which emanate from outside the organization – for example, through business press and media reports on success of other organizations and the direct and indirect promotion of various management fads and fashions.
>
> (1994, pp. 36–7)

References

Abdul Khalid, S. N. (2000), 'An Institutionalist Study of Resistance to Management Accounting Change', unpublished Ph.D. thesis, Manchester School of Accounting and Finance.

Abernethy, M. A. and Chua, W. F. (1996), 'A field study of control systems "redesign": the impact of institutional *processes* on strategic choice', *Contemporary Accounting Research*, 13: 569–606.

Amburgey, T. L. and Dacin, M. T. (1994), 'As the left foot follows the right? The dynamics of strategic and structural change', *Academy of Management Journal*, 37(6): 1427–52.

Barley, S. R. and Tolbert, P. S. (1997), 'Institutionalization and structuration: studying the links between action and institution', *Organization Studies,* 18(1): 93–117.

Baum, J. A. C. (1996), 'Organizational ecology'. in S. R. Clegg, C. Hardy and W. Nord (eds), *Handbook of Organization Studies,* London: Sage, pp. 77–114.

Baxter, J. and Chua, W. F. (2003), 'Alternative management accounting research – whence and whither', *Accounting, Organisations and Society,* 28: 97–126.

Burns, J. (2000a), 'The dynamics of accounting change: inter-play between new practices, routines, institutions, power and politics', *Accounting, Auditing and Accountability Journal,* 13(5): 566–96.

—— (2000b), 'Institutional theory in management accounting research: the past, the present, and the future', Paper presented in ENROAC Conference, Oslo.

—— (2001), 'Institutional theory in management accounting research: towards more pluralistic dialogue in conceptualising management accounting change', working paper.

Burns, J. and Scapens, R. W. (2000), 'Conceptualizing management accounting change: an institutional framework', *Management Accounting Research,* 11: 3–25.

Burns, J., Ezzamel, M. and Scapens, R. W. (2003), 'The challenge of management accounting change: behavioural and cultural aspects of change management', CIMA monograph.

Carmona, S., Ezzamel, M. and Gutiérrez, F. (1998), 'Towards an institutional analysis of accounting change in the Royal Tobacco Factory of Seville', *Accounting Historians Journal,* 25(1): 115–47.

Carpenter, V. L. and Feroz, E. H. (1992), 'GAAP as a symbol of legitimacy: New York State's decision to adopt generally accepted accounting principles for external financial reporting', *Accounting, Organisations and Society,* 17(7): 613–43.

—— (2001), 'Institutional theory and accounting rule choice: an analysis of four US state governments' decisions to adopt generally accepted accounting principles', *Accounting, Organizations and Society,* 26: 565–96.

Carruthers, B. G. (1995), 'Accounting, ambiguity, and the new institutionalism', *Accounting, Organizations and Society,* 20(4): 313–28.

Child, J. (1972), 'Organizational structure, environment and performance: the role of strategic choice', *Sociology,* 6: 1–22.

Collier, P. M. (2001), 'The power of accounting: a field study of local financial management in a police force', *Management Accounting Research,* 12: 465–86.

Covaleski, M. A. and Dirsmith, M. W. (1988), 'An Institutional perspective on the rise, social transformation, and fall of a university budget category', *Administrative Science Quarterly,* 33: 562–87.

—— (1995), 'The preservation and use of public resources: transforming the immoral into the merely factual', *Accounting, Organizations and Society,* 20(2/3): 147–73.

Covaleski, M., Dirsmith, M. W. and Michelman, J. (1993), 'An Institutional theory perspective on the DRG framework: case-mix accounting systems and health care organizations', *Accounting, Organizations and Society,* 18(1): 65–80.

Dawson, P. (1994), '*Organizational Change: A Processual Approach*', London: Paul Chapman.

DiMaggio, P. (1988), 'Interest and agency in institutional theory' in L. E. Zucker (ed.), *Institutional Patterns and Organizations: Culture and Environment,* Cambridge, MA: Ballinger, pp. 3–21.

DiMaggio, P. J. and Powell, W. W. (1983), 'The iron cage revisited: institutional isomorphism and collective rationality in organizational fields', *American Sociological Review*, 48: 147–60.

—— (1991a), 'Introduction', in W. W. Powell and P. J. DiMaggio (eds), *The New Institutionalism in Organizational Analysis*, Chicago, IL: University of Chicago Press, pp. 1–38.

—— (1991b), 'The iron cage revisited: institutional isomorphism and collective rationality in organizational fields' in W. W. Powell and P. J. DiMaggio (eds), *The New Institutionalism in Organizational Analysis*, Chicago, IL: University of Chicago Press, pp. 63–82.

Dirsmith, M. W., Heian, J. B. and Covaleski, M. A. (1997), 'Structure and agency in an institutionalized setting: the application and social transformation of control in the big six'. *Accounting, Organizations and Society*, 22(1): 1–27.

Dugger, W. and Sherman, H. (1994), 'Comparison of Marxism and institutionalism', *Journal of Economic Issues*, 28(1): 101–27.

Genschel, P. (1997), 'The dynamics of inertia: institutional persistence and change in telecommunications and health Care', *Governance: An International Journal of Policy and Administration*, 10(1): 43–66.

Greenwood, R. and Hinings, C. R. (1996), 'Understanding radical organizational change: bringing together the old and the new institutionalism', *Academy of Management Review*, 21(4): 1022–54.

Gupta, P., Dirsmith, M. W. and Fogarty, T .J. (1994), 'Coordination and control in a government agency: contingency and institutional perspectives on GAO audits', *Administrative Science Quarterly*, 39: 264–84.

Hannan, M. T. and Freeman, J. (1977), 'The population ecology of organizations', *American Journal of Sociology*, 82: 929–64.

—— (1984), 'Structural inertia and organizational change', *American Sociological Review*, 49: 149–64.

Hodgson, G. (1993), 'Institutional economics: surveying the old and the new', *Metroeconomica*, 44: 1–28.

—— (1998), 'The approach of institutional economics', *Journal of Economic Literature*, XXXVI (March): 166–92.

Khalil, E. L. (1999), 'Institutions, naturalism and evolution', *Review of Political Economy*, 11(1): 61–81.

Ledford, G. E., Mohrman, A. M. and Lawler, E. E. (1989), 'The phenomenon of large-scale organizational change', in A. M. Mohrman, S. A. Mohrman, T. G. Ledford, T. G. Cummings, E. E. Lawler and Associates (eds), *Large-Scale Organization Change*, San Francisco, CA: Jossey-Bass, pp. 1–31.

Macintosh, N. and Scapens, R. (1990), 'Structuration theory in management accounting', *Accounting, Organizations and Society*, 15(5): 455–77.

Madhok, A. (1997), 'Cost, value and foreign market entry mode: the transaction and the firm', *Strategic Management Journal*, 18: 39–61.

Major, M. J. M. F. and Hopper, T. (2002), 'Extending new institutional theory: a case study of activity-based costing in the Portuguese telecommunications industry', working paper.

Martinez, R. J. and Dacin, M. T. (1999), 'Efficiency motives and normative forces: combining transactions costs and institutional logic', *Journal of Management*, 25(1), January–February: 75–6.

Mayhew, A. (1987), 'Culture: core concept under attack', *Journal of Economic Issues*, 21: 587–603.

Meyer, A. D., Tsui, A. S. and Hinings, C. R. (1993), 'Configurational approaches to organizational analysis', *Academy of Management Journal*, 11(4–5): 1175–95.

Meyer, J. W. (1986), 'Social environments and organizational accounting', *Accounting, Organizations and Society*, 36(6): 345–56.

Meyer, J. W. and Rowan, B. (1977), 'Institutionalised organisations: formal structures as myth and ceremony', *American Journal of Sociology*, 83: 340–63.

—— (1991), 'Institutionalised organisations: formal structures as myth and ceremony', in A. Powell and P. J. DiMaggio (eds), *The New Institutionalism in Organizational Analysis*, Chicago, IL: University of Chicago Press, pp. 41–62.

Mezias, S. (1990), 'An institutional model of organizational practice: financial reporting at the Fortune 200', *Administrative Science Quarterly*, 35: 431–57.

Miller, D. and Friesen, P. (1984), *Organizations: A Quantum View*, Englewood Cliffs, NJ: Prentice-Hall.

Mintzberg, H. (1979), *The Structuring of Organizations*, Englewood Cliffs, NJ: Prentice-Hall.

—— (1981), 'Organization design: fashion or fit?', *Harward Business Review*, 59: 103–16.

Modell, S. (2001), 'An institutional perspective on cost allocations', paper presented at the third Workshop on Management Accounting Change, Certosa di Pontignano, Siena, 17–19 May.

Neal, W. C. (1987), 'Institutions', *Journal of Economic Issues*, XXI(3): 1177–1206.

Nelson, R. R. (1994), 'Routines', in G. Hodgson, W. Samuels and M. Tool (eds), *The Elgar Companion to Institutional and Evolutionary Economics*, Aldershot: Edward Elgar, L–Z, pp. 249–52.

Nelson, R. R. and Winter, S. G. (1982), *An Evolutionary Theory of Economic Change*, Cambridge, MA: Belknap Press.

Oliver, C. (1991), 'Strategic responses to institutional processes', *Academy of Management Review*, 16(1): 145–79.

—— (1992), 'The Antecedents of deinstitutionalization', *Organization Studies*, 13(4): 563–88.

Perrow, C. (1986), *Complex Organizations*, 3rd edn, New York: Random House.

—— (1991), 'Review essay: overboard with myth and symbols', *American Journal of Sociology*, 91(1): 151–5.

Pfeffer, J. and Salancik, G. R. (1978), *The External Control of Organizations: A Resource Dependence Perspective*, New York: Harper and Row.

Powell, W. W. (1991), 'Expanding the scope of institutional analysis', in W. W. Powell and P. J. DiMaggio (eds), *The New Institutionalism in Organizational Analysis*, Chicago, IL: University of Chicago Press, pp. 183–203.

Preston, A. (1995), 'Budgeting, creativity and culture', in D. Ashton, T. Hopper and R. W. Scapens (eds), *Issues in Management Accounting*, London: Prentice Hall Europe, pp. 273–97.

Romslad, Y. (1996), 'Is a transaction a transaction?', *Journal of Economic Issues*, XXX(2): 413–25.

Scapens, R. W. (1991), *Management Accounting: A Review of Recent Developments*, 2nd edn, London: Macmillan.

—— (1994), 'Never mind the gap: towards an institutional perspective on management accounting practice', *Management Accounting Research*, 5: 301–21.

Schein, E. H. (1992), *Organizational Culture and Leadership*, San Francisco, CA: Jossey-Bass.

Scott, W. R. (1987), 'The adolescence of institutional theory', *Administrative Science Quarterly,* 32: 493–511.

—— (1991), 'Unpacking institutional arguments', in W. W. Powell and P. J. DiMaggio (eds), *The New Institutionalism in Organizational Analysis,* Chicago, IL: University of Chicago Press, pp. 164–82.

—— (1995), *Institutions and Organizations,* Thousand Oaks, CA: Sage.

Scott, W. R. and J. W. Meyer (1983), 'The organization of societal sectors', in J. W. Meyer and W. R. Scott (eds), *Organizational Environments: Ritual and Rationality,* Beverly Hills, CA: Sage, pp. 129–53.

Selznick, P. (1949), *TVA and the Grass Roots Berkeley,* Berkeley, CA: University of California Press.

Soin, K., Seal, W. and Cullen, J. (2002), 'ABC and organizational change: an institutional perspective', *Management Accounting Research,* 13: 249–71.

Strang, D. and Sine, W. D. (2002), 'Interorganizational institutions', in J. Baum (ed.), *Blackwell Companion to Organizations,* London: Blackwell Scientific Publications.

Tolbert, P. S. (1985), 'Resource dependence and institutional environment: sources of administrative structure in institutions of higher education', *Administrative Science Quarterly,* 20: 229–49.

Tolbert, P. S. and Zucker, L. G. (1983), 'Institutional sources of change in the formal structure of organizations: the diffusion of civil service reforms, 1880–1935', *Administrative Science Quarterly,* 28: 22–39.

Veblen, T. (1898), 'Why is economics not an evolutionary science?', *Quarterly Journal of Economics* 12: 373–97.

—— (1909), 'The limitations of marginal utility', *Journal of Political Economy,* 17: 620–36.

—— (1919), *The Place of Science in Modern Civilization and Other Essays,* New York: Huebsch.

Whittington, R. (1992), 'Putting Giddens into action: social systems and managerial agency', *Journal of Management Studies,* 29: 693–712.

Williamson, O. (1975), *Markets and Hierarchies: Analysis and Anti-Trust Implications. A Study in the Economics of Internal Organisation,* New York: Free Press.

—— (1981), 'The modern corporation: origins, evolution, attributes', *Journal of Economic Literature,* 19: 1537–68.

—— (1985), *The Economic Institutions of Capitalism: Firms, Markets, Relational Contracting,* New York: Macmillan.

Yazdifar, H. (2004), 'Insight into the Dynamics of Management Accounting Systems Implementation in Group (Dependent) Organizations: An Institutional Perspective', unpublished Ph.D. thesis, Manchester School of Accounting and Finance.

Zucker, L. G. (1987), 'Institutional theories of organizations', *Annual Review of Sociology,* 13: 443–64.

—— (1991), 'The role of institutionalization in cultural persistence' in W. W. Powell and P. J. DiMaggio (eds), *The New Institutionalism in Organizational Analysis,* Chicago, IL: University of Chicago Press, pp. 83–107.

Part II
The economics of the firm
Change and evolution

6 The evolutionary theory of the firm

Routines, complexity and change

Werner Hölzl

Introduction

The theory of the firm is a central element in modern economics and the firm is one of the central economic institutions of capitalism. There is considerable controversy regarding the relative importance of the techno-functional and institutional foundations of the theory of the firm. An economic explanation of why firms exist – first suggested by Coase (1937) – is because they are efficient. The costs of organizing a transaction within the firm must be less than the costs of using the market for firms to exist. The modern theory of the firm explains the boundaries of the firm based on three major costs of organizing firms: communication and coordination costs (Coase, 1937; Williamson, 1975; Radner, 1992), agency costs (Alchian and Demsetz, 1972) and the hold-up problem (Klein *et al.*, 1978; Williamson, 1985). These costs can be lumped together and viewed as different kinds of transaction costs. However, there is still room for controversy, as Dietrich (2006) suggests: the firm can be conceived primarily as a legal unit, a governance structure or a strategic entity, which has different theoretical implications. However, common to this literature on the theory of the firm is the view that the size of the firm is largely independent of technological considerations which dominate the literature on plant size. The neglect of technology in this literature has been noted by a number of commentators (e.g. Antonelli, 1999; Lindbeck and Snower, 2003). However, most modern developments falling within the rubric of the economic theory of the firm have looked at the firm as a bundle of bilateral contracts. This implies a major neglect of the technological and organizational aspects of production. This view is epitomized by Alchian and Demsetz (1972), who do not see any relevant difference between the relation which occurs between employer and employee and the one between a grocer and his customers.

The evolutionary theory of the firm provides an alternative explanation of the firm based on routines. In a world where agents differ in their perceptions of the environment, and where communication, acquisition of information and computation are limited and costly, coordination can only be achieved by means of the definition of a common set of rules and codes which are understood and shared by the members of the organization involved in economic interaction. While it is true that evolutionary theory focuses especially on the technological aspects of production, it also stresses the cognitive nature of the organizational structure of the firm.

The evolutionary theory of the firm in its original form as proposed by Nelson and Winter (1982) is similar to the 'black-box' view of neoclassical economics as a device to study evolutionary dynamics. This view of the firm does not consider the organization of the firm in an explicit way. However, the firm is described as entity processing, storing and producing knowledge. The evolutionary theory of the firm can be more than a device to study industrial dynamics. Notions like 'corporate coherence' (Teece *et al.*, 1994) or 'routines as truce' (Nelson and Winter, 1982) point in this direction.

Evolutionary economics

Evolutionary economics sees the economy as a scientific domain character-ized by disequilibrium processes in which economic agents create and adapt to novelty through learning rather than a system in equilibrium or resting in a steady state (Witt, 1991; Nelson, 1995; Saviotti, 1997; Foster and Metcalfe, 2001; Fagerberg, 2003; Cantner and Hanusch, 2002). The influence of Schumpeter on evolutionary economics cannot be overstated. The reasons for Schumpeter's appeal to many economists stems from the fact that he stressed the qualitative nature of economic change which revolves around the introduction of new goods with different characteristics, new methods of production, and new methods of organization. Schumpeter was a major influence on the work of Nelson and Winter, whose seminal contribution *An Evolutionary Theory of Economic Change* provided the point of origin for the modern study of the evolutionary behaviour in economic systems. The starting point of Nelson and Winter's contribution is a critique of the standard theory of production. Their emphasis is on learning (mainly technological) and selection among heterogeneous firms. The basic tenets are outlined in Nelson and Winter (1982: 4), as follows:

> [t]he firms in our evolutionary theory will be treated as motivated by profit and engaged in search for ways to improve their profits, but their actions will not be assumed to be profit maximizing over well-defined and exogenously given choice sets ... Our theory emphasizes the tendency for the most profitable firms to drive the less profitable ones out of business; however, we do not focus our analysis on hypothetical states of 'industry equilibrium' in which all the unprofitable firms no longer are in the industry and the profitable ones are at their desired size.

Since Nelson and Winter's contribution it has become more and more customary to equate changes in economic structure, the changing relative frequencies of different actions, behaviours and institutions with evolutionary change, and to attribute the ultimate source of change to the co-existence of rival and different forms of behaviour. Evolution in the context of evolutionary economics means that economic development over time is an open-ended dynamic process over an open state space. This shows that evolutionary economics is not a one-to-one transfer of evolutionary theory or metaphors from biology into economics. Far from that, evolutionary economics takes into account the specificity of the economic sphere. The framework outlined in Nelson and Winter's contribution has proved to be fruitful, especially in the area of the economics of technology and growth theory. Three distinguishing and interrelated traits of evolutionary economics can be identified:

1   While there is disagreement on the specific definitions, there is agreement on the fact that *knowledge and information* are central ingredients of the approach of evolutionary economics. Economic systems are knowledge-based. Economic knowledge is conceived as a set of routines that are reproduced through practice. The processes of knowledge creation and destruction underpin and drive economic growth and qualitative change. The growth of knowledge cannot be meaningfully captured as a constellation of equilibrating forces (Nelson and Winter, 1982; Metcalfe, 1998; Witt, 1997; Foster and Metcalfe, 2001).

2   Evolutionary economics takes a *population approach* instead of a typological approach based on representative agents. The heterogeneity of economic behaviour is based on the distribution of knowledge and information within the economy (Hayek, 1945). Heterogeneity drives economic change, which can be cast in terms of observable changes in the compositions of population of firms, technologies and industries. The decentralized nature of the economic system implies that there is massive parallelism of computation and behaviour within the economic systems. Together with spillovers the decentralized organization creates not only the problem-solving capability of the economic system but also the capability to formulate new problems and new behaviour (Dosi, 1997; Metcalfe, 1998).

3   The *interdependence between selection and development* is a first characteristic of evolutionary economics. Competition as a selection process provides a process structuring economic activity (Metcalfe, 1998) and imposing a requirement of procedural rationality on participants. Selection changes the frequencies of entities (measures them as numbers or market shares) in the population according to rewards. From a perspective of variety generation, markets are institutions which not only coordinate economic behaviour but facilitate change, entrepreneurship and challenges to established behaviours. Selection processes operate on variety: they destroy variety. The generation of variety and the selection of variety interact in the process of development. In order to have economic development, variety needs to be re-created.

The outcome of the operation of an evolutionary process is adaptation: the fit of entities in consideration with the properties of the selection environment. In this respect, it has to be noted that evolutionary processes are not compatible with completely random behaviour. Every notion of evolution which postulates that behaviour is random ignores the requirement of *inertia* of any evolutionary argument. In other words, there must be some degree of heredity of behavioural routines, technologies and attributes in the economic system. The inertia argument implies that the behavioural characteristics of the agents and units of selection must be correlated over time. This suggests that constructed 'random' worlds may change over time but not evolve in an evolutionary sense. This means, in order to construct an evolutionary argument for the economic sphere, it must be ensured that the behaviour of agents and organizations changes more slowly than the rate at which the selection process takes place.

The evolutionary theory of the firm

Nelson and Winter begin with a critique of standard production theory. Standard production theory starts from the set of all technologically feasible technologies and assumes that each firm can operate these technologies if it wishes. Each of the different production techniques available is parameterized by a vector of inputs and outputs corresponding to the productive transformation a firm can accomplish. The set of all optimal techniques which provide the maximum output with given inputs define the production function. Nelson and Winter criticize this conception of production as not depicting the reality of the economic problem of production, where the idea that all technological knowledge is available in an articulate way in a book of blueprints is not met. Especially the implicit assumption that technological knowledge can be written down at a negligible cost is a target of their critique. The existence of universally available technological knowledge implies that technological change is exogenous and the activities of research and development are separated from actual production. They contrast this theory with their own theory of production based on differential capabilities, embedded in the personal and organizational structure of firms. Skills on the personal level and routines at the organizational level form the repository of knowledge which in turn defines the production possibilities of firms. The important aspect for Nelson and Winter was that the theory emphasized 'firm differences'. Thereby Nelson and Winter (1982) proposed an interpretation of production technology as 'production knowledge' including, besides embodied knowledge in equipment and machinery, also tacit knowledge, capabilities, skills and even heuristics for problem-solving. Even if this knowledge is non-excludable in nature, it is not easily transferable between firms. It is stored as routines in the firms. Routines define the technological knowledge of a firm. Following Nelson and Winter, evolutionary theorists base their theories of the firm on bounded rationality (rule-based behaviour) and routines.

The behaviour of firms is characterized in terms of technological capabilities, worker skills and decision rules. The connecting elements are called routines. Routines are the result of past learning efforts and constitute the organizational memory of a firm. As such they are embodied in and link activities with the aim of producing goods or processing information. Routines can be considered to be repositories of knowledge because they connect in a quasi-formal way individual skills. A routine is a sequence of condition-action rules for different tasks which are executed sequentially or in parallel. The evolutionary paradigm of the firm is deeply rooted in the idea of the firm as an information processor that facilitates the firm's capacity to adapt and process new information. Organizational routines are all organizational regularities and standardized processes of production and information processing which describe the behavioural patterns and production techniques of firms. Nelson (1994) stresses that 'a firm can be understood in terms of a hierarchy of practiced organizational routines, which define lower order bureaucratization skills and higher order decision procedures for choosing what is to be done at the lower level'. With the term 'routine' Nelson and Winter describe two different aspects: the cognitive aspects of learning and knowledge on the one hand and the organizational aspects of incentives, monitoring and control on the other hand. From this stems the conceptual difficulty or confusion on the exact definition of what routines are in the literature (Cohen *et al.*, 1996). Routines have a double character as problem-solving skills and as mechanisms of governance.

Organizational traits are closely related to the function of a 'truce' of routines. March and Simon (1993: 2) state: 'organization is the transformation of conflict into cooperation'. In the terminology of game theory this may be expressed as how a prisoner's dilemma can be transformed into a coordination game. Basically, three different mechanisms can be used to achieve this goal: reciprocal altruism, the exclusion of free-riding behaviour, and most importantly the repeated nature of the game within an organization. The folk theorem states that trigger strategies can support any set of payoffs feasible in the underlying game. The selection of equilibria is essentially a coordination problem. No longer are preferences central; the beliefs about how the other players play the game become central. Put in this context a routine is a specific way of playing the organizational coordination game. Routines provide organization-specific conventions. There will be routines within groups, but in an organizational context of firms the rules of the game and the way this game is played between different subgroups (different divisions or departments) of a firm are highly important. Inconsistent conventions lead to frictions in coordination and to losses in performance.

The specific feature of the evolutionary approach is that it explains the adaptive behaviours of firms through the tension between innovation and various selection mechanisms. Coriat and Weinstein (1995) argue that an evolutionary theory of the firm has the advantage, compared to other theories of the firm, of providing an explanation for three issues of importance to understanding the nature of firms:

1   It explains how a firm can be defined, through the set of routines and competencies that the firm encompasses.
2   It explains why firms differ, because they rely on a different set of routines which are firm-specific and cannot be transferred at low cost.
3   It explains the dynamics of firms, through the combined mechanisms of searching and selection and the possibility of transforming a set of secondary routines into the core activity.

The evolutionary theory thus provides a theory of firm differences and dynamic change based on learning and adaptation. Thereby it is a device for studying industrial dynamics. However, even if the evolutionary theory is not primarily focused on the boundaries of the firm, it suggests an alternative approach to this issue – namely that the boundaries of the firm lie where information is most easily codified and a shared context is created which allows the minimization of transaction costs associated with problems of limited (or missing) competence. In this respect it is true that routines may help save transaction costs associated with information processing. But there are distinctive differences between transaction cost theory and the evolutionary approach. The transaction costs approach views the firm as an efficient outcome of market selection processes, which are usually treated as black box. The evolutionary paradigm, in contrast, is based on cumulative processes which do not necessarily ensure the 'survival of the fittest' but advocate a 'weak selection process' that is based on existing structures.

However, there are still a number of open questions which need to be answered for the evolutionary theory to provide a true theory of the firm:

1   The theory of how routines change is not well developed. The internal selection process within the firm needs more empirical and theoretical content.
2   Routines as a truce: the evolutionary firm has little to say regarding the conflicts within firms, e.g. capital–labour conflict or corporate governance. The role of routines as truce is largely unexplored.
3   The evolutionary theory of the firm is largely silent on the issue of entrepreneurship (Witt, 1998).

Among these unsettled questions the issue of how routines change is a very important one. Therefore let us concentrate on this issue, and in order to do this we first need to look in more detail at the foundations of the basic concept of the evolutionary theory of the firm: routines and rule-based behaviour.

Routines and rule-based behaviour

Routines are specific instances of rule-based behaviour at the level of an organization. They are decision processes that require low levels of creative information processing (rules of thumb), but can be complex automatic behaviours which involve high levels of repetitive information processing. Cohen *et al.* (1996: 683) define a routine as 'an executable capability for repeated performance in some context that has been learned by an organization in response to selection pressures'.

However, as a general theory of decision making the concept of routine is not precise enough. A consensus has emerged that routines relate to organizations, whereas rule-based behaviour relates to individuals. Rule-based individual behaviour, it has been argued, may provide the core for an alternative behavioural theory of decision making (Cohen *et al.*, 1996; Heiner, 1988). Like modern rational choice theory modern theorizing on rule-based behaviour is based on firm individualistic foundations. Thereby the concept of rule-based behaviour may form a theoretical basis to explain organizational routines.

Most economic models which involve learning argue that only some well-specified dynamics on the content of the rules are needed, as it is assumed that:

1   the representations of the agent are strict partitions of the states of the world;
2   the set of possible actions is known and relatively trivial, which implies that the known actions do not differ from the possible actions;
3   the interpretations are always true and there is no need for an interpretation. Any real interpretation is redundant as there is transparency, i.e. the agent knows what really happened.

However, as Dosi *et al.* (2004) argue, it might be that another model might well be useful as a first descriptive approximation, where it is assumed that:

1   the action repertoire is fixed;
2   learning is basically about the development of representations and models which map the invariant action repertoire on the payoff.

Behavioural adaptation is learning about the representations of the environment, the appropriateness of rules and the payoff function attached to these rules given the environment. This shows that rule-based behaviour is essentially dynamic, based on behavioural adaptation. The prime difference from rational choice theory is that theories of rule-based behaviour see the adaptiveness at the level of the rules of action. The individuals are not presumed to be case-by-case maximizers, capable of understanding all contingencies of the chosen situation. What is ascribed to them is the capability to change their rules by learning from past experience. Rule-based theorizing attracts attention towards the process of adaptive learning (Vanberg, 1994: 29).

A rule is essentially a condition–action rule applied to chosen situations, which allows individuals to trigger an action when a condition is realized. There is no finite set of alternative rules available from which one is chosen. And it does not make much sense to speak of a 'given best' rule, as the very nature of rules implies that their appropriateness can only be judged by their performance on a longer sequence of applications.[1] This shows that in the context of rule-based behaviour there is more to bounded rationality that costly decision making (Radner, 1996). Costly decision making refers to costly activities related to (i) observation, (ii) information processing that is computing, (iii) memory, and (iv) communication. The last category is especially important in the context of an organization when the decision making process is assigned to a team of individuals. If these costly processes refer to binding constraints they need to be taken in account in the decision makers' optimization problem. If they relate to resource use in time, then extensive decision making causes delay, which may result in the lower effectiveness of the decision.

The same is true for truly bounded rationality in the sense of Radner (1996), who does identify (i) inconsistency, (ii) ambiguity and vagueness, (iii) unawareness and (iv) the failure of logical omniscience as leading to true bounded rationality. Inconsistency may result in the decision maker having inconsistent preferences, as he is forced to articulate preferences about which he is not sure. Ambiguity and vagueness relate to the interpretation of the world, and the learning process relates to revisions of the model the agent holds. The problem is that the agent knows that he will revise the model in future, but he has no ability whatsoever to predict what the revisions will be. Vagueness and ambiguity can refer to the uncertainty of consequences: that is, uncertainty about the payoff function or vagueness about the states of the world. While it may well be that a rational choice theory about learning the model is feasible, the problem of 'failure of logical omniscience' is fundamental, as it refers to the fact that the agent 'does not know all of the relevant logical implications of what he knows' (Radner, 2000: 653). Radner gives examples which illustrate the problem; one of these is: 'Given all that is known, theoretically and empirically, about business organizations in general, and about telecommunications and AT&T in particular, should AT&T reorganize itself internally, and if so, how?' (Radner, 2000: 654).

As Radner remarks, the problem with the 'failure of logical omniscience' for any theory of rational choice including theories of bounded rationality is the meaning of 'rationality' in this specific case. Rule-based behaviour in contrast replaces 'rationality' with adaptability. There are still problems with the formulation of a 'general' theory of behavioural adaptation. In this context the distinction between information and knowledge is extremely useful. Information can be defined as data relating to states of the world and the state-contingent consequences that follow from events. Knowledge in contrast is an information-produced belief (Fransman, 1994): the cognitive frame to interpret information and to transform it into new knowledge. And rules are essentially a specific form of (tacit or formal) knowledge.

Whenever one abandons the most restrictive assumption on information perfection and symmetry among agents, organizational forms do matter because incentives, information flows and behaviour differ according to the particular architecture of rules (corporate culture) of each firm. Routines are not behaviour. They are stored behavioural capabilities. These capabilities involve knowledge and memory, and the firm, by being the storage of routines, is a coordination device for economic, and especially productive, action.

The firm as a collection of organizational routines

Routines are not isolated. They are interdependent within firms. Business firms and other economic organizations are more or less complex networks of routines, where products (also information) of one activity are inputs into another. Some of the ties in this network can be very strong, while others may be weaker. The strength of the connection can result from strict technical complementarities, but also from dynamic complementarities, which capture learning spillovers, synergy effects and other mechanisms generating dynamic complementarities.

The same production activities – for example, the manufacture of cars – can be routinized in different ways, as emphasized by Dosi and Coriat (1998), who compare the different management styles, routines, incentives and control mechanisms in American and Japanese manufacturing. The differences show how knowledge and competence can be allocated in quite different ways. Aoki (1990) has emphasized that this implies different internal architectures with respect to information-processing and incentive governance. The fragmentation of tasks allocated to single workers requires a different control system and system of coordination from the Japanese system based on 'transferable work components' which can be allocated to the workers in a small group. This example shows that routines must fit with each other in order to provide a required performance.

Complementarity is an attribute of elements of a given system (network, production process or firm) and arises if single elements of the systems interact in such a way as to influence the overall performance of the system. An good example is provided by the personal computer: the choice of best components (CPU, motherboard, graphic card, software) does not necessarily imply that this PC is better than all the others. Indeed it might even not work if the 'best' CPU cannot be put on the 'best' motherboard. This shows also that complementarity is deeply connected to the concept of linkages and interfaces, as with an adapter it might be possible to put the CPU on the motherboard. A useful metaphor for thinking about systems with comple-mentarities is Stuart Kauffman's *NK* model (cf. Kauffman, 1993; Hölzl, 2006). The *NK* model presents an intuitive mathematical metaphor for thinking about complementarity. The *NK* model is simple: it presents a system with *N* elements, each of which can take one of *x* possible states, and *K* dependence relations between these elements. The *NK* model can easily be thought of as representing a firm with *N* routines. If a routine is not linked to any other activity then we have perfect separability. Under perfect separ-ability each activity can be changed or even exchanged without compro-mising the working of the system, as the performance of other elements is not influenced. If an element is connected with other activities in the net-work, then its removal affects the performance of the other activities.

Some routines will mediate the interaction between other routines and in this way influence the performance characteristics. These may be viewed as forming the organizational 'core' of a firm. If no such activities existed the firm would just be a collection of unrelated organizational and technological processes not interacting with each other. The interdependencies and com-plementarities between routines form the core of a firm. That means that routines that affect the performance of many other routines are critical. A change in one of those core routines affects the overall performance of the firm to a much larger extent than routines that are peripheral. This implies that complementarity lowers the possibility of controlling perfectly the per-formance of the firm, as small changes may have large effects. Separable routines, which are peripheral, are more likely to be changed, as even negative changes do not have a pervasive effect and can be identified and isolated without affecting many other functions within a firm. A firm con-sisting only of separable activities is perfectly modular. This would allow perfect control of the performance of the firm, but in the end this system is devoid of a formal coordination mechanism relating them to each other. Hence, it would no longer be possible to talk about a firm.

The existence of highly interrelated activities has two implications for the process of organizational and technological search (Hölzl and Reinstaller, 2003; Reinstaller and Hölzl, 2004). First, for core activities there are more tradeoffs between the performance values of other different elements of the organizational system. The risk that the improvements in performance of some routines are offset by reductions in performance of other routines is high. The more complex the organization, the higher the likelihood that a change in one component may conflict with the overall performance. This implies that elements in the core are less likely to be changed. Improvements within the context of an existing organizational core take place by substi-tuting, adding or changing routines that are peripheral. The second implication is that the core reduces uncertainty by representing a stable setup. It represents a organizational design that works, and there is an incentive to keep the core elements of the operating procedures as they are. Together this implies that firms are slow and reluctant to change core routines. Firms are complex multi-dimensional bundles of routines, decision rules and incentive schemes whose interplay is largely unknown to those who manage the organization, since with strong interdependencies the system cannot be optimized by optimizing the separate elements it is made of.

If shocks punctuate evolutionary development and induce radical transformations, the strong complementarities in the core may turn into binding constraints by causing imbalances between activities and hindering adaptation. Then firms have an incentive to break up the constraint posed by complementarities between the different routines forming the core. It is difficult for firms to reinvent themselves. Empirical research shows that changes that require the change of core routines increase organizational mortality (Carroll and Hannan, 2000). This explains why new firms are the carriers of radically new innovations with respect to both technology and organization. Incumbents have an advantage with cumulative changes. Organizational routines, while being an effective way of storing and reproducing organizational knowledge, are by their very nature a source of organizational inertia.

The picture of the firm that emerges is one of relative stability, which forms a focusing device to coordinate the actions of the people involved within the organization. Routines and rule-based behaviour reduce the cognitive distance between the members of the organization (Nooteboom, 1992). The focusing device helps to align perceptions, understandings, goals and motives.

How do routines change?

The firm as a collection of organizational routines is rigid and inert. However, firms do change, and with them their routines. This raises questions about the usefulness of this view of the firm – especially from the perspective of evolutionary economics, where competition does not take the form of pushing prices to marginal costs, but rather replacing products and processes by ones that are better, more efficient or satisfy preferences more closely (Nooteboom, 2001). The question is how routines change and how firms change. This question is far from settled, and is related to the tradeoff between exploration and exploitation in organizations (March, 1991). The tradeoff between efficiency of current production and the exploration of new products and new ways of doing things, related to the uncertainty of innovation, is one of the fundamental questions of the management of change.

Most evolutionary models are based on competitive selection. This model has also been applied to the selection of organizational traits. But in the context of the firm as a network of interdependent routines and activities this model has serious limitations, even if it cannot be denied that the competition between firms should lead to the selection of collections of routines that yield the highest profits (Massini *et al.*, 2002). A strong selection argument is impossible to make as it is the totality of routines that are subject to the 'market screening', rather than individual routines. Increasing the internal efficiency of some routines does not imply that the overall efficiency of the firm needs to increase as well. Outputs are selected by the market, not by individual routines or transactions. Therefore, it is generally very difficult to link the performance of single routines to a firm's overall performance. Competitive selection between firms cannot explain the diffusion of routines.

The replication (copying) of organizational practices is a second mechanism (Hodgson and Knudsen, 2004). For this reason, in organization science the idea of internal or managerial selection is dominant. Let us first consider the creation of a pool of variety for selection internal to the firm. This relates to the duplication of subsidiaries, divisions or departments. This redundancy is inefficient and difficult to manage (Nooteboom, 2001). This possibility is open only to very large firms which have both the managerial and financial resources for the creation of internal variety of routines. Moreover, if we consider multinational firms, the subsidiaries are embedded in different economic and cultural environments, which may make it difficult to compare the efficiencies of routines or collection of routines. Even if it is difficult to obtain a clear picture of the contribution of each routine to the firm's overall performance, it is only possible to consider routine bundles related to identifiable and measurable activities such as total quality management or sales or logistic systems (Lazaric and Denis, 2001). The internal selection of routines by management fiat is related to learning, imitation and local adaptation. However, there is a fundamental problem related to the managerial selection and local adaptation. The link between internal selection processes and environmental pressures need not be strong. It might well be that internal selection environments become divorced from external pressures leading to maladaptation (Sorenson and Stuart, 2000). The incremental nature of local learning processes increases the effectiveness of operating routines and production processes. But these improvements are realized in the neighbourhood of the firm's existing activities, thus increasing the possibility that the local adaptation becomes divorced from the selection environment, leading to an obsolescence of underlying routines.

As noted in the literature on the diffusion of organizational practices, examples of successful routine replication exist, as do examples of successful reinvention of firms, such as the transformation of Preussag, a diversified national mining company since 1923, into TUI (its new name adopted in 2002), now a leader in the European tourism market. Critical in this respect is the capacity of the organization to absorb the new practices and to integrate them into the existing organizational context. This is an easier task for large firms with appropriate managerial and financial resources such as Preussag than for small firms, as refocusing through acquisition is much easier than reconfiguring an existing organizational structure. The interdependency of routines implies that a change of routine not only alters the performance of other routines but more importantly it also predetermines the type of other routines. This implies that firms cannot easily be decomposed into their individual components. The structures and routines within firms normally share the fate of the firm itself. While individual skills and physical capital can be moved to alternative uses, idiosyncratic structures and routines are usually specific to the firm itself (Winter, 1988). Most of the firm's routines share the fate of the firm in which they were created (Hodgson and Knudsen, 2004). This suggests that entrepreneurial action in response to firm exit may be an important element changing the pool of routines in an economy. The skills and physical resources released are released for alternative uses in existing and new firms, where they can be routinized in new and more efficient ways.

Concluding remarks

The specific feature of the evolutionary approach is that it explains the adaptive behaviours of firms through the tension between innovation and various selection mechanisms. It shows that rule-based behaviour and routines can provide a useful basis for a theory of the firm which is concerned with change over time and development. However, the evolutionary theory of the firm is still basically a theory of why firms differ and provides a device for the study of industrial dynamics and evolutionary growth.

The discussion of the firm as a collection of organizational routines and the change of routines has shown that an evolutionary theory of the firm need not be restricted to the definition of innovation possibility frontiers. An evolutionary theory of the firm may be able to provide a theoretical framework for the analysis of organizational boundaries and change. The understanding of how routines are formed and change is central and needed as the foundation for an evolutionary theory of the firm that integrates the views of the firm as a repository of knowledge and as a network of incentives and power.

Note

1 A question which is debated in the literature is whether rule-following behaviour is a subset of rational choice theory: that is, whether it can be rationally chosen to follow a rule. This question seems to be innocent, but it boils down to the question: can it be assumed that economic actors can choose to switch their rational calculation on and off? This would require some kind of 'meta-rationality' and a two-step procedure of rational choice. In the first stage the decision maker decides rationally whether he decides on a rule or whether he makes a choice. In the second stage he follows the rule or makes a rational choice. However, such a theory would not be much different from an adaptive learning process about rules: that is, about evaluating rules *ex post* and adjusting the rule.

References

Alchian, A. A. and Demsetz, H. (1972), 'Production, information costs, and economic organization', *American Economic Review*, 62(5): 777–95.

Antonelli, C. (1999), 'The organization of production', *Metroeconomica*, 50: 234–59.

Aoki, M. (1990), 'Towards an economic model of the Japanese firm', *Journal of Economic Literature*, 28(1): 1–27.

Cantner, U. and Hanusch, H. (2002), 'Evolutionary economics, its basic concepts and methods', in H. Lim, U. K. Park and G. C. Harcourt (eds), *Editing Economics*, London: Routledge, pp. 182–207.

Carroll, G. and Hannan, M. (2000), *The Demography of Corporations and Industries*, Princeton, NJ: Princeton University Press.

Coase, R. H. (1937), 'The nature of the firm', *Economica*, 4: 386–405.

Cohen, M., Burkhart, G., Dosi, M., Egidi, M., Marengo, L., Wargilen, M. and Winter, S. (1996), 'Routines and other recurring action patterns of organisations: contemporary research issues', *Industrial and Corporate Change*, 5(3): 653–98.

Coriat, B. and Weinstein, O. (1995), *Les nouvelles théories de l'Entreprise*, Paris: Livre de Poche.

Dietrich, M. (2006), 'The nature of the firm revisited', this volume, ch. 2.

Dosi, G. (1997), 'Opportunities, incentives and the collective patterns of technological change', *Economic Journal*, 107: 1530–47.

Dosi, G. and Coriat, B. (1998), 'Learning how to govern and learning how to solve problems: on the coevolution of competences, conflicts and organisational routines', in A. D. Chandler, P. Hagstrom and Ö. Sovell (eds), *The Dynamic Firm: The Role of Technology, Strategy, Organization, and Regions*, Oxford: Oxford University Press.

Dosi, G., Marengo, L. and Fagiolo, G. (2004), 'Learning in an evolutionary environment', in K. Dopfer (ed.), *The Evolutionary Principles of Economics*, Cambridge: Cambridge University Press.

Fagerberg, J. (2003), 'Schumpeter and the revival of evolutionary economics: an appraisal of the literature', *Journal of Evolutionary Economics*, 13: 125–59.

Foster, J. and Metcalfe, J. S. (eds) (2001), *Frontiers of Evolutionary Economics*, Cheltenham: Edward Elgar.

Fransman, M. (1994), 'Information, knowledge, vision and theories of the firm', *Industrial and Corporate Change*, 3: 713–57.

Hayek, F. A. (1945), 'The use of knowledge in society', *American Economic Review*, 34(4): 519–30.

Heiner, R. A. (1988), 'Imperfect decisions, routinized behaviour and inertial technical change', in G. Dosi, C. Freeman, R. Nelson, L. Soete and G. Silverberg (eds), *Technical Change and Economic Theory*, London: Pinter.

Hodgson, G. M. and Knudsen, T. (2004), 'The firm as an interactor: firms as vehicles for habits and routines', *Journal of Evolutionary Economics*, 14(3): 281–307.

Hölzl, W. (2006), 'The convergence of financial systems: towards an evolutionary perspective', forthcoming *Journal of Institutional Economics*.

Hölzl, W. and Reinstaller, A. (2003), 'The Babbage principle after evolutionary economics', Discussion Paper 2003–13, MERIT, Maastricht University.

Kauffman, S. A. (1993), *The Origins of Order*, Oxford: Oxford University Press.

Klein, B., Crawford, R. A. and Alchian, A. A. (1978), 'Vertical integration, appropriable rents, and the competitive contracting practice', *Journal of Law and Economics*, 21: 297–326.

Lazaric, N. and Denis, B. (2001), 'Why and how routines change', *Economies and Societes*, 6: 585–611.

Lindbeck, A., and Snower, D. J. (2003), 'The firm as a pool of factor complementarities', IUI Working Paper No 598, Stockholm.

March, J. (1991), 'Explorations and exploitation in organizational learning', *Organization Science*, 2(1): 71–87.

March, J. and H. Simon (1993 [1958]), *Organizations*, 2nd edn, Oxford: Blackwell.

Massini, S., Lewin, A. Y., Numagami, T. and Pettigrew, A. M. (2002), 'The evolution of organizational routines among large western and Japanese firms', *Research Policy*, 31(8–9): 1333–48.

Metcalfe, J. S. (1998), *Evolutionary Economics*, London: Routledge.

Nelson, R. R. (1994), 'The co-evolution of technology, industrial structure and supporting institutions', *Industrial and Corporate Change*, 3(1): 47–64.

—— (1995), 'Recent evolutionary theorizing about economic change', *Journal of Economic Literature*, 33: 48–90.

Nelson, R. R. and Winter, S. (1982), *An Evolutionary Theory of Economic Change*, Cambridge, MA: Belknap Press.

Nooteboom, B. (1992), 'Towards a dynamic theory of transactions', *Journal of Evolutionary Economics*, 2: 281–99.

—— (2001), *Learning and Innovation in Organizations and Economies*, Oxford: Oxford University Press.

Radner, R. (1992), 'Hierarchy, the economics of managing', *Journal of Economic Literature*, 30(3): 1382–1415.

—— (1996), 'Bounded rationality, indeterminacy, and the theory of the firm', *Economic Journal*, 106: 1360–73.

—— (2000), 'Costly and bounded rationality in individual and team decision-making', *Industrial and Corporate Change*, 9(4): 623–58.

Reinstaller, A. and Hölzl, W. (2004), 'Complementarity constraints and induced innovation: some evidence from the first IT regime', in J. Foster, and W. Hölzl (eds), *Applied Evolutionary Economics and Complex Systems*, Cheltenham: Edward Elgar.

Saviotti, P. (1997), *Technological Evolution, Variety and the Economy*, Cheltenham: Edward Elgar.

Sorenson, J. and Stuart, T. (2000), 'Aging, obsolescence and organizational innovation', *Administrative Sciences Quarterly*, 45: 81–112.

Teece, D. J., Rummelt, R., Dosi, G. and Winter, S. (1994), 'Understanding corporate coherence: theory and evidence', *Journal of Economic Behaviour and Organization*, 23(1): 1–30.

Vanberg, V. J. (1994), *Rules and Choice in Economics*, London: Routledge.

Williamson, O. E. (1975), *Markets and Hierarchies: Analysis and Antitrust Implications*, New York: Free Press.

—— (1985), *The Economic Institutions of Capitalism*, New York: Free Press.

Winter, S. (1988), 'On Coase, competence, and the corporation', *Journal of Law, Economics, and Organization*, 4: 163–80.

Witt, U. (1991), 'Reflections on the present state of evolutionary economic theory', in G. M. Hodgson and E. Screpanti (eds), *Rethinking Economics: Markets, Technology and Economic Evolution*, Aldershot: Edward Elgar, pp. 83–102.

—— (1997), 'Self-organization and economics – what is new?' *Structural Change and Economic Dynamics*, 8: 489–507.

—— (1998), 'Imagination and leadership – the neglected dimension of an evolution-ary theory of the firm', *Journal of Economic Behaviour and Organization*, 35: 161–77.

7 Insights into the self-reproduction of the firm with the Von Neumann automaton model

Pavel Luksha

Self-reproduction of the firm: introduction of the model

The self-reproduction problem in the context of theories of the firm

The enterprise, or the firm, is a key (and the ubiquitous) element of economic life. Debates over its structure and functions have lasted a long time, and there is hardly a unified theory (Hodgson, 1999). Intuitively, the following general description is accepted: the firm is envisaged as an entrepreneurial or corporate enterprise for manufacturing or/and commercial activities. Yet, regarding properties of the firm or the peculiarities that may distinguish it from any other social institution, various and often contradictory suggestions have been made (see, for example, reviews by Machlup, 1967; Hodgson, 1994).

Scholars considering technological perspectives on the firm focus on the economic issues of production technology, participation in the supplier–consumer value-added chain, and profit generation through market activity. These issues constitute the core of the neoclassical theory of the firm and the theory of industrial organization. The firm is considered, in these theories, as a kind of 'black box' that transforms input resources into output products with its technologies, without any concern for its internal structure. As a consequence, it is suggested that, in order to describe any firm, it is sufficient to characterize its cost and production functions, subject to which (and with a consideration for the market industrial structure) the firm maximizes its profit. It is suggested that the 'black box' increases its efficiency through market specialization and (consequently) through scale economies. The key task (and thus the main question of the theory) is to ensure the efficient allocation of resources: it is suggested that firms exist to combine (mobile and easily available) factors of production and to choose the optimal production schedule. Accordingly, a technological perspective taken by classical/neoclassical researchers proposes a theory of market allocation rather than a detailed theory of individual firms (Spulber, 1992). Industrial market and industrial organization theory can complement this approach with a notion of 'competitive strategy'; however, the internal organization of the firm is left unattended to. Within the technological perspective, industries and firms are considered as given entities that exist in near equilibrium (stable) states; the issue of firm self-reproduction is left beyond the scope of researchers.

In organizational (and institutional) perspectives, attention is paid to rules and relations between the subjects of economic processes. It is suggested that the firm is an alternative way of allocating scarce resources, as is the market. Accordingly, inside the 'black box', the coordination of agency is taking place, which may have different levels of efficiency in comparison with market coordination. Rationally behaving individuals tend to minimize uncertainty (and thereby emerging transaction costs). The firm is envisaged as a set of non-market transactions (Foss, 2000) or a bundle of contracts (Williamson, 1985); it is structured, and then maintained, through contractual relationships. Organizational theories attempt to look inside the 'black box'. However, the main concern of these theories remains the cause and boundaries of the firm. Little attention is paid to the generation of resources by which the firm exists, the preservation of its key capabilities and the maintenance of its competitive advantages.

Evolutionary and resource perspectives admit that firms are not only contractual bundles but unique combinations of specific resources and competences, generated in the course of production activities through innovation and knowledge accumulation. Firms are not only adapting to their environment, but also actively transforming it to their own benefit. Accordingly, in market-type societies, the firm has been largely recognized as the cornerstone of socio-economic evolution (Knudsen, 2002). However, the theory elaborates little on one of the prerequisites of evolutionary processes, namely the self-reproduction of the firm in its socio-economic environment. The ability to self-reproduce has emerged as a major type of self-sustenance for complex dynamic systems in highly turbulent environments, as a way to retain their function and structure (Kaufmann, 1993). Thus the issue of the self-reproduction of the firm (as an entity subject both to destructive impacts from the environment and to internal processes of degradation) is relevant for evolutionary studies of the firm. As economic science strives to build a structured evolutionary theory of the firm (Rahmeyer, 2003), it cannot omit the aspect of self-reproduction. It is widely recognized that the firm should be treated as an evolving whole, a complex adaptive system (Montresor and Romagnioli, 2003; Morgan, 1997). The purpose of this chapter is to discuss possible mechanisms by which firms (as systems) may reproduce themselves, and consider the implications of this.

Self-reproduction in the evolutionary context

The firm, considered as an evolving entity, has notable similarities in its evolutionary mechanics to biological systems, although Lamarckian evolution plays a more important role here than it does in nature (Saviotti and

Metcalfe, 1991). From the contemporary Darwinian point of view, three basic principles are sufficient to describe the process of evolution as constant change and the emergence of new species (Smith, 1977; Mayr, 1978). These principles, also known as the three pillars of evolutionary approach, include:

1 reproduction of an evolving entity (or principle of heredity): that is, temporal persistence of its key characters in the 'population' of physical systems of the same class through production of their copies;
2 variability: that is, maintenance of a range of available variants of each key character;
3 selection: that is, persistence of a variant of a key character that 'better fits' the environment or physical systems of the same class.

Socio-economic evolution occurs typically through reproduction of the firm in accordance with some 'genome' and further selection in its market (those that are unfit, i.e. non-competitive, disappear, and those that are fit survive) (Nelson and Winter, 1982; Nelson, 1995). The genome of the firm is represented by the informational content of routines (see Chapter 6 in this volume): standardized activities and procedures inside the firm (according to Hodgson and Knudsen (2003), deeply rooted habits and behavioural patterns form the 'genetic basis' of organizations). In fact, this is the codified (explicit) and non-codified (tacit) knowledge and competences of firms that are translated into the daily activities of their participants. Similar to biology, the genotype determines the phenotype, i.e. everyday practices. The self-reproduction of biological systems allows them to perpetuate their informational basis (potentially to infinity), while individual organisms are prone to senescence and death. Similarly, the informational basis of the firm, the content of its routines, is retained throughout the self-reproduction process.

One of the requisites for evolution is 'genome' change. Accordingly, a bundle of routines evolves through R&D and internal optimization, but also frequently through acquisition of new staff bringing in new corporate habits and behavioural practices (as in mergers and acquisitions). In general, the firm may evolve:

- either through internally caused changes in technologies and practices: technological 'mutations' (including rationalization activity and R&D), or the distribution of best practices;
- or through externally caused changes in technologies and practices: informational exchange with other firms (technological 'crossing-over'), or the inclusion of newly acquired practices (patents, licences and consultancy, as well as the recruitment of qualified staff).

It is evident that, in a socio-economic context, self-reproduction should be understood in its broad meaning: the production of system copies, known as 'outer' self-reproduction, and the replacement of all elements inside the system, or 'inner' self-reproduction. Processes of both outer and inner self-reproduction have similar mechanics: the latter can be represented as the production of a copy at exactly the location of an original. In a socio-economic context, self-reproduction of the firm has to be understood in a broader sense: the production of system copies ('external' self-reproduction) and the replacement of all elements inside the same system ('internal' self-reproduction). These two types of reproduction have similar mechanisms; the latter can be envisaged as the production of the system copy in exactly the same location as the original.

Self-reproduction of firms and other socio-economic institutions is an intermediate layer between the reproduction of socio-economic individuals and that of societies (as described, for example, in Luksha, 2001). Society self-reproduction requires the simultaneous mass-like actions of large socio-economic groups, i.e. the attainment of a certain level of social order. Yet this social order cannot emerge by itself, but only as a result of ordering at lower organizational levels. Accordingly, in a modern 'economy-based' society, where individualism is praised and social independency and flexibility are promoted, social self-reproduction can only be accomplished through 'isles' of organized and manageable socio-economic life, such as firms, organizations and other institutions. If free economic exchange were the dominating form of socio-economic interaction, then contacts between any individuals would always be sporadic and occasional, and social binding and structures could not be sustained – and thus no regular social self-reproduction would be possible.

The firm is, therefore, metaphorically speaking, a 'cell' of a social 'macro-organism': only through self-reproduction of its 'cells' can an organism maintain itself as a whole. Evidently, much like different types of cells that have developed to accomplish specific functions in organisms, different kinds of organizations have emerged that support various social activities – and so the firm is not a unique type of institution that has to reproduce (other such institutions may include governmental bodies, religious and charity organizations, etc. and also non-organizational forms of institutions). The focus of this chapter is on the self-reproduction of the firm; however, other types of social institutions have similar mechanisms of self-reproduction.

Key elements of the firm that accomplish self-reproduction

In order to recognize the key elements of the firm that support its self-reproduction, it is possible to apply the general principles of the theory of self-reproductive automata (see, for example, Sipper *et al.*, 1998). In particular, it is adequate to use the general model of a self-reproducing automaton that was suggested by von Neumann (von Neumann, 1966), with amendments from the present author (Luksha, 2006). It is worth noting that, in recent years, scholars of the firm, especially those in management and organizational science, have shifted away from a firm-as-machine metaphor towards a metaphor of organization as a living, organic system. Treating organizations as automata has been criticized for insufficient humanity and lack of consideration for the 'soft' properties of any system consisting of human beings (Morgan, 1997). Nevertheless, the use of an 'automaton' notion in the present chapter is judged valid for two reasons. First, some authors argue that the machine metaphor should not be abandoned, since organizations are complex entities that have both mechanistic and organic properties (Connor and Napolitano, 2005). Second, and more importantly, the model proposed by von Neumann, was intended to study qualities of living matter, and it was one of the first attempts to tackle organism-type systems with mathematical formalism. The validity of von Neumann's model for both the modelling of life and constructing artificial self-replicators is now widely accepted (Freitas and Merkle, 2004).

Von Neumann proposed in his report (an extended version of which is published in Von Neumann, 1966) that a self-reproducing automaton (JVN automaton) must incorporate four key elements in its structure, namely (see also Figure 7.1):

A   instructions that describe the way to reconstruct the structure and processes of an automaton;
B   a copying unit, that is capable of reading and copying instructions A: it copies instructions into a new automaton, and also translates them as directions for production unit C;
C   a production unit, that builds a new automaton based on instructions A supplied by a copying unit B; and
D   a controller, which coordinates the other three units and ensures that both a new automaton is built and instructions are copied. This unit (as suggested by later scholars) can be optional, as coordination between units A, B and C can be intrinsic.

As proposed by the present author (Luksha, 2006), any natural system which is built or is working according to JVN automaton principles, must also ensure a stable inflow of construction materials and energy. Thus, it is required to have:

E   a resource extractor, that supplies matter and energy resources into a JVN automaton for production unit C and copying unit B operations.

An important feature of a JVN automaton is that it is the simplest structure capable not only of reproducing itself, but also of producing any additional components (that are potentially constructible), or performing any additional operations (that are potentially realizable given the construction of the automaton), if relevant instructions are provided for them. But a JVN automaton has an additional characteristic. Von Neumann was particularly

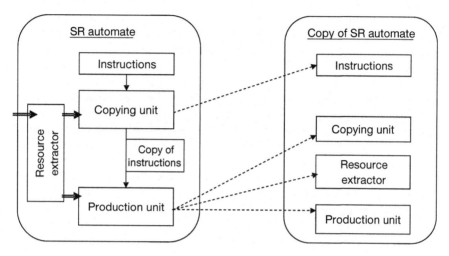

Figure 7.1 Structure and operation of a JVN automate as in Luksha (2006).

interested in designing such a complicated model (as, evidently, more basic models of self-reproduction exist) for the reason that he wanted to scrutinize a system that was capable of evolving; and it has been shown that a JVN automaton is such a system. This is why this model should be considered more useful for economic systems that exhibit evolution.

It is evident that the firm, much like the JVN automaton, possesses the following properties:

1   The firm reproduces itself:

- *temporarily*: many companies exist for decades and even centuries (e.g. the oldest family company in the world, Kongo Gumi from Japan, has existed since AD 578, i.e. over fourteen centuries). Evidently, in such companies no single person is left from when they were founded, and yet the company's key knowledge is retained, such as its brand and its self-identification ('corporate spirit').
- *spatially*: companies develop not only by increasing the number of their employees in a single office or factory, but also by spreading in space: for example, opening representative offices in new locations, frequently in other countries, and establishing the same standards and organizational routines through these units.

2   The process of self-reproduction is based primarily upon the translation of the 'genome' (the core knowledge and competencies of the firm) to new employees that replace, or add to, existing ones (Senge and Sternman, 1992; Bessy, 2000).

3   The firm is capable of handling functions and maintaining structures

that are not related to a self-reproduction function, and which yet are preserved in the course of self-reproduction.

4   The firm is an evolving entity that transforms primarily through changes, both purposeful and unintended, in its 'genome' (its core knowledge and competencies).

5   The firm organizes the collective activities of a multiplicity of people, and thus it exists (most frequently, though not exclusively) on the biological substrate of their bodies. Also, the firm usually transforms matter and energy as a result of its operations. Accordingly, the firm is always a matter-and-energy system that is prone to degradation. It can maintain itself as other complex material systems do: through self-reproduction of some kind.

These properties of the firm make it evident that it is feasible to apply a JVN automaton model to it. The model allows for elements that are requisite for the self-reproduction of the firm and what functions they can accomplish in the course of the self-reproduction. A minimal self-reproducing structure of the firm, by analogy, should then include:

A   'technologies': a body of knowledge, skills, norms, values and other information (including machine codes) necessary for primary and supporting activities (including self-reproduction); this information may appear in codified (explicit) as well as in uncodified, intuitively mastered (implicit) form (Antonelli, 1999);

B   'tutors', responsible for the instruction of technologies A to implementers C; they can take various forms within the firm, such as:

   – experienced workers, educating new ones;
   – training specialists;
   – corporate knowledge databases for self-education and reference;
   – control centres for machinery code replication;

C   'implementers': workers and/or machines (devices, IT, robotics) performing their activities in accordance with technologies;

D   the 'controller': an executive, or an entrepreneur, or even an automatic device (for instance, a robotic plant control centre), that coordinates the activities of implementers and tutors;

E   'resource suppliers': all employees and groups thereof (as well as mechanisms), that search, in the environment of the firm, and supply the firm with all the resources necessary for its self-maintenance and self-reproduction. In a contemporary firm, these functions are undertaken by its HR department and also by units serving its value-added chain (drawing material and financial resources into the firm).

Elements of a self-reproducing firm, corresponding to JVN automaton units, are presented in Table 7.1. This table describes the minimal structure

Table 7.1 Analogies between a JVN automate and a self-reproducing firm

Element of the JVN automate	Element of the SR firm	Function of the element
A Instructions	Technologies	A body of core knowledge and competences (procedures, strategies, know-how, etc.) defining a range of firm's activities
B Production unit	Implementers	Actors implementing a body of knowledge and competences in regularly repeated activities (routines)
C Copying unit	Tutors	Actors establishing transfer of technologies to new and existing implementers
D Controller	Coordinators	Actors establishing coordination of other actors' activities in order to ensure consistency and synchronization
E Resource extractor	Resource suppliers	Actors establishing inflow of resources necessary for self-reproduction

of any firm capable of self-reproduction. Certainly, when a material production sphere is introduced, the firm would also require means of production, i.e. 'implementers' are not only workers, but workers *and* machines, equipment, etc. This table does not only describe the firms of today. One could suppose that certain functions could be delegated to automatic and robotic devices (as they gradually have been, since the beginning of Industrial Revolution). Then, firms of the future could also be envisaged: fully automated self-reproducing and self-maintaining plants, with elements that are not humans and human knowledge, but machines and codes. Projects such as a Moon colony (Freitas and Gilbreath, 1982) or a flying plant (Moore, 1956) were suggested as engineering projects in the past; debates over these ideas continue. However, since an enterprise remains embedded in society, and it presumably will do so in the future, the replacement of all its human elements by machines is doubtful. Despite a tremendous growth in mechanization over the last century, some essential human characteristics, such as creativity, are judged to be impossible to implement in machinery (Penrose, 1994).

Another important issue is whether an entrepreneurial function could be replaced, in part or as a whole, by machinery. Seeing the entrepreneur as a 'creative destructor' (Schumpeter, 1934), one could say that entrepreneurs do exactly what machines cannot do. However, a substantial part of entrepreneurial activity is about 'transforming uncertainty into risk' (Casson, 1982), which implies that rational choices and algorithms are applied throughout an organization, especially when management of already existing organizations (and not the formation of new ones) is considered. Entrepreneurial work requires a substantial amount of information gathering and processing; many of the decision making rules are standardized as relations between informational inputs and outputs. Consequently, entrepreneurs are not only dealing with circumstances of the environment, but also coping with situations inside the organization. To the extent that the environment of the firm can be standardized, digitized and rationalized, it is possible to support entrepreneurship with information processing machinery. One could not go as far as to suggest the elimination of entrepreneurs completely, because of their ability to cope with 'unknown unknowns', to take irrational but working actions, and to make efficient moves where they seem impossible (Low and MacMillan, 1988).

Functions of key elements of the firm

The key elements of the contemporary firm's self-reproductive structure are soft (in terms of Checkland (1981), they are 'soft systems'): that is, a network of human relations and roles. An implementer role is typically performed by key and supporting personnel (in material production, it is equipped with machinery and tools). Technologies, as mentioned before, can be seen as the 'information substance' (explicit and implicit knowledge) of organizational routines (as discussed in evolutionary economics). They necessarily include a 'description' of (or rather an instruction for) the primary processes, supporting processes, and management procedures. Apart from that, they can also include (explicit and implicit) descriptions of corporate identity (or 'corporate culture'), of relationships within an organization, etc. (Wilderom and Berg, 2001). In terms of a general framework for social self-reproduction analysis, set out by the present author (Luksha, 2001), technologies represent stratified social memory distributed between different groups of enterprise employees and managers.

With regard to the function of tutors (as a 'copying unit' for the firm), it can be noted (based on a JVN automaton analogy) that:

1   Tutors do not necessarily master all information relevant to organizational functioning, as their main function is only to transfer instructions stored elsewhere (e.g. in corporate books of standards or technological guidelines) to implementers, since the copying unit itself does not 'remember' instructions.
2   Tutors can transfer instructions to implementers simply by guiding/ controlling them, as the copying unit transmits a copy of instructions to the production unit. Then there is no need for an explicit function of tutors in the firm capable of self-reproduction. This function can be performed by middle management acting as both supervisors and mentors, directing and educating the skeleton staff of implementers.

In a JVN automaton, it is assumed that each unit is programmed (or determined) to accomplish its action in accordance with instructions. In the firm, the human element allows for malfunctioning or opportunism: employees may not always implement working routines in a proper manner. Thus, the importance of conveying instructions, motivating employees to follow them, and reacting to employees' deviant behaviour is introduced. Thus it is necessary to have mechanisms for steering, which are undertaken by junior and middle managerial staff. The function of an overall coordinator is also important, although a lot of activities can be synchronized through self-steering ('automatic' synchronizing of implementers). This function becomes critical in large organizations, where the number of implementers and other staff is great. The controller function is then taken over by a CEO and senior managerial staff that establish coordination of units' activities.

Classes of firms by self-reproduction type

A general classification of self-reproducing systems, based on the comparative complexity of the system and its environment, has been proposed by the present author (Luksha, 2002). It follows from the formal definition of self-reproduction by Löfgren (1972) as 'the entity producing entity in the given environment'. It is possible to point out that, for different classes of self-reproducers, the complexity of the environment relative to the entity can be different. 'Environment' here means not all the possible elements of physical space outside the entity, but only those elements relevant to the entity's operations (niche in terms of evolutionary biology, or the 'own world' (*Umwelt*) of von Uexküll (1957)). A virus using a cell as its host and all the mechanics of cell duplication is evidently less complex than the environment necessary for its reproduction (and even more so is a computer virus, which is but a line of programming code, relative to a computer); hence such a type is a quasi-self-reproducer. To the contrary, a bacterium reassembles itself from comparatively simple 'construction elements' of organic compounds (carbohydrates, amino acids, nucleic acids, lipids, etc.), and thus it is more complex than the environment where it reproduces, so it is called a fully capable self-reproducer. A bacterium may also exchange part of its genetic material with other bacteria: that is a system of comparable complexity; this act is not necessary for reproduction, although it is advantageous for evolution. Sexually reproducing species, requiring a sexual partner, an entity of comparable complexity, are something in between – hence semi-dependent self-reproducers. The strict application of this classification would require the elaboration of a formal complexity measure (Edmonds, 1999); yet, intuitively it appears feasible.

Using this classification, it is possible to derive major types of self-reproducing firms (see Table 7.2), characterized by different levels of complexity compared to their environment. Three such types can be identified: an entrepreneurial idea, an enterprise, and a self-reproducing corporation.

From a business perspective, quasi-self-reproducers rely heavily on external resources: start-ups, small and extra small enterprises. At this level, entrepreneurs try to use personnel with a variety of skills (capable of acting as 'jacks of all trades'). They exploit many non-business facilities (e.g.

Table 7.2 Classification of self-reproducing firms

Type of enterprise	Formal class (Luksha, 2002)	Description
Entrepreneurial idea	Quasi-self-reproducer: no formal internal structure responsible for reproductive function (system is simpler than its environment). Example: virus	An individual, or a group of people, united around an idea or a commercial intent (small/extra-small enterprises, start-ups)
Company, also member of SR firm network	Semi-dependent self-reproducer: depends on internal reproductive structures as much as on outside structures (system is comparable in complexity with its environment). Example: organism of species with sexual divergence	An enterprise, operating through certain (formal or informal) processes, concentrated on certain core competencies and reproduction of core knowledge (small to medium and medium enterprises)
SR corporation, or self-reproducing firm network	Fully capable self-reproducer: produces many of its components inside itself, internalizes some functions of its environment (system is more complex than its environment). Example: bacteria	An enterprise, which in-sources many technological stages and takes over some social functions (e.g. recreation and social memory replication for its personnel) (large companies, often MNCs)

personal living quarters), and procure most necessary goods and services instead of producing them internally. This is, so to speak, one extreme of the classification scale.

At the other extreme, fully capable self-reproducers correspond to large-scale business, such as town- and region-forming enterprises, and many multinational companies. Frequently they create specific business units instead of outsourcing to the market. Many examples of this type of enterprise are observed in former socialist economies: a city could grow around a single enterprise, and this enterprise would be responsible for education, healthcare, leisure and the other needs of workers and their families. Other examples are found in developed capitalistic states. For example, Hershey, Pennsylvania, is a town of chocolate factory workers that has every facility for life and recreation: cottages, schools, hospitals and entertainment zones; the location has a large candy plant with a full cycle of production. Another example, Ford's River Rouge complex in Detroit, operated much in the same manner (*Forbes*, 1998), being technically capable of producing anything from glass and steel to complete cars and battleships.

Most enterprises, however, are not too small to outsource their reproductive functions to other institutions, nor are they big enough to internalize these functions. They are in between, reproducing the company-specific knowledge and competencies within themselves, and placing anything else outside (biological reproduction, general education of employees, etc.). Compared in their complexity with any other institution they depend upon, such firms can be called semi-dependent self-reproducers.

All these types of firms reproduce themselves in a similar manner, by translating their core knowledge and competence to new staff, and thus they should have similar structural elements. Yet, for some of them, these elements can be poly-functional, and some of their key functions can be placed outside the system. Generally, fully capable self-reproducers internalize reproduction processes (as bacteria do), and quasi-self-reproducers externalize them (as viruses do).

Self-reproduction as the process in the firm

Self-reproduction of the firm: relevant theories

Firm self-reproduction was initially emphasized in resource-based and evolutionary theories of a firm: firms survive in competition, and they reproduce through routine retranslation, as envisaged in one of the key publications by Nelson and Winter (1982). Yet Nelson and Winter do not focus particularly on routine reproduction; nor is this accomplished explicitly in subsequent papers.

The resource-based paradigm and its dynamic version (the dynamic capability approach) admits that each firm has certain relatively stable properties that lead to its consistent heterogeneity regarding market performance. The firm is viewed as a bundle of productive physical and human resources (stocks) capable of internal development; results produced by these resources can be used for manufacturing purposes and the distribution of outputs. The creation, use and dissemination of individual and organizational knowledge, accordingly, is the most important task of the firm. Issues of resource reproduction and of means through which it is established (i.e. market strategy, internal management and organizational structure, and specific competencies and capabilities) are central to this approach (Penrose, 1959). Furthermore, this approach can be extended to say that the firm is primarily a knowledge-integrating institution (Grant, 1996).

It is worth emphasizing that evolution occurs primarily through the individual survival of similar entities constituting a population: in this case the population of firms in the industry. Nelson (1995) recognizes that forces of persistence retain continuity in respect to which features survive in the selection process. Thus, concepts of survival and the transfer of key characters (hence self-reproduction) have prime importance. It could be argued that the process of self-reproduction could be understood in a broader context. Apart from the transfer of knowledge and competencies (and, accordingly, the reproduction of activities, roles and organizational structures), for the majority of firms, issues of working capital reproduction, reproduction of long-term capital (physical, intellectual and social) and of the work force, are all relevant.

The enterprise therefore can be envisaged as a set of interdependent processes directed towards reproduction of the 'whole'. An idea that the firm tries to mitigate all disturbances through 'negative feedback loops', has previously been approached by Beer (1988), who suggested his notion of the 'cybernetic firm', built in accordance with a homeostatic principle. Proposals to consider the firm as a self-sustaining and self-maintaining system have also been considered in autopoietic theory (Bednarz, 1988). However, the firm represented in these theories appears as a structure of social relations that are maintained through regularly reproduced social interactions. To the present author, this is but one aspect of the self-reproduction of the firm. Attention has to be paid also to physical 'substances' of self-reproduction: stability of material processes and entities that underlie the firm. There is also one key difference that distinguishes firms, as self-reproducing systems, from other systems of this class (e.g. living systems such as organisms), and thus limits application of an autopoietic approach. The firm can only exist as a complex of hierarchically organized social processes. Its main 'goal of operation' (production/commercial activities beneficial to the owner) emerges and exists 'outside' of itself, in the field of the institutions of market society (money, wealth, market exchange, etc.). Self-reproduction appears to be only a 'supporting' process (although, as we shall see below, the opposite perspective is also possible). Conversely, biological self-reproduction has no other goal than itself. Living systems do not live 'for something', they just live. In this sense, the firm is not 'autopoietic' in the same sense as living organisms.

The process-based view of the firm

The firm incorporates a multiplicity of simultaneous processes in the system of socio-economic relations. Extending the process-based approach (Porter, 1985), three major types of processes can be identified in any firm, that include:

- A 'main' process (known also as 'primary activities'): manufacturing/ commercial activity, intended to be beneficial to a firm's owners.
- A self-maintenance/self-reproduction process (part of what is known as 'supporting activities'): resource restoration activities, costly to a firm's owners.
- 'Through' processes (also considered 'supporting activities'): processes of management regulation and control accomplished through information processing and exchange: e.g. finance, administration, IT, legal processes, etc.

The 'main' process corresponds to the manufacturing and distribution chain of the product (good or service). A self-reproduction process moves 'backwards'; means generated through sales of goods/services are then spent to restore resources expended by the firm. 'Through' processes, that present with comparable intensity in all spheres of the firm's activity, are organized 'perpendicularly', i.e. they penetrate all processes of production and reproduction. These processes are repeatedly accomplished by any firm within the set-up of relations with its environment: clientele, suppliers, workforce and stakeholders (see Figure 7.2). The result of 'useful work' by the firm, from the owners' point of view, is the benefit of its main process less the costs of its supporting processes (reproduction and management).

The firm may exist without achieving any 'useful work' (as malfunctioning firms sometimes do). But it will not exist without self-maintenance/self-reproduction activities. From this perspective, self-reproduction could be considered to be the process which is central to any firm. As the firm is primarily a self-reproducer, it is a tool for collective survival in a capitalistic social world (including the survival of capital owners), and only then is it a tool to produce any additional benefits. Metaphorically, the firm is a type of social group sustenance in an aggressive environment. Thus, a certain analogy can be seen between the tribal life of ancient people, and the modern joining up into firms and other organizations. Initially the firm is created as a project with an 'external' purpose to bring benefits to its owners. Once it starts to self-reproduce, however, new meanings emerge in this organization relevant to its maintenance. Evidently, successfully self-reproducing firms must operate at least at the break-even point; otherwise they will not have sufficient resources to restore their internal structure. Thus, any such firm also has to be a profit-maker; although its target may not be profit-making

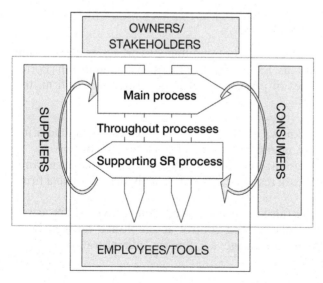

Figure 7.2 Processes of an enterprise.

per se (and certainly not profit maximization), but a maximal timespan of its own existence. Dutta and Radner (1996) demonstrate that, in a world of uncertainty, decision rules for the firm that maximize the probability of its long-run survival are not those that maximize its expected profits. It may be argued that firms just try to survive, and their best survival strategy is that of extended reproduction, or growth.

Implications of firm self-reproduction

Major implications of understanding the firm as a self-reproducing system can be structured into three groups: internal factors (the organization and structure of the firm), external factors (interactions with the environment), and changes in the firm's structure.

Internal aspects are related to the structure and dynamics of the firm.

1   Personnel hiring. Contemporary production has become increasingly knowledge-intense, with qualified workers becoming the key and the most valuable manufacturing resource of the firm (Sveiby, 1997). If the classic firm of the nineteenth and early twentieth centuries was a purchaser of unskilled labour from households (and so it enters theoretical models), this is no longer the case. Firms require workers with better qualifications and more specific competencies, and this forces them to establish and maintain the process of competence management. As such competencies can frequently be a unique match, firms seek ways to retain competent employees (either by bounding contracts or by incentive programmes).

2   Knowledge transfer. As a consequence of technological specialization (or knowledge heterogeneity), firms have to get involved in personnel development: training, coaching, and the building of intellectual and social capital. Expenditures on this activity for many companies in developed countries are comparable with the payroll (Cortada and Woods, 1999). This implies that firms are driven to become more explicitly focused on their own self-reproduction. Accordingly, firms gradually shift from the role model of aggressive profit-makers towards partnership relations with their socio-economic environment.

3   Incorporation of social functions into the firm. Contemporary firms often take over certain 'social' functions such as the education (social reproduction) and even the recreation (social self-maintenance) of their employees. Examples of this kind of firm may include Japanese companies ('company-family' model), or transnational consulting companies, trying to preserve competencies embedded in their employees (such as the Big Four, international management/ IT consultants, and others).

External aspects of firm dynamics are related to interactions with the business environment (buyers, suppliers, communities, etc.).

1   Integration with suppliers and buyers into self-reproducing networks. Business thinking may still occur within a 'technological' or 'neo-institutional' paradigm, assuming that either scale effects must be achieved, hence enlargement and specialization, or that efficiency of production should be comparable with market leaders, hence size reduction and outsourcing (Slywotzky *et al.*, 1998). As a consequence, firms tend to simply exploit human capital and knowledge, presuming that other institutions will be capable of producing them (much as natural resources are exploited), treating knowledge production as part of the external environment. Suppliers and consumers, another important source of relevant business knowledge and important elements of a firm's activity coordination, are also addressed as external. In recent years, new processes have begun, which can be called 'environment interiorization'. It has been recognized that outsourcing per se has no value. Enterprises have to establish long-term partnership relations extending beyond market contracts, and even though they might have different owners, they have to coordinate activities so tightly that in fact they act as a whole. Firms, especially those in highly technological industries (automotive, space and aircraft, computer and electronics, etc.), tend to integrate (at least through information and resource exchange) with their customers and suppliers. Customers become a part of the self-reproducing 'base' (through demand generation and management); firms are also informed of their future needs by establishing feedbacks. Similarly, suppliers become informed about the needs of the firm, and joint programmes are developed to satisfy these needs (e.g. in machinery production, a substantial part of the designing activity often goes on in parallel at both the premises of the supplier and of the manufacturer). Firms may in-source various activities that are important from a long-term perspective, instead of dropping them because of the short-term benefits. Limits to such in-sourcing will be determined by the ability to remain in the market. Industrial structure will then be transformed from a range of independent market players into interdependent self-reproducing networks of suppliers and consumers.

2   Integration into society. Since qualified personnel become the key production factor, enterprises tend to enter into long-term partnership relations with producers of new qualified labour (such as universities), and institutions of recreation and health restoration (such as communities with budget-financed hospitals and cultural institutions, or commercial healthcare/recreation companies, both public and private). Social responsibility standards are introduced in many of the largest companies, and a growing number of companies certify matching international social standards (such as SA8000).

Aspects of structural change in the firm are related to intra-firm change processes.

1   Knowledge preservation in the course of change. Because firms are prone to change, one of their major problems is to preserve their key resources and capabilities. Companies have realized that, with time passing, staff leaving and structures changing, it is possible lose key knowledge without even realizing that it has happened. This has been called the 'boiled frog problem', since a frog can slowly get boiled without noticing it (Hoffman and Hanes, 2003). It is evident that informational storage of firm technologies (e.g. corporate knowledge databases) and processes of technology translation (e.g. corporate training) are both critical for consistent self-reproduction. To emphasize this recognition, and to facilitate the process of knowledge preservation, many companies have even introduced a position of Chief Knowledge Officer (or Chief Learning Officer) (Pringle, 2003).

2   Knowledge transfer in the course of organizational design. The proper identification of 'tutors' has to be a key step of any organizational re-engineering. Until tutors start to replicate newly redesigned practices, the firm may keep on reproducing old procedures and old corporate cultural elements which organizational engineers try to eliminate.

Concluding remarks

The notion that certain processes in the enterprise serve its self-maintenance and self-reproduction is not new to economic and management theory. It was the resource-based approach that emphasized the reproduction of a firm's key capabilities and resources. The model outlined in this chapter allows detailed consideration of how this reproduction is accomplished. Identification of the main elements of self-reproduction processes, and major types of self-reproducing entities, might have interesting implications for the understanding of both a firm's routinized dynamics and its evolution. In turn, the general theory of self-reproduction, a part of modern complexity theory, finds interesting groundings in a subject that has been traditionally alien to it: theoretical economics and organization theory.

References

Antonelli, C. (1999), 'The evolution of the industrial organization of the production of knowledge', *Cambridge Journal of Economics*, 23: 243–60.

Bednarz, J. (1988), 'Autopoiesis: the organizational closure of social systems', *Systems Research*, 5(1): 57–64.

Beer, S. (1988), *Brain of the Firm*, 2nd edn, London: John Wiley.

Bessy, C. (2000), 'Is the reproduction of expertise limited by tacit knowledge?' *Proceedings of the Danish Research Unit for Industrial Dynamics Conference on Learning Economics,* Aalborg.

Casson, M. (1982), *The Entrepreneur: An Economic Theory*, Totowa, NJ: Barnes and Noble.

Checkland, P. B. (1981), *Systems Thinking, Systems Practice*. Chichester: John Wiley.

Connor, P. and Napolitano, C. (2005), 'Machines or Gardens ... Or Both?', in K. Richardson (ed.), *Managing the Complex: Philosophy, Theory and Practice*, vol. 1, Greenwich, CT: Information Age Publishing Inc.

Cortada, J. W. and Woods, J. A. (eds) (1999), *The Knowledge Management Yearbook 1999–2000*, Woburn, MA: Butterworth-Heinemann.

Dutta, P. and Radner, R. (1996), *Profit Maximization and the Market Selection Hypothesis*, New York: New York University Press.

Edmonds, B. (1999), 'Syntactic Measures of Complexity', Ph.D. thesis, University of Manchester.

Foss, N. (2000), 'The theory of the firm. an introduction to themes and contributions', in N. Foss (ed.), *The Theory of the Firm: Critical Perspectives on Business and Management*, London, Routledge, vol. 1, pp. XV–LXI.

Freitas, R. and Gilbreath, W. (eds) (1982), *Advanced Automation for Space Missions*, Proceedings of the 1980 NASA/ASEE Summer Study, University of Santa Clara, California, 23 June–29 August, NASA Conference Publication CP-2255 (N83-15348). Also available at http://www.islandone.org/mmsg/aasm.

Freitas, R. and Merkle, R. (2004), *Kinematic Self-Replicating Machines*, Georgetown, TX: Landes Bioscience.

Grant, R. (1996), 'Toward a knowledge-based theory of the firm'. *Strategic Management Journal*, 17: 109–22.

Hodgson, G. M. (1994), 'Optimization and evolution: Winter's critique of Friedman revisited'. *Cambridge Journal of Economics*, 18(4): 413–30.

—— (1999), *Evolution and Institutions. On Evolutionary Economics and Evolution of Economics*. Cheltenham: Edward Elgar.

Hodgson, G. M. and Knudsen T. (2003), 'Firm-specific learning and the nature of the firm: why transaction costs may provide an incomplete explanation', working paper.

Hoffman, R. and Hanes, L. (2003), '"The boiled frog problem": Human-centered computing', *IEEE Intelligent Systems*, August–September: 68–71.

Kaufmann, S. (1993), *The Origins of Order: Self-Organization and Selection in Evolution*, New York: Oxford University Press

Knudsen, T. (2002), 'Economic selection theory', *Journal of Evolutionary Economics*, 12: 443–70.

Löfgren, L. (1972), 'Relative explanations of systems', in G. J. Klir (ed.), *Trends in General Systems Theory*. New York: John Wiley.

Low, M. B. and MacMillan, I. C. (1988), 'Entrepreneurship: past research and future challenges', *Journal of Management*, 14: 139–61.

Luksha, P. (2001), 'Society as a self-reproducing system', *Journal of Sociocybernetics*, 2(2): 13–36.

—— (2002), 'Formal definitions of self-reproductive systems', *Proceedings of the Eighth Artificial Life World Conference*, Sydney, Australia.

—— (2006), *Features of Socio-Economic Self-Reproduction* (in Russian: 'Osobennosti samovosproizvodstva sotsialno-ekonomikeskih sistem'), Moscow: Central Economics and Mathematics Institute.

Machlup, F. (1967), 'Theories of the firm: marginalist, behavioral, managerial', *American Economic Review*, 57: 1–33.

Mayr, E. (1978), 'Evolution', *Scientific American*, 239(3): 46–55.

Montresor, S. and Romagnioli, A. (2003), 'Modeling firms from a system perspective: some methodological insights', PRIN Working Paper AT1 5/2003.

Moore, E. (1956), 'Artificial living plants', *Scientific American*, 195: 118–26.

Morgan, G. (1997), *Images of Organisation*, London: Sage Publications.

Nelson, R. (1995), 'Recent evolutionary theorizing about economic change', *Journal of Economic Literature*, 33: 48–90.

Nelson, R. and Winter, S. (1982), *The Evolutionary Theory of Economic Change*, Cambridge, MA: Harvard University Press.

Penrose, E. (1959), *The Theory of the Growth of the Firm*, New York: John Wiley.

Penrose, R. (1994), *Shadows of the Mind*, Oxford: Oxford University Press.

Porter, M. (1985), *Competitive Advantage*, New York: Free Press.

Pringle, D. (2003), 'Learning gurus adapt to escape corporate axes', *Wall Street Journal*, 7 January, p. B1.

Rahmeyer, F. (2003), 'Towards an evolutionary theory of the firm', *Proceedings of the Third European Meeting of Applied Evolutionary Economics*.

Saviotti, P. and Metcalfe, J. (1991), 'Present development and trends in evolutionary economics', in P. Saviotti and J. Metcalfe (eds), *Evolutionary Theories of Economics and Cultural Change*, Chur, Switzerland: Harwood Academic, pp. 1–30.

Schumpeter, J. A. (1934), *The Theory of Economic Development*, Cambridge, MA: Harvard University Press.

Senge, P. and Sternman, J. (1992), 'Systems thinking and organizational learning: acting locally and thinking globally in the organization of the future', *European Journal of Operations Research*, 59(1): 137–50.

Sipper, M., Tempesti, G., Mange, D. and Sanchez, E. (eds) (1998), *Artificial Life: Special Issue on Self-Replication*, 4(3).

Slywotzky, A., Morrison, D. and Quella, J. (1998), 'Achieving sustained shareholder value growth', *Mercer Management Journal*, 10: 7–22.

Smith, J. M. (1977), *The Theory of Evolution*, Harmondsworth: Penguin.

Spulber, D. (1992), 'Economic analysis and management strategy: a survey', *Journal of Economic and Management Strategy*, 1: 509–33.

Sveiby, K.-E. (1997), *The New Organizational Wealth: Measuring and Managing Knowledge-Based Assets*, San Francisco, CA: Berrett-Koehler Publishers.

Uexküll, J. von (1957), 'A stroll through the worlds of animals and men. A picture book of invisible worlds', in C. H. Schiller (ed.), *Instinctive Behavior. The Development of a Modern Concept*, New York: International Universities Press, pp. 5–80.

Von Neumann, J. (1966), *Theory of Self-Reproducing Automata*, ed. A. W. Burks, Urbana, IL: University of Illinois Press.

Wilderom, C. and Berg, P. van den (2001), 'Firm culture and leadership as firm performance predictors: a resource-based perspective', discussion paper no. 0003, Center for Economic Research.

Williamson, O. (1985), *The Economic Institutions of Capitalism*, New York: The Free Press.

8 A Penrosean theory of the firm

Implications and applications for the study of the growth of young firms

Erik Stam, Elizabeth Garnsey and Paul Heffernan[1]

Introduction

Western countries are said to be experiencing a shift from a managerial to an entrepreneurial economy (Audretsch and Thurik, 2001), implying that we are currently in the age of the young firm (Jovanovic, 2001). If young firms play the part in economic renewal currently attributed to them, the study of their growth needs a sound conceptual base for empirical research. However, we know remarkable little about this category of young firms. Most theories of the firm are built on evidence of the long-established large managerial firm (cf. Chandler, 1990; Jensen and Meckling, 1976; Williamson, 1985). A theory of the growth of the new entrepreneurial firm has hardly been developed. There has been some fragmented research on new and young firms: in industrial economics on the post-entry performance of firms (e.g. Audretsch and Mata, 1995; Caves, 1998), in small business economics on the determinants of small firm growth (e.g. Barkham *et al.*, 1996; Storey, 1997a; Almus and Nerlinger, 1999), and in organization studies on the life cycle of firms (Greiner, 1972; Kazanjian and Drazin, 1989). However, empirical studies on firm growth and theoretical studies on life cycles of firms over-determine the explanation of (young) firm growth. This is in contrast to studies that are based on neoclassical theories of the firm, which regard corporate growth as random. Based on the standard textbook (neoclassical, production-function-based) theories of the firm, we should expect random corporate growth rates. Predictions on the size (and growth) of the firm are conditional on various exogenous variables, and it follows that variations in the latter over time drive variations in the former (Geroski, 2005). Even if we assume rational expectations, the essential randomness of environmental changes will cause changes in firm size that are largely, if not completely, unpredictable (Geroski, 2005). If firm size follows a random walk, firm growth is random and unpredictable (Geroski, 2005). This is supported by several empirical studies that appear to confirm Gibrat's Law of Proportionate Growth (see Gibrat, 1931; Sutton, 1997), a descriptive relationship between size and growth. It holds that the size of units and measures of percentage growth are statistically independent. In the context of industrial organization this means that growth rates should be independent of firm size. But there are many disparities in the empirical findings on Gibrat's Law, which make the assumed randomness of corporate growth less indisputable than neoclassical theories propose (Botazzi *et al.*, 2002; Reichstein and Dahl, 2004).

The occurrence of random events – making it difficult to predict the magnitude, effects, and timing of growth (Geroski, 2005) – does not mean that we have to leave firm growth as the unexplained outcome of 'exogenous effects'. In the first place, randomness may be treated as a default explanation when determinants are too complex to unravel. Complexity theory proposes that the workings of complex dynamic processes offer the appearance of randomness because of measurement difficulties (Prigogine and Stengers, 1984), e.g. where path-dependent systemic factors cannot be captured by cross-sectional aggregate methodologies. Outcomes may be systemic rather than purely random when chance is the source of new structural factors. To follow the interaction of chance and determinism there is a need to trace the complex feedback effects that explain developments. But even apart from this radical reappraisal of randomness, there is a need for a systematic analysis of firms' ability to resist external shocks: 'If there is a high probability of any negative event occurring and the hardship it imposes are generic, then one can incorporate the effect of random events through the venture's capacity for withstanding a common set of probable difficulties' (Woo *et al.*, 1994: 520). Such an analysis would, for example, imply a focus on pre-emptive and remedial measures to deal with uncertainty and on the various buffers which enable young firms to reduce or cope with the impact of random jolts. Another research strategy would be to focus on the developmental processes that are common in young entrepreneurial firms and examine whether these developmental processes create patterns of growth that can be detected from aggregate data. These patterns could be used to identify systemic features of the growth paths of populations of new firms that are consistent with theoretical explanation at the firm level.

The study of young firm growth has suffered from an absence of conceptual models that can link research at different levels of analysis so that consistent inferences can be drawn from one level to another. Such connections are necessary in order to understand economic change at the macro and the micro level (cf. Porter, 1998; Mathews, 2003). Our focus here is on the microfoundations. In this paper we propose an account of young firm growth built on a Penrosean theory of the firm (Penrose, 1955; 1960; 1995) and explore available data on the growth paths of young firms. We have constructed five measurable propositions based on the Penrosean theory of the firm. These propositions are examined in the light of empirical data on the growth paths of young firms in three countries. We find that the growth of these firms is non-linear and prone to interruptions and setbacks to an extent overlooked in the literature. However, this accords with what a Penrosean theory of the firm would lead us to expect.

This chapter starts with an introduction of the theory of the firm and how this connects to young firm growth. In the subsequent section we introduce a Penrosean theory of the firm and discuss its use for the analysis of young firm growth. After this we present the methods and data of our empirical research. This is followed by an empirical exploration of the growth paths of young firms in three countries. The chapter ends with some concluding remarks.

The theory of the firm and young firm growth

Traditionally the theory of the firm has sought to answer the following questions (Holmström and Tirole, 1989; Foss, 2000):

1   Why do firms exist?
2   What factors determine their boundaries relative to markets?
3   What determines the firms' internal organization?

These questions involve a (comparative) static analysis of the firm. More dynamic analyses of the firm require additional questions such as (Casson, 2000; Rathe and Witt, 2001):

4   What guides the creation of firms?
5   How do firms, and the markets in which they operate, co-evolve, and how is the boundary between them affected?
6   What regular paths of internal, organizational development can be identified, and what contingencies determine which of the paths is likely to be taken?

We are particularly interested in the theory of the *entrepreneurial* firm, as our object of research is a nascent or proto-firm (cf. Langlois, 2005). For some, entrepreneurship and the firm are inextricable connected to each other. The firm exists because of entrepreneurship (Langlois, 2005) and entrepreneurs need firms (Witt, 1998a). For the study of these entrepreneurial firms, or more specifically young firm growth, questions 4–5 and especially question 6 are highly relevant.

The entrepreneurial firm is a dynamic entity, and needs to be studied in a longitudinal perspective. Certain *developmental processes* are common in entrepreneurial firms: to operate in a capitalist economy, they must mobilize resources to form a resource base capable of generating market returns. The building of different kinds of resource base involves different kinds of activity. It may be necessary to lay down infrastructure before facilities can be used, or, at the other extreme, resources may be rapidly mobilized to create a base for consultancy using current knowledge. Problems may be addressed in parallel, or may recur. Firm founders may or may not inherit a resource base from another organization through spin-out (Klepper, 2001). Evidence does not support the notion that there are invariant *phases of activity* in young firm development, as the firm life cycle literature assumes (Greiner, 1972; Kazanjian and Drazin, 1989), because different problems arise in different kinds of ventures and are addressed in different ways. Nevertheless, those young firms that face and solve similar developmental problems in sequence will go through similar phases of activity; firms with business models that require an in-house production facility, for example, have to build this before they can organize productive activity (Garnsey, 1998). Firm life cycle approaches often fail to note differences that stem from the type of activity and business model. However, they do have the merit of making observations of a firm's internal dynamics. Without observations at the firm level, the mechanisms and processes of growth remain obscure, however sophisticated the regressions and cross-sectional analysis of variance used (Mohr, 1982). Measures of attributes drawn even from comparable firms cannot reveal the underlying mechanisms and processes that give rise to young firm growth. Argenti (1976: 121) articulated the problem in connection with firm failure: 'a mere list of causes and symptoms, no matter how coherent and comprehensive it may be, is not enough. What is missing from such an inventory – and indeed from all previous work in this field – is the dynamics ... the sequencing of events'. Moreover it is essential to have related explanatory concepts to guide inquiry and make sense of evidence. A mass of undigested empirical findings can be misleading. For example, evidence that outstanding growth occurs among only a few firms has been used as a rationale for investing in fast-growth firms. Databases are created to identify such firms, but by excluding firms from fast-track databases as soon as their performance falters, the very evidence required to understand the experience of fast growth in a firm's development is eliminated.

In brief, the study of young firm growth suffers from an absence of conceptual models that can filter and assimilate diachronic evidence (on change over time) at the firm level and interpret this in terms of a shared discourse (a theory of the firm). Conceptual models are needed to build on prior work and make connections between related fields of study.

A Penrosean theory of the firm

Penrose found a middle way between description and unsubstantiated generalization in her book on the growth of the firm (1995; cf. Best and Garnsey, 1999; Kor and Mahoney, 2000; Pitelis, 2002). She identified dynamic processes by inference from detailed observation, drawing together her inferences to build an account of the interconnected causes of growth in established manufacturing firms. Penrose did not write about young firms, but dynamic processes operate in young firms as they do in established firms, and shape early growth experience, but with distinctive effects that reflect the liabilities of newness (Hugo and Garnsey, 2005).

Penrose (1995) saw growth as a cumulative process in which the members of a firm build knowledge and competence. Firm growth is 'a result of a *process* of development ... in which an interacting series of internal changes leads to increases in size accompanied by changes in the characteristics of the growing object' (Penrose, 1995: 1).[2] Penrose derived her evidence from detailed study of the history of particular firms, but was able to provide an analysis going beyond the firm-specific context. She retained her focus on internal processes of change while emphasizing the importance of the firm's positioning in its industrial environment. Firm growth is driven by a 'productive opportunity' (Penrose, 1995) in a cumulative process of interaction between the firm's productive base and market opportunities. For Penrose, entrepreneurs seek to realize a 'productive opportunity' which comprises 'all of the productive possibilities that its "entrepreneurs" see and can take advantage of' (Penrose, 1995: 31). This productive opportunity exists in the imaginations of entrepreneurs (cf. Shackle, 1979). Imagination widens the range of investment opportunities for firms (Penrose, 1955: 540). Entrepreneurs do not just perceive opportunities which already exist, as consequences of changes in preferences, prices or technology which have already taken place (Kirzner, 1973): opportunities may also be created (cf. Sarasvathy *et al.*, 2003). The entrepreneurial literature which focuses on opportunity recognition fails to emphasize, for example, the creation of resources *de novo* in which the entrepreneur often engages, which in turn create opportunities.

To realize an opportunity it is necessary to organize business activity, which calls for some kind of resource base. The young firm may aim at a productive base that is very simple, as in the case of a research services company, or very complex, as in the case of a plant or other installation. Penrose (1995) was dealing with mature firms that already had a base of this kind. The young firm, in contrast, rarely starts out with a productive base, except in special cases such as de-merger or endowed spin-out, but has to build one from the resources the entrepreneurs mobilize. Penrose stressed the way entrepreneurial managers match up opportunities and resources: 'The continual change in the productive services and knowledge within a firm along with the continual change in external circumstances present the firm with a continually changing productive opportunity' (Penrose, 1995: 150). As it grows, the firm's resources may come to support a variety of productive bases (diversification based on economies of scope), but Penrose pointed out that: 'movement into a new base requires a firm to achieve competence in some significantly different area of technology' (1995: 110). However, growth and diversification are not inextricably linked (Teece, 1982).

Process-based analysis of the kind we have in mind engages in reasoning about interconnected causes of change and growth, and attempts to identify mechanisms and drivers of change in relation to timing and sequence (cf. McKelvey, 2004). Mohr (1982) argued that process theories embody a flow of action in which the time ordering of events is of critical importance. In contrast 'in a variance theory the ordering of two direct causes, X_1 and X_2, is immaterial in the sense that each has an independent effect on Y with the other held constant' (Mohr, 1982: 60). Many studies that attempt to account for variance do not inquire into the influence of timing and sequencing on causal processes. The importance of timing is conveyed in Penrose's dictum that 'history matters' in the growth of the firm ('path dependence'). Although useful attempts have recently been made to apply resource-based theory to new firms (Alvarez and Busenitz, 2001; Brush *et al.*, 2001; Lichtenstein and Brush, 2001), the potential of Penrose's original dynamic process approach to take into account feedback effects remains to be explored. In the next sub-section we draw inferences from Penrose's work (1995) pointing to non-linearities in new firms' growth paths.

Liabilities of newness

Penrose explored the dynamic processes taking place in established firms that achieved sustained growth. She identified the key to sustained growth as the ability to build a resource base and adapt this base to respond to new opportunities as these arose. Because markets and opportunities undergo change, she argued that there could be no state of rest in the firm. Young firms must mobilize resources for and generate returns from the 'particular productive activities ... chosen from among the alternatives suitable to the abilities, finance and preferences of the entrepreneur' (Penrose, 1995: 82). But, in practice, abilities and preferences may not include responsiveness to new opportunities. Indeed most small firms are run by people with modest expectations and limited access to resources who fail to recognize or pursue new opportunities (cf. Davidsson, 1989).

It follows that if the firm is started by entrepreneurs who settle for low or no growth, its sales and inputs are threatened as soon as the conditions in which it operates change. Cash constraints are a likely outcome of low or no growth in revenues. Young firms are at risk before they have been able to build the resource base.[3] In contrast, more established firms are more likely to have 'organizational slack' (cf. Cyert and March, 1963) that acts as a buffer to deal with growth interruptions and for the exploitation of new opportunities. Unless they can finance the building of a resource base themselves, young firms that run out of cash have to turn to the capital market, which imposes criteria they may be unable to meet. Young firms often close before they have built a sustainable resource base. This leads us to our first proposition:

Proposition 1: Young firms that do not grow are more likely to close.

Dynamic instability

If failure to grow makes firms vulnerable, those that do grow are continually challenged by the demands of coordinating growth. Both growth-inducing and growth-limiting factors create coordination problems. Penrose explicitly rejected equilibrium theories of the firm (cf. Foss, 1997: 363). She pointed out (Penrose, 1995: 68) that:

> The attainment of such a 'state of rest' is precluded by three significant obstacles: those arising from the familiar difficulties posed by the indivisibility of resources; those arising from the fact that the same resources can be used differently under different circumstances, and in particular, in a 'specialized' manner; and those arising because in the ordinary processes of operation and expansion new productive services are continuously being created.

In some cases, asynchronies of this kind can actually stimulate growth by spurring action to remedy deficits or surpluses – either by building new resources internally or by obtaining complementary resources externally. Obtaining or creating complementary resources are solutions that enlarge the firm's knowledge base, from which new opportunities can be pursued (Penrose, 1995: 54). The learning process that young firms go through may result in non-linear and discontinuous growth paths in which sudden spurts of growth are followed by periods of stagnation.

Dynamic processes continually alter the resource mix. Under-utilized resources are an unacceptable opportunity cost for entrepreneurial managers intent on the pursuit of growth. Those who find ways to exploit under-used resources to realize new opportunities are more likely to sustain growth (cf. Wiklund and Shepherd, 2003). But once growth prospects are actively pursued, asynchronies arise again, possibly giving rise to the perverse effects of growth.

According to Penrose, growing firms tend to experience a critical resource deficit in the capacity of decision makers to deal with the demands of growth (the so-called 'Penrose effect': see Marris, 1964; Slater, 1980; Tan and Mahoney, 2005). Managers with inside knowledge, experience and authority cannot be recruited in the market (Penrose, 1995: 45). Other kinds of resource deficit are common and have to be dealt with by acquiring external or building internal resources.[4] This occurs sequentially as growth exerts uneven pressures on resources and hence on requirements for matching resources to remedy deficits or complement surpluses. If firms do not create or acquire the complementary resources required, their growth will be inhibited and a period of 'stagnation' may follow (Penrose, 1995: 47). This applies not only to those faced with capacity shortages, but also to those who allow some of the resources they have to remain unused. They are failing to exploit a key growth mechanism, the building of complementary resources.

The mismatch between available resources and required resources 'limits the amount of expansion that can be undertaken at any given time' (Penrose 1955: 532). If we apply these insights to the case of the rapidly growing young firm, we can foresee the perverse effects of early growth. The growing firm must draw in new resources to support growth, but it faces planning delays and coordination problems because it is impossible to synchronize resources to requirements precisely in a dynamic system. The need for internal coordination sets a brake on the rate at which market opportunities can be pursued (Penrose, 1995: 44–54).

Early growth may have dangerous consequences in young firms still lacking reserves. The rate at which new resources are effectively mobilized may be insufficient to keep up with the pressures of growth on resources. Growth may consequently stall and bottlenecks can move growth into reverse. Penrose was concerned with firms of the kind that had built up sufficient reserves to carry them through short-term crises, and did not examine situations of this kind. But if we apply her dynamic analysis to the young firm that has achieved early growth but still has an immature resource base, we see that crises are a likely outcome of uncontrolled early growth. This effect can tip previously growing firms out of the growth league and into the faltering or declining categories.

The dynamic instability of young growing firms is represented in proposition 2 and specified in propositions 2a and 2b:

Proposition 2: Young firm growth is uneven.
Proposition 2a: There are turning points in young firms' growth paths.
Proposition 2b: Early growth is liable to reversal.

Economies of growth

The relatively few firms that overcome the difficulties inhibiting early growth are those that experience growth-reinforcing processes. Expanding firms of this kind – sufficiently well resourced to take over competitors and complementary firms – are likely to become major employers. Acquisition offers ownership of a resource base created elsewhere. A firm's expanding resource base allows it to respond to changes in opportunity structure without succumbing to resource shortages but, as Penrose emphasized, it is necessary to perceive and act on the need for such reorientation. She also emphasized the need for the firm to be continually adjusting its activities to the shift in opportunities consequent on changes in technology and preferences. This ability to respond to a new market is also key in current debates on dynamic capabilities (Dosi *et al.*, 2000). Penrose identified prospects for new firms to grow in interstices, with expanding opportunities in new growth industries (cf. Hugo and Garnsey, 2002).

There was great interest during the technology boom in fast-growth firms that become major employers. These are often contemporary versions of Penrose's successful entrepreneurial firm that can embark on a process of resource accumulation (Ghoshal *et al.*, 2000; 2001), further enhancing their market position: 'past success is a powerful aid to future progress' (Penrose, 1995: 205). This phenomenon of autocorrelated growth was early recognized by Ijiri and Simon (1967) and has recently been formalized by Botazzi and Secchi (2003) who consider this to be a self-reinforcing or 'positive feedback' effect (cf. Arthur, 1994; Antonelli, 1997) in a process whereby the probability of a given firm being able to exploit new opportunities depends on the number of opportunities already captured. They regard economies of scale, economies of scope, network externalities and knowledge accumulation as possible underlying economic mechanisms that explain this process (Botazzi and Secchi, 2003: 417), while Chandler (1990) regards the interaction between economies of scale and economies of scope as the basic engine of economies of growth. Economies of growth may be important in explaining growth paths of (young) firms, hence:

Proposition 3: Growth is conducive to further growth.

Dynamic processes and growth indicators

In this chapter, our aim is to use the Penrosean model outlined above to connect mechanisms of growth at the level of the individual firm to evidence on growth among populations of firms. The dynamic processes Penrose analysed are not directly measurable by growth indicators. Rich case data is required to identify and explore the way they operate (cf. Hugo and Garnsey, 2005). However, growth metrics can be used to invalidate or support our inferences from Penrose on the development of young firms. For example, if there are few signs of unsteady growth, interrupted growth, or growth surges and reversals, our argument that asynchronies are endemic in young firms and result in performance fluctuations would be in question. We present evidence in support of these non-linearities of growth among young firms.

The following section explores new ways of identifying and comparing diachronic features of young firms' growth that are obscured by the standard synchronic measures. Cross-sectional attributes cannot capture the growth paths of young firms or represent the surges, interruptions and reversals which are to be expected from the operation of dynamic processes. This chapter is an exercise in theory building, not theory testing. We are not carrying out variance analysis to compare the growth rates and performance of young firms, nor formally testing associations among episodes of experience. The study aimed to draw quantifiable propositions from the Penrosean theory of the firm and to see if these are consistent with aggregate data on young firm growth. This required collecting data of a specific kind and using new methods to represent evidence on the growth paths of young firms.

Methods and data to explore young firm growth paths

Non-linear phenomena are usually modelled as if they were linear in order to make them more tractable. Aggregate behaviour is analysed as though produced by individual entities which all exhibit average behaviour (cf. Anderson *et al.*, 1999). But standard cross-sectional measures and average growth rates fail to capture important features of the course of growth in firms.[5] Little evidence is available on the growth paths of firms over time. Standard cross-sectional attribute measures and average growth rates are unable to convey the cumulative process of new firm growth. It was therefore necessary to collect and analyse new data for this purpose and to devise methods for representing this evidence. Since standard descriptive statistical methods were unsuitable for our purpose we used a form of exploratory data analysis (EDA) which seeks to find patterns in data that are of empirical and conceptual interest (Tukey, 1977; Marsh, 1988). In the empirical part of this paper we explore these issues by investigating the growth paths of several longitudinal samples of young firms. The Penrosean theory of the firm provided guidance on causal factors and pointed to the kinds of patterns in growth paths to look for.[6] From the Penrosean theory of the firm outlined above we draw measurable inferences about the extent, direction, and discontinuities in firms' growth over time. Our data analysis was exploratory in that we had no prior conceptions as to how to recognize or represent evidence relevant to our dynamic model of young firm growth. We had to find new graphical methods to represent sequences of growth behaviour.

We applied sequence analysis (i.e. the temporal ordering of events, which mark the transitions of one phase state into another: see Abbott, 1995) in a novel way to uncover growth episodes and turning points during the early life course of firms. For this purpose, the data points making up the growth paths are compressed and coded for a reduction in a growth indicator, for an increase, and for no change or negligible change. The resulting measures, examined below, were thus coded to represent key turning points in the firms' growth paths. Sequences such as 'plateau following growth', 'growth following plateau', and 'reversal following growth' can be identified in the samples. The interval between turning points (inflections) is measured over time; the period between inflections is a *growth episode*. Growth inflections are not unique but recurrent, i.e. a firm may face some turning points more than once in the course of its existence.

Measuring young firm growth

To represent and compare young firms' growth experience, it is necessary to conceptualize the growth of a young firm in ways that can be measured. According to Penrose (1995: 25):

> Ideally, the size of firm for our purposes should be measured with respect to the present value of the total of its resources (including its personnel) used for its own productive purposes. This is almost impossible to discover in practice, and in the absence of any really satisfactory measure of size we have a wide choice depending on our purpose.

Penrose was sceptical of measuring firm attributes that are unique to individual firms; these may not be 'reducible to any common denominator and are therefore incapable of quantitative treatment' (Penrose, 1995: 199). But she recognized the need to measure growth performance on some basis, for example in terms of the growth of fixed assets (Penrose, 1995: 25). Some such measures are needed for the purpose of comparing the growth experience of firms. A firm's growth can be measured in terms of *inputs* (investment funds, employees), in terms of the *value* of the firm (assets, market capitalization, economic value added) or *outputs* (sales revenues, profits). Each of the measures illustrates some feature of growth and each is subject to limitations as a growth indicator (cf. Delmar *et al.*, 2003). Input, output and value growth in a firm may not be aligned, and so diverse growth measures should not be expected to correlate[7] (see Wiklund and Shepherd, 2005). The relationship between the growth, size and age of firms is very sensitive with respect to the definition of growth and size (Heshmati, 2001).

Tracking growth measures over time (instead of taking average measures of growth rates) is a way of approaching growth in a diachronic way. It is clear that growth indicators reflect the outcomes of many different interacting causes that influence young firm growth paths. Before the relationships between cause and effect can be meaningfully explored, there is groundwork to be done on ways of representing firm growth without losing diachronic information that conveys the path of growth over time.

A firm's growth can be thought of as following one among multiple possible paths (Garnsey, 1998). The actual path can be traced by a variety of growth measures at varying intervals. Slope and change in slope are the elemental components of a firm's growth path. It is axiomatic that at any point in time, the metrics of firm size change will show the firm undergoing growth, stability or decline. Fluctuations may occur at any time and on any scale. As in other fractal phenomena, fluctuations give the appearance of being smoothed out when measures are taken at wider intervals. The series of intervals at which measures are taken along the x-axis determines how many of such fluctuations are captured in the data. The representation of growth paths also depends on measures used. We have chosen the standard indicator, namely employment, which is the most comparable.[8] Changes in the number of employees are a conservative measure for investigating the instability of growth in comparison to more rapidly changing figures such as sales or capital valuation. In our analysis, employment growth has been used for the construction of *growth episodes* and the operational definition of *turning points*. We converted firms' growth over time from interval to nominal scales. These represented types of growth episodes experienced, according to the rate of growth over that episode. A sequence of summarized growth episodes was used to depict turning points in growth paths.

Research samples

Longitudinal samples of young firms which were diverse in some respects but shared enough common features to allow meaningful comparison were needed as a research base for the empirical investigation of early paths of growth over at least five years. We aimed to examine firms founded in the same place and year so that the firms in the sample would experience similar macro-economic effects as they aged. We wanted to investigate the growth of a cohort of young firms drawn from a coherent population of firms. The group of firms investigated should not be in zero-sum competition for customers, i.e. should have their own competitive niche. Technology-based firms founded in the Cambridge (UK) area met these criteria. Data on growth performance over a 10-year period were compiled for 237 firms founded in 1990. The inquiry was replicated and refined using a quota sample of 136 German technology-based firms surviving over seven years from 1991–2 and a sample of 25 young fast-growing firms from the Netherlands surviving over at least five years from 1990 to 1995. The characteristics of the three research samples are summarized in Table 8.1.

The data were compressed in two ways. First, interval scale data were reduced to nominal scales by converting employment level to direction of change from previous period. Data points in the samples were coded for growth reduction greater than 5 per cent, for increase greater than 5 per cent, and for change in either direction of less than 5 per cent. In a subsequent compression, the resulting measures were coded according to key turning points in evidence. Growth paths are categorized by dominant turning point(s), presented as archetypes in Figure 8.3. In what follows propositions from the model of dynamic processes are examined in the light of evidence on growth paths.

Table 8.1 Characteristics of the research samples

Region	Sampling	Data
Cambridgeshire (UK)	Population of 237 technology-based firms founded in 1990 (93 survived over 10 years)	Biennial data on employment
Germany	Sample of 136 technology-based firms founded in 1991/92 and surviving over 8 years	Annual employment and sales data (and 15 qualitative case studies)
Netherlands	Sample of 25 young fast-growing firms founded in 1990/95 and surviving at least 5 years	Annual employment data (and all 25 qualitative case studies)

Young firm development explored: growth paths

In this section we will apply the propositions that are drawn from the Penrosean model to the three research samples.

Proposition 1: Young firms that do not grow are more likely to close.

Young firms that experience little growth are less likely to build up reserves to tide them over the resource asynchronies experienced by most young firms. Because firms need a continuous inflow of resources in order to trade and survive, those that are not growing and expanding productive activity are particularly vulnerable to environmental change.[9] If their environment shifts, the revenues on which they depend for inputs are threatened. Figure 8.1 shows that firms that had grown less than the mean growth of firms in their sector were more likely to be closed.[10] This is consistent with Kirchhoff's findings for high-tech firms, that firms with a better growth record were more likely to survive (Kirchhoff, 1994: 184; see also Phillips and Kirchhoff, 1989; Wagner, 1994; Mata *et al.*, 1995; Cosh and Hughes, 2000), and relates to the conclusion by Audretsch and Mahmood (1995: 97) that 'one of the most striking stylized facts regarding the dynamics of industries, that has emerged from empirical studies, is that the survival rates of businesses are positively related both to establishment size and age' (see also Dunne *et al.*, 1989; Evans, 1987).

Growth creates problems. Reynolds and White (1997: 122, 215) found that in their large new firm samples from the United States, 'firms with more [growth] potential reported more problems of every kind'. But the problems accompanying growth are less dangerous to a firm's survival than the absence of growth.[11]

Our approach is particularly useful for inquiry into growth paths, as discussed under propositions 2, 2a, 2b, and 3 below.

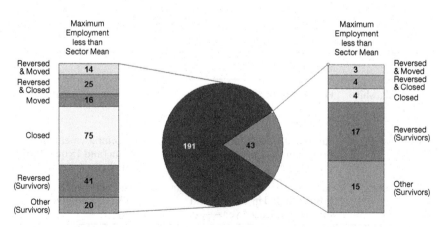

Figure 8.1 Growth and non-growth by age of firm, Cambridgeshire cohort.

Proposition 2: Young firm growth is uneven.

Delay, interruptions and surges of growth are likely in young firms as resource problems arise and are resolved, and opportunities shift for resource-constrained young firms. Dynamic processes of this kind are likely to result in variations in the timing, magnitude, duration and rate of change of growth as between firms and in the same firm over time. For example, difficulties regarding the recognition of the 'productive opportunity' and of building a productive base will result in differences in the onset of growth, with some young firms showing a slow start and growth picking up as the productive base becomes operational.

The growth paths of the firms demonstrated an uneven record. In Figure 8.2, rate of growth is shown by slope, extent of growth by the scale used. Figure 8.2 illustrates growth discontinuities for several of the firms that survived over a 10-year period. They include variations in the timing of the onset of growth, interruptions in the form of growth plateaux and growth reversal. Sustained growth among the young firms was rare. This relates to the findings in studies on growth rates of firms that found a systematic tendency for the variance in growth rates to be larger for small (and often young) firms than in it is for large firms (Hymer and Pashigan, 1962; Amaral *et al.*, 1997; Wilson and Morris, 2000).

Proposition 2a: There are turning points in young firms' growth paths.

This is a specification of proposition 2. Dynamic processes provoke interruptions and setbacks. These discontinuities imply turning points marking changes in growth trajectories in terms of rate and duration. Summary measures, graphics and equations did not readily capture relevant information from growth path data of the kind illustrated in Figure 8.2. Standard measures of growth rates lost the information we sought. For example, if we look at Figure 8.2, cross-sectional measures could assign firms A and C to the same growth category if the age of nine years is taken as the second time point, while a diachronic comparison of the growth paths with EDA would lead to assigning firms A and B to the same category. The same argument could be made in the lower graphic: if the age of three years is taken as a second time point, all three firms would be assigned to the same growth category, while we would classify firm E in another category, due to the setback it had faced in this period. If we take the age of 10 as an end point, cross-sectional approaches would assign firms E and F to the same growth category, while EDA shows that firm F was a slow but steady grower, and that firm E faced several setbacks over the whole period.

Proposition 2b: Early growth is liable to reversal

The tendency for early growth that is interrupted to spiral into decline or reversal is a dynamic process discussed in the explanatory model. Figure 8.3

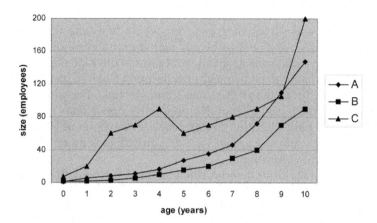

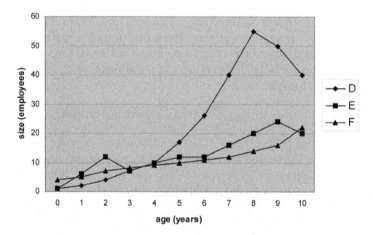

Figure 8.2 Growth paths of new firms, Netherlands sample.

shows that, in the Cambridge data set, only 6 per cent of the surviving firms grew continuously over the 10 years, with another 14 per cent growing continuously after a delay or preparatory period. Another 24 per cent stagnated after an initial growth period, while 37 per cent faced growth setbacks during their early life course. Figure 8.3 summarizes turning points for the 93 firms founded in 1990, which survived 10 years and remained in Cambridge. These firms are those with the best survival record in a cohort of technology-based firms.

The revenue growth record of a cohort of survivors in the German sample shows that only 4 per cent of the firms experienced continuous growth, while 59 per cent experienced at least one episode of decline and 88 per cent experienced at least one episode of stagnation. Employment growth data produces a similar picture, with only 1 per cent of all firms having grown

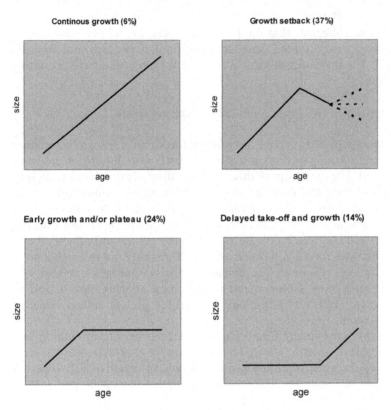

Figure 8.3 Turning points among Cambridgeshire firms founded in 1990, surviving 10 years.

continuously, while 49 per cent experienced at least one period of decline. The firms making up the Netherlands sample revealed, as could be expected from a sample selected for growth record, a higher proportion than the other samples of continuous growth paths (36 per cent of the firms) and a much lower incidence of setbacks (only 16 per cent of the firms in the sample faced a setback during their early life course). This sample included only those that had at least 20 employees within the first 10 years. Even in this sample, 24 per cent of the firms experienced delayed growth and 24 per cent had an initial growth period followed by a plateau period.

There is evidence from other sources that the rapid growth of young firms is hard to sustain. This resembles the 'regression to the mean' phenomenon that is well known in the industrial organization literature (Caves, 1998). In one study of fast-growth firms, among the fastest 10 per cent of growth companies, one fifth show a decline in performance within four years (Storey 1997b: 6). A more recent study analysing these 'Ten Percenters' over a decade shows that the gazelle-like growth behaviour of these firms is very fragile, as their average growth slowed dramatically after their initial fast-growth period (Parker *et al.*, 2005). An earlier study had cited 'empirical evidence which suggests that the financial structures and performances of high performers and failing firms are very similar' (Keasey and Watson, 1993: 112). The pressures of growth take a toll even of the most promising young firms.

> Proposition 3: Growth is conducive to further growth.

The advantages of early growth are internal (economies of scale, economies of scope, and learning effects) as well as external (market position, network externalities). The data from all three samples showed growth more likely to follow growth than to follow an episode of plateau or decline. This is consistent with other work showing that growth is more likely among growth firms (e.g. Wagner, 1992; Stanley *et al.*, 1996; Blanchflower and Burgess, 1996; Cosh and Hughes, 2000). According to our results and others', therefore, growth rates for a given firm from year to year are not independent, as assumed by Gibrat's Law. The dynamic process approach explains why conditions for growth reinforcement are not created during stasis or decline phases; growth is more propitious for further growth unless resource constraints set in.

In both the German and Cambridge samples the 'growth-growth' formation, i.e. a year of growth followed by another year of growth, was the most common sequence, representing 30 per cent and 28 per cent of all two-period sequences in the samples. Expressed differently, around 60 per cent of sequences beginning with an incidence of growth were followed by a second period of growth, whereas only 36–39 per cent of sequences beginning with a plateau were followed by growth. In the German case 58 per cent of growth sequences were followed by another period of growth, compared with 59 per cent in the Cambridge cohort. The plateau–growth sequence was found in 36 per cent of the sequences in the German sample and 39 per cent in the sequences of the Cambridge cohort. In the sample of successful firms from the Netherlands the 'growth–growth' formation was even more pronounced: 85 per cent of all two-period sequences. Even more of the sequences beginning with an incidence of growth were followed by a second period of growth (93 per cent), while only 52 per cent of sequences beginning with a plateau were followed by growth.

Concluding remarks

The Penrosean theory of the firm presented here explains why it is to be expected that firms that achieve early rapid growth often run into resource shortage and other growth-induced problems, while the relatively fewer firms that overcome these endemic difficulties move onto an improved growth trajectory. A diachronic approach to young firm growth reveals dynamic processes at work as the young firms develop. This provides a theoretically grounded basis for interpreting case study evidence at the firm level. Detailed case studies of young firms can be carried out to explore the operation of dynamic processes of the kind set out above. We have shown that many of the dynamic processes that Penrose identified in mature growing firms can be seen to occur in young firms and to shape their development experience. The proposed approach is most fruitful for the analysis of those relatively young firms that operate in industries where there is enough space to grow without intensive competition with incumbents: i.e. where the processes of value creation through opportunity identification and resource mobilization are more likely to result in value capture by the originators._

The methods we propose provide a way of comparing the growth paths of young firms and identifying key differences calling for explanation from case evidence. Moreover, instead of the disjuncture often found in the literature between research on development processes in the individual firm and generalizations about growth rates in populations of (young) firms, analysis at the two levels can be mutually supportive. The Penrosean theory of the firm makes sense of the non-linearities we have discovered in the growth paths of young firms illustrated by three longitudinal samples of young firms. Standard cross-sectional attribute/performance correlations and average growth rates fail to capture important features of the course of growth in firms. The exploratory analysis has shown that there are recurring patterns in the growth of young firms associated with typical developmental experiences. These systemic features of the growth paths of populations of new firms are consistent with theoretical explanation at the firm level, and disconfirm the assumed randomness of corporate growth.

Notes

1 This chapter is partly based on an article published in *Industry and Innovation* (Garnsey *et al.*, 2006).
2 The theory of cognitive leadership by Witt (1998b; 2000) is complementary to this approach, because it analyses the effects of growth (increasing size) on the development of the firm (governance and leadership).
3 Initial resource endowments – the stocks of resources that entrepreneurs contribute to their new firms at the time of founding – may explain the different life chances of new firms during start-up (cf. Bhidé, 2000; Klepper, 2001); in that way certain firms (e.g. spin-offs or firms of serial entrepreneurs) already control a relatively large productive base and some financial reserves at the start.
4 Penrose (1960) examined this in the case study of Hercules Powder, the Dupont de-merger whose unused resources opened new opportunities, which, however, required further complementary resources to overcome resource deficits.
5 In their exhaustive overview of organizational growth studies, Weinzimmer *et al.* (1998) show that these studies are dominated by formulae using manipulations of first-year (t_0) and last-year (t_f) size to measure growth, either as absolute growth or as growth rate. They acknowledge that these studies 'ignore valuable information concerning the middle years of a study, and thus fail to capture the dynamic properties of growth. This may result in either weak models and/or misspecified results and interpretations' (Weinzimmer *et al.*, 1998: 238). However, they leave the issue of growth processes aside in the rest of their article.

6 In contrast to the traditional research design, EDA need not start with a fully specified research problem since it involves an open-minded inductive approach, exploring what is to be found in the data, whether or not anticipated. This exploratory research generates questions that can be answered by analysing contrasting cases with regard to interesting features of the data, for example why certain firms initially follow the same growth path but bifurcate after a certain moment in time. Unlike some investigators using EDA, we had interpretive guidance from our model.

7 Agarwal (1979) suggests that size measures such as employment, assets and sales are likely to be correlated and have a proportional effect on organization structure measures ('span of control', 'functional differentiation', 'spatial diversity', and 'vertical differentiation') within an industry, but not between industries.

8 The German sample has parallel data for sales and employment, enabling us to identify discrepancies between the two sets of measures.

9 An alternative explanation is given by industrial economists with the notion of 'minimum efficient scale': new firms that do not grow in order to attain the minimum efficient scale that is required in their industry will not become profitable and are thus more likely to close (see e.g. Audretsch *et al.*, 2004).

10 It is possible that in some firms the decision to lay off employees would have been planned and desired, e.g. through the sale of a division. But firms would not have intended cutbacks that increased their vulnerability to closure.

11 Across all sectors, the well-endowed start-up and initial large team is less likely to lose impetus (Reynolds and White, 1997). In technology-based ventures, large team start-ups are often the result of de-mergers or groups of people leaving earlier employment together in spin-outs. Where they have experience and access to a resource base this enables the 'new' firm to achieve revenues early on.

References

Abbott, A. (1995), 'A primer on sequence methods', in G. P. Huber and Van de Ven (eds), *Longitudinal Field Research Methods*, Thousand Oaks, CA: Sage, pp. 204–27.

Agarwal, N. C. (1979), 'On the interchangeability of size measures', *Academy of Management Journal*, 22(2): 404–9.

Almus, M. and Nerlinger, E. A. (1999), 'Growth of new technology-based firms: which factors matter?', *Small Business Economics*, 13: 141–54.

Alvarez, S. A. and Busenitz, L. W. (2001), 'The entrepreneurship of resource-based theory', *Journal of Management*, 27: 755–75.

Amaral, L. A. N., Buldyrev, S. V., Havlin, S., Maass, P., Salinger, M A., Stanley, H.E. and Stanley, M. H. R. (1997), 'Scaling behavior in economics: the problem of quantifying company growth', *Physica A*, 244(1–4): 1–24.

Anderson, P., Meyer, A., Eisenhardt, K., Carley, K. and Pettigrew, A. (1999), 'Introduction to the special issue: applications of complexity theory to organization science', *Organization Science*, 10(3): 233–6.

Antonelli, C. (1997), 'The economics of path-dependence in industrial organization', *International Journal of Industrial Organization*, 15: 643–75.

Argenti, J. (1976), *Corporate Collapse – The Causes and Symptoms*, London: McGraw-Hill.

Arthur, B. W. (1994), *Increasing Returns and Path Dependence in the Economy*, Ann Arbor, MI: University of Michigan Press.

Audretsch, D. B. and Mahmood, T. (1995), 'New firm survival – new results using a hazard function', *Review of Economics and Statistics*, 77(1): 97–103.

Audretsch, D. B. and Mata, J. (1995), 'The post-entry performance of firms: introduction', *International Journal of Industrial Organization*, 14: 413–19.

Audretsch, D. B. and Thurik, A. R. (2001), 'What's new about the new economy? Sources of growth in the managed and entrepreneurial economies', *Industrial and Corporate Change*, 10(1): 267–325.

Audretsch, D. B., Klomp, L., Santarelli, E. and Thurik, A. R. (2004), 'Gibrat's law: are the services different?', *Review of Industrial Organization*, 24(3): 301–24.

Barkham, R., Gudgin, G., Hart, M. and Hanvey, E. (1996), *The Determinants of Small Firm Growth: An Inter-Regional Study in the UK 1986–1990*, London: Jessica Kingsley Publishers.

Best, M. H. and Garnsey, E. (1999), 'Edith Penrose, 1914–1996', *Economic Journal*, 109(453): 187–201.

Bhidé, A. (2000), *The Origin and Evolution of New Businesses*, Oxford: Oxford University Press.

Blanchflower, D. G. and Burgess, S. M. (1996), 'Job creation and job destruction in Great Britain in the 1980s', *Industrial and Labor Relations Review*, 50(1): 17–38.

Botazzi, G. and Secchi, A. (2003), 'Why are distributions of firm growth rates tent-shaped?', *Economics Letters*, 80: 415–20.

Botazzi, G., Cefis, E. and Dosi, G. (2002), 'Corporate growth and industrial structure. Some evidence from the Italian manufacturing industry', *Industrial and Corporate Change*, 11: 705–23.

Brush, C. G., Greene, P. G. and Hart, M. M. (2001), 'From initial idea to unique advantage: the entrepreneurial challenge of constructing a resource base', *Academy of Management Executive*, 15(1): 64–78.

Casson, M. C. (2000), 'An entrepreneurial theory of the firm' in N. Foss and V. Mahnke (eds), *Competence, Governance and Entrepreneurship, Advances in Economic Strategy Research*, Oxford: Oxford University Press, pp. 116–46.

Caves, R. E. (1998), 'Industrial organization and new findings on the turnover and mobility of firms', *Journal of Economic Literature*, 36: 1947–82.

Chandler, A. D. (1990), *Scale and Scope: The Dynamics of Industrial Capitalism*, Cambridge, MA: Harvard University Press.

Cosh, A. and Hughes, A. (2000), *British Enterprise in Transition*, Cambridge: ESRC Centre for Business Research.

Cyert, R. M. and March, J. G. (1963), *A Behavioral Theory of the Firm*, Englewood Cliffs, NJ: Prentice-Hall.

Davidsson, P. (1989), 'Entrepreneurship – and after? A study of growth willingness in small firms', *Journal of Business Venturing*, 4: 211–26.

Delmar, F., Davidsson, P. and Gartner, W. B. (2003), 'Arriving at the high-growth firm', *Journal of Business Venturing*, 18, 189–216.

Dosi, G., Nelson, R. R. and Winter, S. G. (2000), *The Nature and Dynamics of Organizational Capabilities*, Oxford: Oxford University Press.

Dunne, T., Roberts, M. and Samuelson, L. (1989), 'The growth and failure of US manufacturing plants', *Quarterly Journal of Economics*, 104(4): 671–98.

Evans, D. S. (1987), 'The relationship between firm growth, size, and age: estimates for 100 manufacturing industries' *Journal of Industrial Economics*, 35: 567–81.

Foss, N. J. (1997), 'Resources and strategy: problems, open issues, and ways ahead', in N. J. Foss (ed.), *Resources, Firms, and Strategies. A Reader in the Resource-Based Perspective*, Oxford: Oxford University Press, pp. 345–65.

—— (2000), 'The theory of the firm: an introduction to themes and contributions', in

N. J. Foss (ed.), *The Theory of the Firm. Critical Perspectives on Business and Management*, London: Routledge, pp. xv–lxi.

Garnsey, E. (1998), 'A theory of the early growth of the firm', *Industrial and Corporate Change*, 3: 523–56.

Garnsey, E., Stam, E. and Heffernan, P. (2006), 'New firm growth: exploring processes and paths', *Industry and Innovation*, 13(1): 1–20.

Geroski, P. A. (2005), 'Understanding the implications of empirical work on corporate growth rates', *Managerial and Decision Economics*, 26(2): 129–38.

Ghoshal, S., Hahn, M. and Moran, P. (2000), 'Organizing for firm growth: the interaction between resource-accumulating and organizing processes', in N. J. Foss and V. Mahnke (eds), *Competence, Governance and Entrepreneurship, Advances in Economic Strategy Research*, Oxford: Oxford University Press, pp. 146–67.

—— (2001), 'Management competence, firm growth, and economic progress', in C. Pitelis (ed.), *The Growth of the Firm; The Legacy of Edith Penrose*, Oxford: Oxford University Press, pp. 279–308.

Gibrat, R. (1931), *Les inégalités économiques*, Paris: Librairie du Recueil Sirey.

Greiner, L. E. (1972), 'Evolution and revolution as organizations grow', *Harvard Business Review*, July–August: 37–46.

Heshmati, A. (2001), 'On the growth of micro and small firms: evidence from Sweden', *Small Business Economics*, 17(3): 213–28.

Holmström, B. and Tirole, J. (1989), 'The theory of the firm', in R. Schmalensee and R. D. Willig (eds), *Handbook of Industrial Organization*, vol. I, Amsterdam: North Holland, pp. 63–133.

Hugo, O. and Garnsey, E. (2002), 'Hotmail & Co.: the emergence of electronic messaging and the growth of four entrepreneurial entrants', in R. Oakey (ed.), *New Technology-Based Firms in the New Millennium*. Amsterdam: Pergamon Press.

—— (2005), 'Problem-solving and competence creation in new firms', *Managerial and Decision Economics*, 26: 139–48.

Hymer, S. and Pashigan, O. (1962), 'Firm size and rate of growth', *Journal of Political Economy*, 70: 556–69.

Ijiri, Y. and Simon, H. (1967), 'A model of business firm growth', *Econometrica*, 35(2): 348–55.

Jensen, M. C. and Meckling, W. (1976), 'Theory of the firm: managerial behavior, agency costs, and ownership structure', *Journal of Financial Economics*, 3: 305–60.

Jovanovic, B. (2001), 'New technology and the small firm', *Small Business Economics*, 16(1): 53–56.

Kazanjian, R. K. and Drazin, R. (1989), 'An empirical test of a stage of growth progression model', *Management Science*, 35(12): 1489–1503.

Keasey, K. and Watson, R. (1993), *Small Firm Management: Ownership, Finance and Performance*, Oxford: Blackwell.

Kirchhoff, B. (1994), *Entrepreneurship and Dynamic Capitalism: The Economics of Business Firm Formation and Growth*, Westport, CT: Praeger Publishers.

Kirzner, I. M. (1973), *Competition and Entrepreneurship*, Chicago, IL: University of Chicago Press.

Klepper, S. (2001), 'Employee start-ups in high tech industries', *Industrial and Corporate Change*, 10(3): 639–74.

Kor, Y. Y. and Mahoney, J. T. (2000), 'Penrose's resource-based approach: the process and product of research activity', *Journal of Management Studies*, 37(1): 109–39.

Langlois, R. N. (2005), 'The entrepreneurial theory of the firm and the theory of the entrepreneurial firm', Department of Economics Working Paper 2005–27, University of Connecticut.

Lichtenstein, B. M. B. and Brush, C. G. (2001), 'How do "resource bundles" develop and change in new ventures? A dynamic model and longitudinal exploration', *Entrepreneurship Theory and Practice*, 25(3): 37–58.

McKelvey, B. (2004), 'Toward a complexity science of entrepreneurship', *Journal of Business Venturing*, 19: 313–41.

Marris, R. (1964), *The Economic Theory of Managerial Capitalism*, London: Macmillan.

Marsh, C. (1988), *Exploring Data*, Cambridge: Polity Press.

Mata, J., Portugal, P. and Guimaraes, P. (1995), 'The survival of new plants: start-up conditions and post-entry evolution', *International Journal of Industrial Organization*, 13(4): 459–81.

Mathews, J. (2003), 'Competitive dynamics and economic learning: an extended resource-based view', *Industrial and Corporate Change*, 12(1): 115–45.

Mohr, L. B. (1982), *Explaining Organizational Behavior*, London: Jossey-Bass.

Parker, S.C., Storey, D. J. and Van Witteloostuijn, A. (2005), 'What happens to gazelles? The importance of dynamic management strategy', Paper presented at ERIM workshop 'Perspectives on the Longitudinal Analysis of New Firm Growth' 18–19 May, Erasmus University, Rotterdam.

Penrose, E. (1955), 'Research on the business firm: limits to growth and size of firms', *American Economic Review*, 45(2): 531–43.

—— (1960), 'The growth of the firm – a case study: the Hercules Powder Company', *Business History Review*, 34(1): 1–23.

—— (1995), *The Theory of the Growth of the Firm*, 3rd edn, Oxford: Oxford University Press.

Phillips, B. D. and Kirchhoff, B. A. (1989), 'Formation, growth, and survival: small firm dynamics in the US economy', *Small Business Economics*, 1(1): 65–74.

Pitelis, C. (2002), *The Growth of the Firm; The Legacy of Edith Penrose*, Oxford: Oxford University Press.

Porter, M. (1998), 'The Adam Smith address: location, clusters, and the "new" microeconomics of competition', *Business Economics*, 33(1): 7–13.

Prigogine, I. and Stengers, I. (1984), *Order Out of Chaos: Man's New Dialogue with Nature*, New York: Bantam.

Rathe, K. and Witt, U. (2001), 'The nature of the firm – static versus developmental interpretations', *Journal of Management and Governance*, 5: 331–51.

Reichstein, T. and Dahl, M. S. (2004), 'Are firm growth rates random? Analysing patterns and dependencies', *International Review of Applied Economics*, 18: 225–46.

Reynolds, P. and White, S. (1997), *The Entrepreneurial Process*, Westport, CT: Quorum Books.

Sarasvathy, S. D., Dew, N., Velamuri, S. R. and Venkataraman, S. (2003), 'Three views of entrepreneurial opportunity', in Z. J. Acs and D. B. Audretsch (eds), *Handbook of Entrepreneurship Research. An Interdisciplinary Survey and Introduction*. Boston, MA: Kluwer, pp. 141–60.

Shackle, G. L. S. (1979), *Imagination and the Nature of Choice*, Edinburgh: Edinburgh University Press.

Slater, M. (1980), 'The managerial limitation to a firm's rate of growth', *Economic Journal*, 90: 520–28.

Stanley, M. H. R., Amaral, L. A. N., Buldyrev, S. V., Havlin, S., Leschhorn, H., Maass, P., Salinger, M. A. and Stanley, H. E. (1996), 'Scaling behaviour in the growth of companies', *Nature*, 379(6568): 804–6.

Storey, D. (1997a), *Understanding the Small Business Sector*, London: Thomson.

—— (1997b), *The Ten Percenters, Fast Growing SMES in Great Britain*, Second Report, London: Deloitte Touche Tohmatzu International.

Sutton, J. (1997), 'Gibrat's legacy', *Journal of Economic Literature*, 35: 40–59.

Tan, D. and Mahoney, J. T. (2005), 'Examining the Penrose effect in an international business context: the dynamics of Japanese firm growth in the US industries', *Managerial and Decision Economics*, 26: 113–27.

Teece, D. J. (1982), 'Towards an economic theory of the multiproduct firm', *Journal of Economic Behavior and Organization*, 3: 39–63.

Tukey, J. W. (1977), *Exploratory Data Analysis*, Reading, MA: Addison-Wesley.

Wagner, J. (1992), 'Firm size, firm growth, and persistence of chance – testing Gibrat's law with establishment data from Lower Saxony, 1978–1989', *Small Business Economics*, 4(2): 125–31.

—— (1994), 'The post-entry performance of new small firms in German manufacturing industries', *Journal of Industrial Economics*, 42(2): 141–54.

Weinzimmer, L. G., Nystrom, P. C. and Freeman, S. J. (1998), 'Measuring organizational growth: issues, consequences and guidelines' *Journal of Management*, 24(2): 235–62.

Wiklund, J. and Shepherd, D. (2003), 'Knowledge-based resources, entrepreneurial orientation, and the performance of small and medium-sized businesses', *Strategic Management Journal*, 24: 1307–14.

—— (2005), 'Knowledge accumulation in growth studies: the consequences of methodological choices', paper presented at ERIM workshop 'Perspectives on the Longitudinal Analysis of New Firm Growth', 18–19 May, Erasmus University Rotterdam.

Williamson, O. E. (1985), *The Economic Institutions of Capitalism: Firms, Markets, Relational Contracting*, New York: The Free Press.

Wilson, J. O. S. and Morris, J. E. (2000), 'The size and growth of UK manufacturing and service firms', *Service Industries Journal*, 20(2): 25–38.

Witt, U. (1998a), 'Do entrepreneurs need firms? A contribution to a missing chapter in Austrian economics', *Review of Austrian Economics*, 11: 99–109.

—— (1998b), 'Imagination and leadership: the neglected dimension of an evolutionary theory of the firm', *Journal of Economic Behavior and Organization*, 35: 161–77.

—— (2000), 'Changing cognitive frames – changing organizational forms: an entrepreneurial theory of organizational development', *Industrial and Corporate Change*, 9(4): 733–55.

Woo, C. Y., Daellenbach, U. and Nicholls-Nixon. C. (1994), 'Theory building in the presence of "randomness": the case of venture creation and performance', *Journal of Management Studies*, 31(4): 507–24.

9 Entrepreneurship and corporate ownership

An Austrian view

Stavros Ioannides

Introduction

Modern research on the theory of the firm is described as belonging to one of two perspectives. The first, which is usually referred to as 'contractual', stems from the work of Coase (1937), Alchian and Demsetz (1972), Williamson (1975, 1985) and Hart (1995), and it views the firm as a set of optimal contracts that bind together the assets it employs. The second perspective comprises the 'capabilities' theories of the firm that stem from the work of Penrose (1959), Richardson (1972) and Nelson and Winter (1982). These theories view the firm as a bundle of capabilities, which are largely tacit and shared by the human assets that constitute it. The two perspectives place emphasis on different aspects of the firm as an organization. Contractual theories address questions such as the existence, boundaries and internal organization of firms, while the capabilities perspective adopts a developmental approach that puts emphasis on how economic organization changes through time.[1]

The application of Austrian ideas to the theory of economic organization is quite a recent development.[2] Most contributors to this growing literature make the concept of *entrepreneurship* the starting point of their analyses. The open-ended approach of Austrian economics depicts the entrepreneur as a creative actor, in contrast to the static context of contractual theories that view agents as passive 'contract takers'.[3] On the other hand, the idea of the firm as a cognitive entity, the emphasis on tacit knowledge and the evolutionary account of the processes of business organizations – i.e. the major ideas of the capabilities perspective – are viewed as implying open-endedness and, thus, as more receptive to the Austrian notion of entrepreneurship.

We argue here that the Austrian concept of entrepreneurship offers a conceptual framework in which ideas from both perspectives may be combined in order to explore one central issue in the theory of economic organization: corporate ownership. We take our lead from Foss and Foss (2002: 103), who argue that the entrepreneurial approach to economic organization sees that 'the productive opportunities that can be realized is a function of economic organization. Thus, one property rights arrangement may stimulate entrepreneurial discovery to a greater extent than another.' On these grounds, we argue that Israel Kirzner's theory of entrepreneurship can help us understand under what circumstances a bundle of cooperating resources will remain independent – e.g. in a joint venture – and under what circumstances they will be jointly owned by the legal person of the corporate firm. A by-product of our analysis is that it may lead to a reconsideration of the significance of Kirzner's concept of entrepreneurship, by legitimizing its linking to ownership under the circumstances we will describe.

The next section of the chapter presents the major elements of Israel Kirzner's theory of entrepreneurship. Following this we attempt to show why an entrepreneurial understanding of business organization must conceive of it as a collection of assets assembled through market exchange. Then we explore the relation between the firm and joint venture forms of organization. The following section analyses the way that the passage of time affects the context in which entrepreneurial behaviour occurs. Then we set forth the conditions under which the merging of resources may develop out of entrepreneurial action. Finally, we summarize our conclusions.

Israel Kirzner's theory of entrepreneurship[4]

In contrast to the standard neoclassical conception of optimization within a given ends–means framework, Kirzner (1973: 35) insists that the most important aspect of human behaviour is *entrepreneurial* activity: choosing among alternative, and hitherto unimagined, frameworks. As the present author has argued (Ioannides 1999a: 79), the fact that entrepreneurship is conceived as one aspect of the universal category of human action infuses the concept with an anthropological quality, as it implies that entrepreneurial activity is part of human nature and, as such, independent of the social context in which it occurs.[5]

There is one notion that captures this anthropological dimension of entrepreneurship: *alertness.* According to Kirzner (1976: 129–30), entrepreneurial behaviour entails alertness to market *errors*, i.e. instances where the structure of relative prices reflects unexploited trading margins. In the market process, the ends–means frameworks upon which the agent reflects are constantly reshaped by the actions of other agents. At the same time, by choosing to operate within a specific ends–means framework, the agent simultaneously reshuffles the environment in which all other agents act. Therefore, the market process constantly reproduces the agent's *ignorance* of the entire market configuration, thus reproducing the possibility of errors.

Since the discovery of error is the object of entrepreneurial activity, the actual exercise of entrepreneurship must be understood as eradicating precisely those errors that gave rise to it in the first place. The exploitation of an entrepreneurial idea reveals the relative possibility to market participants, thus attracting competitors and diluting the profit that flows from it as time evolves. Thus, unlike the Schumpeterian (1934) entrepreneur who constantly destabilizes the system by introducing new ways of doing things,[6] Kirzner's entrepreneur promotes market equilibration.[7]

Kirzner maintains that entrepreneurial discovery is conceptually inseparable from action aiming to take advantage of it.[8] Importantly for our argument here, however, his notion of entrepreneurship is entirely unrelated to factor ownership. On the one hand, the perception of market errors does not require the expenditure of any resources. On the other, entrepreneurial discovery should not itself be seen as a factor of production, since it is a kind of knowledge of which the individual is not even aware prior to its discovery. Thus Kirzner (1973: 48) introduces the concept of *pure* entrepreneurship: the activity of discovering profit opportunities without having to expend any resources.

However, Kirzner (1974: 101) maintains that, while a pure entrepreneur need not be a capitalist, a capitalist cannot but be an entrepreneur. An individual who discovers a profit opportunity that requires resources that the entrepreneur does not initially possess must convince a capitalist to supply the capital. One possible outcome of such a negotiation is that the two parties will jointly assume the entrepreneurship involved in the specific discovery, and jointly reap the profit. In Kirzner's view, this is precisely the way in which the partnership between capitalists and prospective entrepreneurs works in the framework of the modem corporation, where the shareholders hire would-be entrepreneurs as corporate executives.

This brief account of Kirzner's theory of entrepreneurship reveals the fact that it may combine insights from both the contractual and the capabilities perspectives. The affinity with the latter stems from the fact that the theory emphasizes issues such as knowledge, uncertainty and coordination. On the other hand, instead of depicting agents as choosing among a set of clearly defined and fully known alternatives, Kirzner describes how the agent structures the environment within which s/he is to take action. Therefore, the contractual character of business organization is shaped by entrepreneurial activity. However, in contrast to contractual theories that view contracts as symmetrical relations between agents, Kirzner's theory allows us to view these deals as *asymmetrical,* where one party – the entrepreneur – has the leading role.[9]

Productive organization as a collection of assets

Following Kirzner, we can now describe the entrepreneurial process as involving two distinct instances: the *discovery* and the *implementation* of an entrepreneurial idea. Assume that the entrepreneurial vision of an alert agent E at time t_0 is that, by deploying assets $x_1, x_2, \ldots x_n$, s/he can produce a new product y, such that, when sold at price p_y, the following holds:

(1a) $\quad y^0 p_y^{\ 0} > \sum_{i=1}^{n} x_i^0 p_i^{\ 0}$

The superscripts denote the fact that the above relation describes the way agent E perceives the situation at time t_0, i.e. *ex ante*.[10] This entrepreneurial discovery is thus motivated by a profit (K):

$$(1b) \quad K^0 = y^0 p_y{}^0 - \sum_{i=1}^{n} x_i^0 p_i^0$$

The above is merely a description of the initial 'discovery' phase of entrepreneurial action. However, we have seen that, in Kirzner's schema, entrepreneurial action consists both in the discovery and, at the same time, the implementation of an entrepreneurial idea. So the analysis must turn to how the entrepreneur will obtain the resources needed for implementation.

Surely, it is not plausible to imagine that agent E possesses all the non-human resources that are required for the realization of the entrepreneurial project – assuming, at the same time, that no human assets are needed except E's own human capital.[11] That could be the case only in enterprises of very limited size and complexity. However, there is an even more important consideration here. In the entrepreneurial account of business organization we are developing, a one-person entity would imply that the discovery of profit opportunities is always restricted to those that the entrepreneur can perceive and exploit through the utilization of the resources already possessed, thus collapsing the function of entrepreneurship to that of factor ownership. That would amount to a major contradiction of Kirzner's conception of entrepreneurial behaviour. More importantly, it would violate the aspect of entrepreneurial action that we have described as 'anthropological', as it would imply that entrepreneurship is entirely conditioned by the resources in one's possession, rather than by alertness to profit opportunities at large.[12]

As we want to focus here on the distinction between the instances of discovery and implementation, we now assume that the agent that discovers the profit opportunity does not possess the resources required for the implementation of the entrepreneurial idea. How then are these resources to be obtained?

Obviously, as many as possible of the x_i resources must be obtained through market exchange, if the dilution of the entrepreneurial profit is to be avoided. On the other hand, however, some resources will not be possible for the entrepreneur to obtain in this way, since s/he does not have the means to guarantee payment. In this case the entrepreneur has to share the entrepreneurial discovery, i.e. the profit, with them. Thus the initial entrepreneurial profit is now shared between the entrepreneur (E) who earns only a part of it, and those resource owners – let us refer to them collectively as the 'capitalist' (C) – who now share the entrepreneurial role:

$$(2a) \quad K_E^0 = \lambda \left(y^0 p_y{}^0 - \sum_{i=1}^{n} x_i^0 p_i^0 \right)$$

$$(2b) \quad K_C^0 = (1 - \lambda) \left(y^0 p_y{}^0 - \sum_{i=1}^{n} x_i^0 p_i^0 \right)$$

Again, superscripts denote the fact that these relations refer to the situation at time t_0. K_E^0 and K_C^0 are the parts of the entrepreneurial profit that accrue to the pure entrepreneur and the capitalist respectively, while λ denotes the distribution rule, with values $1 \leq \lambda \leq 0$. Note that, in line with Kirzner's discussion of the relation between the pure entrepreneur and the capitalist, K_E^0 and K_C^0 must be considered as pure entrepreneurial profits: outcomes of an entrepreneurial discovery now shared by the two parties.[13] We must also stress that, although this formal description of the distribution rule between the entrepreneur and the capitalist implies symmetry, it is the entrepreneur's role that is the causal factor. This stems from the fact that 'discovery' is what sets the entrepreneurial process in motion.

Note that K_E^0 and K_C^0 are entirely subjective estimates of the venture's profit in the next period; thus one party's estimates of these two variables may be very different from the other's. Of course, what both have to agree on in order for the contract between them to be viable is λ.[14] The actual value of λ will be determined in the process of negotiation between the pure entrepreneur and the capitalist, as described by Kirzner, and is thus indeterminate theoretically. However, it is important to briefly discuss its economic significance. A value of $\lambda = 1$ means that the pure entrepreneur reaps the whole profit that was initially discovered, a situation that is conceivable either if the start-up capital is already owned – thus violating the assumption that the entrepreneur is propertyless – or if this agent is in a position to obtain all the resources required at their going market rates, i.e. without having to share the entrepreneurial role. On the other hand, a value of $\lambda = 0$ means that the whole entrepreneurial profit is reaped by the capitalist, i.e. the latter must be viewed as the only party that acts entrepreneurially. But we have already assumed that the initial discovery originated from the pure entrepreneur. Therefore, a value of $\lambda = 0$ really amounts to a pure sale of the entrepreneurial idea to the capitalist, whereby the entrepreneurial role is entirely assumed by the latter.[15]

Firm or joint venture?

Let us pause for a moment to consider what the organization that this entrepreneurial action has set up looks like. First of all, agents E and C are the locus of entrepreneurship of this venture, as they now share the original entrepreneurial discovery. Notice that relations 2a and 2b above only refer to the distribution of the entrepreneurial profit between agents E and C, and must not be taken, at least not for the time being, to mean that a joint locus of ownership has been created. It must also be remembered that our agent C merely refers to the function of the 'capitalist'; thus it may not be one individual but many.

This organization is not yet a firm, because the fact that what is discovered is a price discrepancy between inputs and outputs implies that entrepreneurial action is a sort of activity that is, in a sense, self-defeating. Recall

Kirzner's insistence on the fact that entrepreneurial behaviour tends to eradicate the profit opportunity that gave rise to it. Thus the business organization that is set up in order to exploit such an opportunity will be a temporary arrangement.

In actual fact, this productive organization looks more like a temporary alliance between the set of agents that constitute it rather than a conventional firm.[16] What is crucial here is the restricted time horizon of the arrangement that follows from the fact that it is set up to take advantage of a specific profit opportunity. Of course, the longer this horizon, the more likely it is that fresh profit opportunities will be discovered. However, there is nothing that makes it necessary that the *locus of discovery* is the organization as such, rather than the participating entities individually. Oliver Williamson (1996: 118) makes a similar point in his discussion of joint ventures:

> joint ventures are sometimes described as hybrids. If, however, joint ventures are temporary forms of organization that support quick responsiveness, and if that is their primary purpose, then both successful and unsuccessful joint ventures will commonly be terminated when contracts expire. Successful joint ventures will be terminated because success will often mean that each of the parties, who chose not to merge but, instead, decided to combine their respective strengths in a selective and timely way, will have learned enough to go it alone. Unsuccessful joint ventures will be terminated because the opportunity to participate will have passed them by.

There are a number of points that need to be stressed in regard to this quotation. In contrast to Williamson, our argument does not rest on whether the joint venture is successful or not. In our framework, even successful ventures will have a limited time horizon, because of the very nature of entrepreneurial action: the eradication of the profit that it inevitably entails. However, the argument here is close to Williamson in that a joint venture is by its nature a temporary form of organization that will be dissolved at some point in the future. Furthermore, and in agreement with Williamson, our framework allows individual resources to 'learn' while cooperating with others. Again in agreement with Williamson, we lay special importance on whether this learning is individual or organizational. Obviously, while the former can take place within an organizational form like a joint venture, the latter requires a rather different organizational arrangement.

Finally, in this quotation Williamson offers a major criterion on whether a group of cooperating resources can be considered as a joint venture or a firm. This is whether resources are *merged* or not. In this account, therefore, it is not enough that a group of resources cooperate in the context of a productive organization to allow us to describe the latter as a firm. For that, merged ownership is essential. Thus we come to the core question that we have set out to explore in this chapter: whether the concept of entrepreneurship can account for the major attribute of the corporate form of business organization in other words that it is a locus of ownership.

Time

Assume now that the productive organization we have described so far – i.e. both the entrepreneurial discovery summarized by relations 1a and 1b as well as the distribution rule (2a and 2b) – is in fact a joint venture. Consider how the situation changes at time t_1. First of all, note that the venture's locus of entrepreneurship – agents E and C – is constituted around the pursuit of a specific entrepreneurial vision. Therefore, the fact that we have assumed that our productive organization has the character of a joint venture means that it is an organization that is 'frozen' in time, in the sense that the original entrepreneurial idea fully specifies and exhausts its function and scope. The organization will continue to exist only for as long as 1a holds.

However, both agents E and C and the x_i resources do not remain unaffected by their involvement in the first period of the venture's operation, as they have acquired new *capabilities*.[17] It is useful to categorize these capabilities into two broad classes. The first includes those that agents acquire individually. Williamson's reference to the learning by agents, which, very importantly as we will see below, may help them 'go it alone', is a case in point. The second class includes the capabilities that are organization-specific, in the sense that they arise from the fact that the specific resources operate jointly in the context of the organization, thus giving rise to positive externalities.[18]

The operation of the organization changes significantly the scope of entrepreneurial action. The fact that some agents now operate within the context of an organization means that their entrepreneurial discoveries will inevitably be affected by their participation in the organization. This realization provides the basis for a distinction between the concepts of *outward* and *inward* entrepreneurship, which the author has introduced elsewhere (Ioannides, 1999a: 91). Very briefly, the former refers to the exercise of entrepreneurship outside the organization, while the latter refers to profit opportunities that agents perceive within it.

The concepts of outward and inward entrepreneurship may help us understand the behaviour of both the locus of entrepreneurship and of the x_i resources. We start from the outward and inward entrepreneurship of the venture's entrepreneurs (agents E and C). The fact that the organization describes a joint venture means that the entrepreneurial behaviour of agents E and C is greatly restricted: their outward entrepreneurship is, as we have referred to it, 'frozen' to the pursuit of the original entrepreneurial idea. On the other hand, their inward entrepreneurship is very active, as they must strive for two things. First, they must monitor the behaviour of the x_i resources, in order to make sure that they perform according to contract. The idea here is identical to the approach to 'monitoring' of Alchian and

Demsetz (1972). Second, agents E and C acquire new knowledge during the operation of the organization about the best possible way to produce y.

The owners of the x_i resources also continue to behave entrepreneurially. They obtain new knowledge during the production of y, thus increasing their productivity as well as their value. Therefore, outward entrepreneurship encompasses all discoveries of a resource owner that lie outside the organization itself. The second category comprises all entrepreneurial discoveries that allow agents to reap entrepreneurial profits 'within' the organization, i.e. well beyond the remuneration initially contracted for. Shirking and free riding are cases in point. What this analysis suggests is that both the locus of entrepreneurship – agents E and C – as well as the owners of the x_i, resources who do not share the entrepreneurial role, exercise both outward and inward entrepreneurship.[19]

We can express these ideas more formally. Assume that the entrepreneurial profit described by relation 1b is actually realized in the time period that immediately follows the original discovery. Assume also that the locus of entrepreneurship – i.e. agents E and C – discover during the first period that the organization can produce the same quantity and quality of output y by using fewer resources than originally deployed. In other words, y can be produced with savings of x_h resources, where x_h is a subset of x_i, and h ranges from 1 to k ($k \leq n$). Superscripts denote the fact that the new entrepreneurial discovery takes place at time t_1. The relations that now describe this new discovery and the entrepreneurial profit that it entails are:

$$(3a) \quad y^1 p_y^{\ 1} > \sum_{i=1}^{n} x_i^{\ 1} p_i^{\ 1} - \sum_{h=1}^{k} x_h^{\ 1} p_h^{\ 1}$$

and

$$(3b) \quad K^1 = y^1 p_y^{\ 1} - \left(\sum_{i=1}^{n} x_i^{\ 1} p_i^{\ 1} - \sum_{h=1}^{k} x_h^{\ 1} p_h^{\ 1} \right)$$

Note that, although y has a time dimension, we have assumed that in terms of both quantity and quality y remains unchanged from the previous period, (i.e. $y^1 = y^0$). Of course, it is important that input and output prices have a time dimension. This venture may have attracted imitators; thus we generally expect that $p_y^{\ 1} < p_y^{\ 0}$ and $p_i^{\ 1} > p_i^{\ 0}$. On the other hand, the time dimension of inputs reflects their higher productivity, which stems from the fact that the output can now be obtained by less inputs. This means that the process of production that the entrepreneur envisages at t_1 is superior to that of time t_0, in terms of *technical* efficiency.[20]

Joint ownership and the changing character of entrepreneurship

But there is an even more important conclusion from the above analysis. The fact that at time t_1 a more technically efficient production process is discovered means that the x_h, resources – which were originally employed by the venture – are now 'set free' and their owners can deploy them elsewhere.[21] Compare this with the situation that would emerge should the non-human resources of the x_h set be *owned* by the organization. In that case, their redeployment would be the responsibility of the organization itself.[22]

The issue of ownership has remained so far in the exclusive domain of contractual theories, with the different strands of this perspective explaining ownership in different ways. Thus, for transaction cost economics, joint ownership constitutes an efficient governance structure that is capable of mitigating the effects of opportunism and bounded rationality that arise in conditions of asset specificity (Williamson, 1975 and 1985). For the 'nexus of contracts' approach to the firm, ownership is merely one of the possible contractual relations with the firm, which is linked to the function of risk bearing (Fama, 1980). Finally, for the 'incomplete contracts approach' (Hart, 1995), ownership is viewed as the residual right of control over assets.

Our entrepreneurial account of business organization leads to a different explanation of joint ownership, which rests on the trade-off implied by relations 3a and 3b. An organization in which joint ownership is absent – e.g. a joint venture – is able to achieve savings of $\sum x_h^1 p_h^1$ at time t_1. However, this is achieved at the cost of restricting its entrepreneurial scope to the pursuit of the original profit opportunity, thus restricting its outward entrepreneurship. On the other hand, an organization with joint ownership has higher costs, as it cannot release the x_h resources. But it can extend its entrepreneurial scope to new projects utilizing these resources, i.e. its outward entrepreneurship is enhanced.

In the framework we have developed, joint ownership conveys the commitment of assets to use whatever learning they acquire during the production process to mutual advantage: not for the benefit of the individual asset owner but for that of the firm as a whole. Note that it is precisely because the organization is now transformed into a locus of ownership that we can refer to it as a corporate *firm*. This analysis leads to the conclusion that ownership of resources by the organization is less likely when the entrepreneurial vision is specific and unchanging over time, thus when new learning is minimal. In such circumstances, dispersed ownership coordinated through arm's length contracts suffices to ensure that the organization will have at its disposal all the assets required. By contrast, when the entrepreneurial discovery is less clear or is initially perceived as changeable over time, i.e. when the learning that is obtained during the venture's operation is expected to be significant, ownership may be essential for the project's long-term prospects.

However, the process that brings about the corporate firm as a locus of ownership has profound implications for the nature of the entrepreneurial function. Unlike the simple entrepreneurial discoveries we have considered so far, what motivates entrepreneurial activity now is not the discovery of specific profit opportunities but, rather, the realization that a group of assets, if exploited entrepreneurially, may yield high profits in the future.

The owners of the firm lose control of their specific assets; thus there is a reduction in their entrepreneurial role. By abandoning control over specific resources, they lose the possibility to exercise inward entrepreneurship: the ability to discover profit opportunities within the organization. Moreover, the nature of the profit opportunities they may discover now changes – outward entrepreneurship – for it ceases to stem from the firm's ability to generate entrepreneurial profits and turns to how the value of the firm is estimated by markets vis-à-vis the value of other firms. In other words, their entrepreneurial role ceases to be firm-specific and is transformed, instead, to the entrepreneurial role of any holder of assets in the market system at large.[23]

By contrast, the entrepreneurial role of the organization's management is now greatly enhanced and, at the same time, transformed. It is enhanced because it now assumes the entrepreneurial deployment of the assets that previously belonged to specific owners. But it is also transformed because of the changes in the exercise of both inward and outward entrepreneurship that now occur. The change in the former stems from the fact that the management of the corporation may discover profit opportunities within the firm, mainly in the form of new and enhanced capabilities.[24]

There is an even more important change in the firm's outward entrepreneurship. The firm must now use entrepreneurially all assets under its ownership. In other words, the mere fact of ownership now enlarges the scope of entrepreneurial actions that the firm seeks to undertake and, at the same time, links them directly to the set of assets of which the firm is the legal owner. In fact, the entrepreneurial success of the firm now largely depends on its management's ability to coordinate effectively inward with outward entrepreneurship, i.e. to coordinate its capabilities in order to take advantage of profit opportunities.

The important conclusion that this analysis leads to is that, in its corporate form, the firm represents a reversal of the entrepreneurial process, as described by Kirzner in the context of individual action. Relations 1a and 1b continue to describe the entrepreneurial action. However, the process itself is now reversed, in the sense that the capitalist C must now be thought of as seeking a pure entrepreneur E in order to assign to him/her the entrepreneurial management of the resources under C's ownership. In other words, it is the 'capitalist's' action that is now the causal factor in setting up a locus of entrepreneurship, rather than the discovery of a profit opportunity by a pure entrepreneur. Therefore, the corporate firm represents a form of business organization in which entrepreneurship, contrary to the original formulation of the concept by Kirzner, stems from factor ownership.

Concluding remarks

We have attempted in this chapter to develop an analytical framework based on Israel Kirzner's theory of entrepreneurship that can address the phenomenon of corporate ownership. More specifically, we have argued that this line of analysis can help us understand under what circumstances a bundle of cooperating resources will remain independent – e.g. in a joint venture – and under what circumstances they will be jointly owned by the legal person of the corporate firm. Israel Kirzner has never attempted to extend his concept of entrepreneurship towards the study of economic organization, as he has chosen to focus on the entrepreneurial behaviour of individual agents acting in the market process. However, his insistence on the notion of pure entrepreneurship opens up the question of how the resources required for the implementation of an entrepreneurial idea may be assembled. It is his ideas on that issue that provide the building blocks for our analysis here.

A bundle of resources devoted to the implementation of an entrepreneurial project may cooperate under a variety of ownership regimes. From a static point of view, it is impossible to judge which regime will be actually chosen. However, when real time is introduced into the analysis, we have shown that different ownership regimes may be linked to different visions of future entrepreneurial activity. Thus, we have argued that corporate ownership is less likely when the entrepreneurial vision is specific and unchanging over time, i.e. when new learning is minimal. In such circumstances, dispersed ownership coordinated through arm's length contracts suffices to ensure that the organization will have at its disposal all the assets required. By contrast, when the entrepreneurial discovery is less clear or is initially perceived as changeable over time, i.e. when the learning that is obtained during the venture's operation is expected to be significant, ownership may be essential for the project's long-term prospects.

There are at least two directions for future research that this analysis leads to. The first is the further exploration of whether Austrian economics – and especially Austrian ideas on entrepreneurship – can indeed provide a framework in which ideas from both the contractual and the capabilities perspectives can be utilized for the study of economic organization, as we have hinted in this paper. Second, Austrian ideas on entrepreneurship and concepts from the property rights approach to organization may be applied jointly to discriminate among different ownership regimes in terms of their effects in the field of corporate financial structure and corporate governance. In our view, it is in that direction that Austrian economics may be expected to make its most valuable contribution to the theory of economic organization.

Notes

1 See Winter (1991: 188): 'orthodoxy and transaction costs economics, place deal-structuring at center stage, and cast the economics of production and cost in a supporting role'.

2 Indeed, the theory of economic organization seems to constitute *the* growth area of Austrian economics, as illustrated by the following non-exhaustive list of recent

works: Dulbecco and Garrouste (1999), Foss (1994, 1998), Foss and Foss (2002) – and other works in Foss and Klein (2002) –, Ioannides (1999a, 1999b, 2002a, 2002b, 2003a, 2003b), Klein (1996, 1999), Langlois (1992, 1995), Lewin and Phelan (2000), Sautet (2000), Witt (1992, 1999).

3 As noted by Foss (1998: 182–3), contractual theories conduct their analyses of economic organization with the tools of neoclassical orthodoxy: a static framework of analysis and strong assumptions about the knowledge possessed by the agents that exercise choice among alternative contractual arrangements.

4 This section draws from Ioannides (1999a).

5 To illustrate this point, Kirzner (1978: 164) maintains that even Robinson Crusoe must be thought of as acting entrepreneurially, to the extent that his activity is not exhausted in trying to optimize on the basis of the means he already possesses, but also includes a reflection on his situation and an effort to imagine new ways of utilizing his resources.

6 See Kirzner (1973: 72–4) for a comparison between his own concept of entrepreneurial action and that of Schumpeter. However, see also Kirzner (1999), where the sharpness of the original distinction between the two concepts is somewhat qualified.

7 We do not need to address here the controversy within the Austrian school, on whether the exercise of entrepreneurship is equilibrating or not. See O'Driscoll and Rizzo (1985), Vaughn (1992) and Ioannides (1992) for references. See also how Kirzner himself (1992b) has attempted to defend a position, which he describes as the 'Austrian middle ground'.

8 Kirzner (1980: 30) writes: 'The existence of an [profit] opportunity implies access to capital, i.e., the discovery of an opportunity includes the discovery of how to raise the necessary capital ... The brilliance of an idea must include the brilliant discovery of how to raise the capital'.

9 The present author has described this asymmetrical quality of entrepreneurial contracting (Ioannides 1999b and 2003) as 'entrepreneurial leadership'.

10 The entrepreneurial project may, after all, be implemented or not, and the profit may be realized or not. According to Kirzner, however, entrepreneurial action has precisely this *ex ante* quality, in the sense that it primarily refers to the discovery of a profit opportunity.

11 The issue of one-person firms is non-trivial as it has given rise to a critique of Coase's theory of the firm on the grounds that it cannot account for this kind of entity. See Fourie (1989).

12 We will later see under what conditions entrepreneurship may be linked to factor ownership. For the time being, however, our analysis proceeds within Kirzner's original formulation of the entrepreneurial process.

13 In turn, this means that the capitalist's payment for the use of his/her resources is already included in the $\sum x_i^0 p_i^0$ part of the relation.

14 There is an important question that must be addressed at this point (the author wishes to thank Ulrich Witt for raising it). In Kirzner's schema, an entrepreneurial idea has the character of the discovery of an already existing profit opportunity. But what is it that prevents the capitalist from getting rid of the 'pure' entrepreneur, once the former has come to share the latter's discovery? In order to preclude such a possibility, we have to assume that part of the entrepreneur's discovery has the character of tacit knowledge of how to organize the x_i; thus his/her continued involvement in the venture is essential for success. The institution of venture capital is of relevance here. Note that all that relations 2a and 2b describe is what the contract between the entrepreneur and the capitalist will look like, *if the parties come to an agreement.* They do not claim that such an agreement will *always* obtain. Thus the argument here is equivalent to Edith

Penrose's (1959) analysis of the growth of the firm. She does not claim that *all* firms will grow but she discusses, instead, what the process of growth entails *for those that do.*

15 See Ioannides (1993) for this scenario.

16 This type of organization resembles somewhat the one that Teece *et al.* (1994) describe as a 'hollow corporation', i.e. a business entity without any capabilities of its own, that relies instead on comprehensive contracting. Of course, in contrast to our argument here, Teece *et al.* focus on whether this organization is a locus of capabilities rather than ownership.

17 Thus, following Penrose (1959), we make the distinction between resources and the services that they are capable of providing.

18 Obviously, it is on this point that the ideas of the capabilities perspective on the firm become most relevant, especially through the concept of routines introduced by Nelson and Winter (1982).

19 Foss and Foss (2002) discuss the difference between 'productive' and 'destructive' entrepreneurship, which hinges on whether employees can use new knowledge for the benefit of the organization (productive) or of their own (destructive). Therefore, there are significant parallels between these concepts and our notions of outward and inward entrepreneurship.

20 Of course, the above analysis suggests that it is impossible to compare K^0 with K^1; i.e. it is impossible to judge whether the entrepreneurial profit envisaged at time t_0, when contemplating to deploy x_i resources, will be higher or lower than the profit at time t_1, when planning to employ $x_i - x_h$ resources. The reason is that it is impossible to know whether the gains from the rise in technical efficiency will necessarily result in a rise in economic efficiency as well. Recall that, according to Kirzner, entrepreneurial profit inevitably tends to diminish over time, due to the competitive market process.

21 In the framework we have developed so far, all resources remain the property of their original owners and are only hired to the venture that the entrepreneur sets up.

22 Note that this would be so even if the agents constituting the locus of entrepreneurship decided just to sell off these 'redundant' assets, i.e. to *divest.*

23 This conclusion should not be taken to mean that their behaviour ceases to have important implications for the evolution of the firm. Obviously, their transactions in the stock market cannot but affect the ability of the firm's locus of entrepreneurship to obtain financing at reasonable terms, thus affecting the firm's development. But the fact remains that they cease to be the creators of profit opportunities; thus their role is now restricted to that of evaluators of the initiatives of others.

24 This line of reasoning brings out an important affinity between the Austrian concept of entrepreneurship and Edith Penrose's insistence that the entrepreneurial capability of its management team constitutes the most crucial factor in the process of growth of the firm.

References

Alchian, A. A. and Demsetz, H. (1972), 'Production, information costs, and economic organisation', *American Economic Review,* 62: 777–95.

Coase, R. H. (1937), 'The nature of the firm', *Economica,* 4: 386–405.

Dulbecco, P. and Garrouste, P. (1999), 'Towards an Austrian theory of the firm', *Review of Austrian Economics,* 12(1): 43–64.

Fama, E. F. (1980), 'Agency problems and the theory of the firm', *Journal of Political Economy,* 88: 288–307.

Foss, K. and Foss, N. J. (2002), 'Economic organization and the trade-offs between productive and destructive entrepreneurship', in N. J. Foss and P. G. Klein (eds), (2002), *Entrepreneurship and the Firm: Austrian Perspectives on Economic Organization,* Aldershot: Edward Elgar.

Foss, N. J. (1994), 'The theory of the firm: the Austrians as precursors and critics of contemporary theory', *Review of Austrian Economics,* 7(3): 1–65.

—— (1998), 'Austrian insights and the theory of the firm', *Advances in Austrian Economics,* 4: 175–98.

Fourie, F. C. v. N. (1989), 'The nature of firms and markets: do transactions approaches help?', *South African Journal of Economics,* 57: 142–60.

Hart, O. (1995), *Firms, Contracts and Financial Structure,* Oxford: Clarendon Press.

Ioannides, S. (1992), *The Market, Competition and Democracy: A Critique of Neo-Austrian Economics,* Aldershot: Edward Elgar.

—— (1993), 'Comment on Israel Kirzner's notion of pure profit', *Journal des Economistes et des Etudes Humaines.* 4: 329–33.

—— (1999a), 'Towards an Austrian perspective on the firm', *Review of Austrian Economics,* 11: 77–97.

—— (1999b), 'The market, the firm, and entrepreneurial leadership: Some Hayekian insights', *Revue d'Economie Politique,* 109(6): 872–83.

—— (2002a), 'Entrepreneurship, contracts and the corporate firm', in N. J. Foss and P. G. Klein (eds) (2002), *Entrepreneurship and the Firm: Austrian Perspectives on Economic Organization,* Aldershot: Edward Elgar.

—— (2002b), 'Owners, managers, and entrepreneurship in the corporate firm', *Journal des Economistes et des Etudes Humaines,* XII(1), March: 107–18.

—— (2003a), 'Orders and organizations: Hayekian insights for a theory of economic organization', *American Journal of Economics and Sociology,* 62(3), July: 533–66.

—— (2003b), 'The business firm as a hybrid Hayekian order: what is the role of the entrepreneur?', *Advances in Austrian Economics,* 6: 153–72.

Kirzner, I. M. (1973), *Competition and Entrepreneurship,* Chicago, IL: University of Chicago Press.

—— (1974), 'Capital, competition, and capitalism', in Kirzner (1979).

—— (1976), 'Economics and error', in Kirzner (1979).

—— (1978), 'Alertness, luck and entrepreneurial profit', in Kirzner (1979).

—— (1979), *Perception, Opportunity and Profit,* Chicago, IL: University of Chicago Press.

—— (1980), 'The primacy of entrepreneurial discovery', in *Prime Mover of Progress* (Readings 23), London: Institute of Economic Affairs.

—— (1992), 'Market process theory: In defense of the Austrian middle ground', in I. M. Kirzner, *The Meaning of Market Process: Essays in the Development of Modern Austrian Economics,* New York: Routledge.

—— (1999), 'Creativity and/or alertness: A reconsideration of the Schumpeterian entrepreneur', *Review of Austrian Economics,* 11: 5–18.

Klein, P. G. (1996), 'Economic calculation and the limits of organization', *Review of Austrian Economics* 9: 3–28.

—— (1999), 'Entrepreneurship and corporate governance', *Quarterly Journal of Austrian Economics,* 2(1): 19–42.

Langlois, R. N. (1992), 'Orders and organizations: toward an Austrian theory of social institutions', in B. J. Caldwell and S. Böhm (eds), (1992), *Austrian Economics: Tensions and New Directions,* Boston, MA: Kluwer.

—— (1995), 'Do firms plan?', *Constitutional Political Economy*, 6: 247–61.

Lewin, P. and Phelan, S. E. (2000), 'An Austrian theory of the firm', *Review of Austrian Economics,* 13: 59–79.

Nelson. R. R. and Winter S. G. (1982), *An Evolutionary Theory of Economic Change,* Cambridge MA: Harvard University Press.

O'Driscoll, G. P. Jr and Rizzo, M. J. (1985), *The Economics of Time and Ignorance,* Oxford: Blackwell.

Penrose, E. T. (1959), *The Theory of the Growth of the Firm,* Oxford: Oxford University Press.

Richardson, G. B. (1972), 'The organisation of industry', *Economic Journal,* 82: 883–96.

Sautet, F. E. (2000), *An Entrepreneurial Theory of the Firm,* London: Routledge.

Schumpeter, J. A. (1934), *The Theory of Economic Development,* Cambridge MA: Harvard University Press.

Teece, D. J., Rumelt, R., Dosi, G. and Winter, S. G. (1994), 'Understanding corporate coherence: theory and evidence', *Journal of Economic Behavior and Organisation,* 23: 1–30.

Vaughn, K. (1992), 'The problem of order in Austrian economics: Kirzner vs. Lachmann', *Review of Political Economy,* 4: 251–74.

Williamson, O. E. (1975), *Markets and Hierarchies: Analysis and Anti-Trust Implications,* New York: Free Press.

—— (1985), *The Economic Institutions of Capitalism,* New York: Free Press.

—— (1996), *The Mechanisms of Governance,* Oxford: Oxford University Press.

Winter, S. G. (1991), 'On Coase, competence, and the corporation', in O. E. Williamson and S. G. Winter (eds), (1991), *The Nature of the Firm,* Oxford: Oxford University Press.

Witt, U. (1992), 'Turning Austrian economics into an evolutionary theory', in B. J. Caldwell and and S. Böhm (eds), (1992), *Austrian Economics: Tensions and New Directions,* Boston: Kluwer.

—— (1999), 'Do entrepreneurs need firms? A contribution to a missing chapter in Austrian economics', *Review of Austrian Economics,* 11: 99–110.

Part III

The economics of the firm

History and organization

10 Business history and the organization of industry

Jackie Krafft

Introduction

Business history emerged in the 1950s as a sub-discipline of economic history, and its initial domain of investigation was the characterization of the evolution of entrepreneurs and firms at the individual level. Progressively, business history became a discipline in itself, enlarging the scope of analysis, and developing closer connections with the broad economic field of industrial organization. With this transformation, business history – now often called 'new business history' – can be defined as the analysis of the evolution of the structures and behaviours of firms and industries over long periods of time, within a framework which explicitly takes into account markets and institutions that shape these structures and behaviours. Today, research programmes mixing business history with the theory of the firm and industrial dynamics are burgeoning.[1] The major goal of these common research programmes is to characterize the robustness of key results obtained in industrial organization on specific periods analysed by business historians, and to generate new propositions, especially on the question of what determines the boundaries of the firm or the boundaries of the industry.

This chapter analyses whether this emerging interdisciplinary connection may or may not contribute to what we already know as economists in the domain of the theory of the firm and industrial dynamics. In this analysis, we think that two conditions can be considered as crucial. First, the appreciation of the value of research into business history should permit one to observe at the same time general results in the theory of the firm and regularities in industrial dynamics that are not determined contextually, but also critical differences and anomalies that, throughout history, make certain firms or industrial patterns of evolution unique. Second, the confirmation of some general conclusions obtained in the theory of the firm or industrial dynamics should not obscure or leave apart some important results extracted from business history. With these conditions in mind, the chapter stresses that, in practice, there are two different trends under which connections between business history and industrial organization were conducted in various interdisciplinary research programmes. The first tendency is to use the data collected by business historians to answer key questions that structure the theory of the firm and industrial dynamics. Here, a selection of economic models on the firm and the industry is operated in order to provide a consistent interpretation of empirical data over the long run. The second tendency proceeds the other way around, since it consists in the questioning of economic results on the firm and the industry by referring to puzzles and questions emerging from business history archives. Here, long-run historical data is generally used as a way to increase the variety of economic models able to understand these questions and puzzles, rather than to select them a priori. The two trends reveal diverging methods to deal with the relation between theoretical and empirical work.

The chapter shows that the first tendency essentially concerns major neo-institutionalist theories of industrial organization, namely transaction costs approaches, agency theories, and property rights analyses.[2] In connection with business history, these theories privilege problems of coordination of information to understand the firm and the industry, but neglect in the meantime other major determinants of their structure and evolution. Alternatively, the second tendency attempts to characterize problems related to the coordination of economic activities that are so central in innovative firms and industries, and often necessitate elaborating new theoretical perspectives on neo-institutionalism, especially by fostering approaches focusing on innovation and competences.

The argument will be grounded on the valuable contributions made by Alfred Chandler on the connections between business history, the theory of the firm and industrial dynamics.[3] In fact, this pioneering work can be exploited according to two alternative interpretations that have structured the literature so far. In this perspective, we show in a first step that the tendency centred on the information coordination is in the line of a Williamsonian interpretation of Chandler, and ends up with a confirmation of existing results in the theory of the firm and industrial dynamics by business history (section 2). In a second step, we show that the tendency centred on productive coordination restores the essential ideas of Chandler on the connection between business history and industrial organization, and ends up with a real confrontation of results between the two disciplines (section 3). In a third step, we derive some new perspectives on business history and the organization of the industry, specifically by focusing on firms composing the automobile sector (section 4).

When business history confirms industrial organization: a focus on the coordination of information

Since the 1980s, neo-institutionalist approaches to the theory of the firm and industrial dynamics offer a basic framework to elaborate connections between business history and industrial organization. Transaction cost approaches, first, have contributed to analysing the emergence and viability of large vertically integrated firms in the United States at the beginning of the twentieth century. Second, agency theory has provided an in-depth analysis of the relationships between shareholders and managers, and potential conflicts between stakeholders. Finally, property rights analysis has significantly refined the analysis on the boundaries of the firm. Despite these advances, key challenges still remain. In fact, the outcome of these different contributions is essentially to show that business history confirms industrial organization on the key problem of the coordination of information.

The coordination of information in the context of opportunism and asset specificity

One of the preliminary connections between business history and industrial organization started with the interpretation of Alfred Chandler by Oliver Williamson in the domain of the theory of the firm. The main object of Chandler in his book *Visible Hand*, published in 1977, is to understand major characteristics of the industrial revolution which started at the end of the nineteenth century in the United States and subsequently shaped the modern industrial system. Chandler focuses on the reasons why the US economy was so dominated by large companies for a major part of the twentieth century. Starting from monographs of significant companies, the projected outcome was to draw the major characteristics of long-term viability companies over large panels of population. Chandler then generated two essential characteristics. The first characteristic was that companies engaged in massively capital intensive activities were generally confronted by a major problem of coordination. This problem was to articulate mass production with mass distribution. The second characteristic was that the problem of coordination of capital-intensive activities could generally not be resolved automatically, relying on market forces alone. Within these capital-intensive industries, vertical integration (backward or forward) could permit firms to avoid bottlenecks on the supply side and to generate new demand opportunities by the coordination of different yet complementary productive units. The argument is that managerial coordination superseded market coordination in industries characterized by high economies of speed, i.e. in which production is sufficiently high and rapid to decrease unit costs. Investment in organizational capacity to manage vertically related units emerged as a key of competitive success. As a matter of fact, companies which did not invest in organizational capacity exited, while companies which invested became the leaders of the industry.

Oliver Williamson, in Chapter 5 of his book *The Economic Institutions of Capitalism* published in 1985, uses the different cases of vertical integration examined by Chandler as empirical evidence of his own theory based on transaction costs. Williamson argues that firms undertake the minimization of transaction costs in specific situations. Firms emerge when investments are characterized by a high degree of asset specificities, since the sunk costs character of these investments generally involve some hold-up behaviours from managers, leading to the expropriation of their rents. In this theoretical framework, the proposition is that the higher (respectively the lower) the transaction costs, the higher the chances to allocate resources within a firm (respectively within a market). In this framework, vertical integration represents a 'paradigmatic problem' (Williamson, 1985: 150) for the theory of the firm based on transaction costs. Williamson acknowledges that the empirical verifications of his own theory on the basis of the monographs done by Chandler are to some extent preliminary and rudimentary. However, the major outcome is that, in most cases, business history on vertical integration supports the theoretical proposition based on transaction cost, and discards the alternative theoretical proposition. In conclusion he stresses that a predictive theory of vertical integration should essentially refer to asset specificity and opportunism.

Three comments result from this connection between business history and the theory of the firm. The first comment is that Williamson derives from this connection the dominant explanation of why the US economy was characterized in the early twentieth century by large, vertically integrated companies. Vertical integration appears as the optimal governance structure (minimizing transaction costs) since opportunism linked up with asset specificity is eliminated. The second comment is that Williamson argues from this connection that the transaction cost theory of the firm is superior to any other theories of the firm developed so far. Former theories of the firm can essentially identify technical determinants explaining basic mechanisms of integration (mundane integration), but sophisticated forms of vertical integration (exotic integration) are explained by the transaction costs approach to the theory of the firm. The reason is that in addition to production costs integrated within traditional theories of the firm, Williamson focuses on the minimization of the sum of production and transaction costs. The third comment concerns economies of speed. This notion leads to erroneous conclusions for Williamson, since it leads to a justification of vertical integration in industries in which there is no asset specificity. This notion introduced by Chandler does not differ from a technical complementarity argument advanced in traditional analysis of the theory of the firm, and as such is not able to capture the large diversity of integration forms.

Many further contributions were developed in this line of reasoning, following the argument provided by Williamson (Wiggins, 1991; Shelanski and Klein, 1995; Ménard, 2000). The measure of transaction costs, or at least their operational characterization in an empirical context, was considered a major problem in the initial steps. Today, the usual method lies in the decomposition of transaction costs into their different core elements (asset specificity, uncertainty, frequency of transactions), and in characterizing the impact of each element on the optimal mode of governance. Even if this method does not correspond to the original Williamsonian frame in which the different elements are intrinsically related, it certainly produced a huge number of new results. As a matter of fact, transaction cost theory has now an operational content which favours empirical developments, including closer connections with business history. A number of contributions were also centred on the generalization of the multidivisional form within companies in the United States, Europe and Asia (Hannah, 1983; Kocka, 1971; Reader, 1975; Wilson, 1968; Grieves, 1989). Business history here is in line with one of the key themes developed by Chandler, i.e. the definition of an internal structure able to collect and diffuse information, and the basic theoretical reference lies in a combination between transaction cost approaches and agency theory.

The coordination of information in the context of asymmetric information and diverging incentives

Asymmetric information and diverging incentives are at the core of agency theory (Tirole, 1988). This theory focuses on how institutions can be efficiently structured and run when information is not equally distributed among the actors. Raff and Temin (1991) analyse the possible links between this theory and the internal organization of firms within business history. The firm is the usual domain of application, since owner–manager relationships, managerial conflict and manager–employee interactions are analysed, but the framework extends also to industrial dynamics on the question of how the boundaries of an industry are modified over time.

Very often, managers and owners have diverging interests, and owners have a limited capacity to observe what managers really do. Agency theory argues that in this context owners have an incentive to invest in monitoring mechanisms to improve their knowledge on the private information of managers, or impose remuneration schemes to motivate managers to act in the owners' interests. In this situation, the main problem is thus to define efficient monitoring and compensation systems. Business history shows that these questions are not purely theoretical questions, since they have largely been observed in many cases throughout history. In addition, mechanisms implemented in practice were not significantly different from the recommendations of agency theory. De Long (1991) shows that the monitoring systems implemented by top managers at the bank JP Morgan have significantly improved the performance of client companies. Lamoreaux (1991) focuses on how these information problems have influenced loan strategies within US banks. Finally, and within a more recent historical period, many of the agency theory recommendations were implemented within firms in order to increase the efficiency of corporate governance (Holmström and Kaplan, 2001; Tirole, 2001; Schleifer and Vishny, 1997; Jenkinson and Mayer, 1992). Asymmetric information alters the contractual terms under which investors are willing to invest, as well as the structure and strategy of firms in terms of mergers and acquisition, buy-outs and downsizing. Asymmetric information also has important consequences on the evolution of the population of firms, since the need of funds varies a lot with the business cycle (Calomiris and Hubbard, 1995).

Agency theory also includes managerial conflicts, and refers also to monitoring and compensation schemes. Carlson (1995) uses these arguments to analyse the case of the Thompson Houston Electric Company which was significantly affected by such conflicts of interests. Even if managers had the same collective goal, namely the success of the company, their ranking within the company and their position within different and unconnected services, drove them to sub-optimal strategies. Johnson (1991) also shows that erroneous interpretations or wrong utilization of financial accounting by senior managers led to great inefficiencies in production.

On manager–employee relationships, Davis (1996) reviews different incentive mechanisms which were implemented by top managers in US companies at the beginning of the twentieth century to stimulate employees. Most of these incentive mechanisms are related to the development of a certain kind of appropriation of the company by the employees. Korczinski (1999) explains that the emergence of trade unions in the United Kingdom over the period 1960–80 can be seen as contributing to the limitation of opportunistic behaviours from the employees.

Finally, asymmetric information and diverging interests can also have an impact beyond the sphere of the firm, involving major industrial restructuring. British colonies used to rely on crown agents to convey luxury goods from the United Kingdom over the period 1880–1914 (Sunderland, 1999). When importers in the colonies realized that crown agents could manipulate information on the quality of goods, a monitoring system was put in place so that British colonies and the United Kingdom could simply trade directly, without any intermediary agent. The outcome of this restructuring was thus the disappearance of a specific intermediary actor which was considered fundamental in the former configuration.

The coordination of information in the context of property rights

Grossman and Hart (1986) and Hart (1995) have defined property as the power to exercise control. For these authors, the theory of the firm is not based on different structures of remuneration for employees and contractual agents, and thus cannot be reduced to agency theory propositions. For these authors too, the boundaries of the firm should not be determined exclusively by the greater advantage to limit opportunism, as in transaction cost theory. In fact, the theory of the firm is here defined in reference to the entity which has the residual rights of control, i.e. the entity which controls the decision variables in the last resort. Contributions in business history have tried to back up this theory with empirical data, though archive material appears to be less numerous and affirmative. Lamoreaux (1998) and (2001) shows that even if this theory is often presented as one of the most appealing and challenging, some important difficulties emerge as soon as empirical verification is implemented. On the basis of organizational choices developed by entrepreneurs in the nineteenth century, Lamoreaux shows that the trade-off between integration and partnership cannot be clearly proved on the pure basis of property rights arguments.

Business history and industrial organization on the coordination of information: summing up

Major neo-institutionalist approaches to industrial organization, namely transaction costs, agency theory and property rights generally play an important role in business history contributions since they offer a simple, suitable framework. Compared to neoclassical theories of the firm, neoinstitutionalist approaches certainly render the connection between the two disciplines possible and apparently straightforward, since they focus on the same object of study: the firm as a complex system of interactions, the boundaries of which may evolve over time. From this perspective, business history contributions have shown that institutional forms are modified over time and that these modifications can be explained by problems of coordination of information, such as private information and opportunism. Imperfection or asymmetry of information in the specification and enforcement of contracts, the appropriation of rents or the behaviour of contracting parties justify in most cases the transformation of market coordination into managerial coordination supporting an integrated structure. Information problems can also be at the origins of entry and exit phenomena shaping the boundaries of the industry.

This connection between business history, the theory of the firm and industrial dynamics seems to be affected, however, by three major limits. The first concerns the reference to the 'comparative analysis of institutions' (Williamson, 1989: 136) which assumes that the definition and the comparison of respective efficiencies of different forms of institutions are possible. With this notion, nothing can be said about the emergence and viability of institutional or industrial forms. The second limitation is connected to the deductive method which is often used in the connection between economic analysis and business history. The third limitation is related to the systematic reduction of complex phenomena involving the coordination of industrial activities to simpler issues such as the imperfection or the asymmetry of information.

Comparative analysis of institutions

This explicitly involves the idea that one can compare different forms of institutions in order to define the optimal structure using the criteria of the minimization of transaction costs. This notion was extensively used in transaction cost analyses, and also in other dominant neo-institutionalist approaches such as agency theory and property rights. In all of these theories, the costs and advantages of alternative forms of institutions (firms, market, cooperation) are evaluated, and this evaluation exhibits an efficient solution solving information and incentive problems. This procedure is not significantly different from intertemporal optimization and even mechanical convergence towards equilibrium, all neoclassical notions that have always been so comprehensively rejected by major authors in business history.[4] The major problem is that the question of the evolution of institutional forms and the progressive predominance of one mode over the other is reduced to the instantaneous calculus of the optimal solution. Temporality, in which actors interact concretely and coordinate progressively, is completely neglected, although it is so central to business history.

Deductive method and confirmation

The relation between theories and facts is always critical.[5] The predominance of a deductive method naturally leads economists to consider real-world phenomena as potential illustrations of their theoretical frame. The sequence of reasoning can be summarized in the following way: theoretical hypotheses are defined → the optimal organizational structure for the firm/industry is determined → empirical applications are defined. But beyond this theme, the question of how interdisciplinarity operates is also concerned. The value of interdisciplinarity is present when each discipline jointly brings in new elements that were not apparent when disciplines were working in isolation (see Chapter 1 of this volume). In the present case, industrial organization brings in theoretical frames, while business history provides data. This division of labour between disciplines is never changed or questioned in the sense of the opportunity for business history itself to generate new theoretical propositions, i.e. propositions that were not already included within industrial organization frames and results. Confirmation of the theory by facts is thus the priority, and not a confrontation between different theories coming either from industrial organization or business history.

Focus on the coordination of information

The focus on information problems is not a problem in itself. Most of the advances in industrial organization since the 1970s are centred on this question. A difficulty emerges, however, when this focus becomes exclusive in that it obscures other questions, such as the coordination of productive activities (Richardson, 1960, 1972; Loasby, 1991). This difficulty is present in business history. For Chandler, the essential determinants of the predominance of vertical integration lie in the coordination of productive activities, and especially in the articulation between mass production and mass distribution. Williamson transforms this former interpretation into a problem of coordination of information. When Williamson interprets Chandler, vertical integration is justified by the existence of opportunistic behaviour in capital-intensive industries where assets are highly specific. The argument of Chandler is significantly modified, and the status of empirical verification advocated by Williamson is closer to a confirmation of his own theory than a real confrontation between industrial organization and business history.

When business history confronts industrial organization: questions and puzzles on the coordination of productive activities

In this section, we show that, in some cases, problems related to the coordination of productive activities are at the centre of business history studies. The main argument is based on the real problematic of Chandler which is not centred on the coordination of information, but the coordination of productive activities in innovative firms. Lazonick first restored the main content of this problematic, and Chandler himself in more recent contributions stressed that the interpretation which is provided by neo-institutionalist approaches to the firm is not adapted to his monographs of innovative firms. The coordination of productive activities requires the development of alternative visions of the firm, such as the ones developed in dynamic capabilities approaches. We suggest thus new interpretations of business history studies on the basis of dynamic capabilities theories of the firm and industry.

The coordination of productive activities: the Chandlerian innovative firm

In his book *Business Organization and the Myth of the Economy* published in 1991, Lazonick criticizes the interpretation provided by Williamson of the work of Chandler. For Lazonick, the Williamson–Chandler relationship is not a pure connection between theory (based on transaction costs) and facts (based on business history). Rather, this relation should be considered as the confrontation between two distinct theories on the specific issue of vertical integration. From this perspective, it appears that Williamson essentially proposes a theory of adaptive firms, i.e. a theory in which the behaviour of firms is constrained by the structure of the environment. On the other hand, Chandler offers advances in the field of innovative firms on the basis of a theory in which the behaviour of firms shapes the structure of their environments.[6]

The argument is the following. First, economies of speed characterized by Chandler cannot be assimilated to pure technical problems as described in Williamson's book. Second, the emergence of vertical integration analysed by Chandler cannot be assimilated as a reaction against opportunistic behaviour which is so central to Williamson. The four essential cases examined by Chandler (Duke, Kodak, Swift and Singer) were concerned with the emergence of a technological innovation, but the essential thing in each of these cases was that new forms of organization were to be elaborated in order to coordinate mass production with mass consumption. Vertical integration dominated because it was one of the possible solutions to this specific problem of coordination of productive activities. In fact, well before the technological innovation came out on the market, production and distribution networks were in development. The implementation of a capital-intensive programme generally required for the company the maintenance of a regular flow of inputs for the effective utilization of productive capacity, as well as a sufficient flow of output structuring the establishment of a market which was formerly non-existent. When these conditions were not observed, the importance of sunk costs generally undermined the viability of the innovative firm.

For Lazonick (1991: 198–9), the essential problem was in the transformation of high fixed costs into low unit costs. Chandler (1992) confirms that economies of speed generally implied a need to strengthen the capacity of production as well as the intensity of utilization of this capacity. In the meantime, the increased fixed and sunk costs required counterbalanced low unit costs in final production. The engagement of a triple investment, i.e. the elaboration of distribution networks, the elaboration of networks in commercialization and marketing, and the definition of a specific organization dedicated to coordinating the different phases of the process of production, was crucial to the coordination of mass production and the mass market. This triple investment was the source of durable competitive advantages. In labour-intensive industries, however, such triple investment was not observed, essentially because in that case investments were neither fixed nor irreversible. With this interpretation, the explanation of the dominance of vertical integration goes largely beyond the problem of opportunism linked with asset specificity.[7]

The coordination of productive activities: the role of competences in the process of innovation

In 1992, Chandler provides a contribution in which he clarifies his position on industrial dynamics and the theory of the firm. To him, the firm is necessarily at the centre stage and its essential functions, i.e. first production and second exchange, require an in-depth investigation. Neoclassical visions of the firm, and also agency and even transaction cost theories, are not of any real help solving this problem (Chandler, 1992, 85–6).[8] Within neoclassical approaches the firm is considered to be a technical unit dedicated to maximizing a specific function on the basis of a closed set of information. This clearly does not correspond to the concrete production problems that a firm has to face throughout business history. Within agency theory and transaction cost theory, the basic unit of analysis is not the firm but rather the transaction or any contractual arrangement. In fact, the empirical evidence

Chandler has collected and analysed are much more in coherence with an analysis in terms of evolution of competences. More specifically, he suggests that the alternative theory of the firm which is more in accordance with his work on business history is certainly an analysis in terms of dynamic competences, the origins of which are in Marshall, Schumpeter, Penrose and more recent developments by Teece, Dosi, Lazonick and Nelson (Chandler, 1992: 86). As a matter of fact, Chandler criticizes some of the utilization of his own work, and especially the interpretation by Williamson which was considered as one of the key ways of connecting business history and the theory of the firm. Another important lesson is that of the emerging collaboration between business history and the theory of dynamic competences.

Production and organization of industry: towards an operational framework

Langlois and Foss (1999) stress that the specificity of analysis in terms of dynamic competences is to give the opportunity of generating a rebirth of a problematic centred on production in a theory of industrial organization dominated so far by an exclusive focus on transaction problems. Referring to Richardson (1960, 1972) who explicitly relates the 'capabilities' that characterize the productive knowledge of firms to the 'activities' that compose the production process, Langlois and Robertson (1995) propose a theory of industrial dynamics. Activities can be similar, i.e. based on the same set of competences; and activities can also be complementary, i.e. related within a process of production.[9] The confrontation of different degrees of similarity with different degrees of complementarity can generate a matrix guiding the choice between different forms of organization of industry. The essential question is to know whether new competences can be acquired externally via the market, inside the firm, or on the basis of inter-firm cooperation. The answer depends on, in the first instance, the structure of competences and the location of the different bits that compose this structure of competences, i.e. inside the firm, via cooperation or via the market. But, in addition, the nature of innovation is important. This involves whether innovation is systemic, and therefore requires a simultaneous change of all the different parts of a production process, or whether innovation is autonomous, and so requires the simultaneous change of some of the different parts of the production process (see also Teece, 1986): see Table 10.1.

In Chandler's cases, some of the companies (Swift and Kodak) decided to adopt a vertical integration strategy very early. In other cases (Duke and Singer), companies first experienced vertical disintegration, leaving distribution networks to operate independently. As a second step, they opted for vertical integration by the internalization of these distribution networks. Swift and Kodak were confronted by systemic innovation coupled with the non-existence of the structure of competences. The innovation in Swift was systemic since the essential activity of this firm (i.e. the production and

Table 10.1 Competence, innovation and the vertical structure of the industry

Structure of competences	Systemic innovation	Autonomous innovation
Do not exist	Vertical integration	Vertical disintegration
Exist	Vertical disintegration	Vertical disintegration

transportation of meat) required the modification of all the different parts of the traditional production and distribution processes. The productive challenge was to elaborate specialized and refrigerated containers that could be transported by railways from one city to the other. The market challenge was to attract a big enough customer base for this new product. In fact the former structure of competences was not adapted to these new challenges, since no one before Swift had decided to engage in such an innovative project. For Kodak, innovation was systemic too. The productive challenge was to generate a new process for the development of photography, replacing the old system based on plates by a new one using rolls of film incorporated within the camera. The market challenge was to attract non-professional photographers to use a simple, integrated product. In this case, also, the structure of competences was non-existent, since Kodak was the first developer of this technology and no other companies could either compete on a similar activity or contribute in a complementary manner to the new photography process. Vertical integration was here the sole organizational mode able to create the new competences involved in the innovation process and transform them into market opportunities. For Duke and Singer, the existence of a network of independent retailers with adequate competences naturally led these companies to disintegrate.

Business history and industrial organization on the coordination of production: summing up

Though less well recognized compared to transaction cost theory, agency theory and property rights theory, the approach in terms of dynamic competences provides a framework of industrial organization able to redefine connections with business history. This approach centres on innovation and the creation, development and accumulation of competences. It restores the vision of the link between business history and industrial organization that was contained in the initial contributions of Chandler. This link is characterized by three new elements.

Diversity and evolution of institutions

Business history and industrial organization, within this vision, have to focus on the way in which the activities undertaken are divided up among firms, namely why and how some firms embrace many different activities while for others the range is narrowly circumscribed; why and how some firms are large and others small; why and how some firms are vertically related and others not. Business history and industrial organization have to describe and analyse how the firm and the industry are organized now, but also how they differ from what they were in earlier periods. The connection between these two disciplines requires an understanding of the forces that were operative in bringing about a given organization at the level of the firm or the industry, and how these forces have changed over time. The two disciplines have to jointly characterize the coherence that exists within a specific firm or industry – for instance what determines the boundaries of the firm and the industry, who does what and why within the firm and the industry, and what forces are crucial to their functioning – as well as the diversity that may exist among different firms or different industries.

Inductive method and confrontation

Business history and industrial organization have to capture regularities in observed phenomena and elaborate on this basis plausible and testable assumptions to understand these regularities. From this perspective, business history and industrial organization have to privilege an analysis of the process by which a given trend of evolution has been achieved, and why some diverging path may also be obtained. The sequence of reasoning is here: observed organizational structures are determined → regularities and anomalies are characterized and confronted to theoretical results → new theoretical propositions are generated. This inductive method restores a real confrontation between the two disciplines by considering that each of them can contribute equally to the observation and analysis of a phenomenon. Both disciplines can provide data and theoretical assumptions that, together, may generate a better understanding of this specific phenomenon.

Focus on the coordination of production

The coordination of productive activities is an essential problem in innovation, but too often neglected. The reintroduction of this key element in the connection between business history and industrial organization is thus an important step in the understanding of innovative firms and industries. However, one should be aware that the exclusive focus on this type of coordination may also generate similar drawbacks as the exclusive focus on the coordination of information. In a sense, the connection between business history and industrial organization should develop on the basis of a new mode of confrontation: not only the traditional confrontation between theories and facts, but also between different theories, some oriented towards the coordination of information, some oriented towards the coordination of production.

Business history and the organization of the automobile industry: new perspectives

In the following section we proceed with the idea of a confrontation between theories to sustain the link between business history and industrial organization. We focus on a specific industry, the automobile industry, one of the most innovative in the twentieth century. On the key questions of the boundaries of the firm and of the industry, we provide new perspectives on the characterization of major determinants, by confronting two distinct theoretical perspectives: one in terms of the coordination of information, the other in terms of the coordination of production.

Innovation and the evolution of the boundaries of the firm

Agency theory explains the boundaries of the firm by the differences in remuneration schemes between the manager and the employees. Differences may be attributable to risk behaviour, the manager being supposed to be risk-neutral while the employees are generally risk-averse. Differences can also be linked to private information that the employees have, and that the managers attempt to make them reveal. Is this vision of the firm applicable to large trends in the evolution of remuneration schemes throughout history?

Some studies in business history have explored this question, especially by focusing on the US car industry during the period 1910–30.[10] The major outcome of the studies is that there are two essential factors that contradict the interpretation provided by agency theory. First, remuneration schemes are directly affected by the way in which the different tasks are coordinated, which ultimately depends on the organization of production. This factor is in favour of the predominance of productive information over transaction information in the explanation of the evolution of the boundaries of the firm and remuneration schemes of employees. Moreover, different modes of production were implemented within firms during this period of time, involving different forms in the coordination of tasks, and this may explain the large diversity in remuneration schemes. The second factor is that innovative firms in the car industry, like Ford, adopted mass production and a remuneration structure per day in 1913 or 1914. These innovative firms co-existed with more passive companies that kept their former structure of competences as well as more traditional remuneration schemes. The generalization of mass production and remuneration per day was only effective in 1920.

In fact, at the origins of the car industry, the process of production was highly decomposable. The automobile is a luxury good and car companies were more assemblers than producers. Within each enterprise, a small group of persons had to proceed to different parts of the car and reassemble them in a process very similar to that formerly implemented in carriage manufacturing. Each assembler was quite independent of the other, and the rhythm of each single worker was unconstrained by the work done by another worker. In this system, the essential requirement was to produce the largest number of parts, and workers with a high productivity were selected and paid more than others. In this system also, owners of the company had no rights to the manufacturing equipment used in car production, since employees came to the workshop with their own tools. For these reasons, it was quite difficult to distinguish an employee and an independent worker, and the boundaries of the firm were quite fuzzy. The mode of payment was directly dependent on the mode of production: quantity was the priority, and workers were paid according to what they manufactured.

The industry further developed and faced two key changes which were initially introduced by Ford. The first important change was the implementation of progressive assembly, a system by which the work continued even when the company generated stocks. The tasks of each individual employee became more interconnected, and it was now necessary to coordinate the rhythm of work of the team. The second important change involved the American-system production of parts, which involved the production of standardized intermediary and final goods. Investment in manufacturing equipment was now made by the company. With these changes, the assembly line was the place where all the inputs and activities had to be narrowly coordinated. When there was excess production as a result of inadequate coordination, this might generate important losses for the company. The boundaries of the firm emerged in this new situation: the firm was a set of activities closely linked both technically and economically, implemented by a population of workers and coordinated by a group of managers. Here, the mode of payment was not determined on the basis of individual/team productivity, but with reference to the global productivity of the enterprise. The achievement of the process of production involved the engagement of all the workers and the remuneration was identical for each type of worker.

The automobile industry was certainly characterized by systemic innovation. All the tasks and the way in which they were coordinated were redefined at this period. However, systemic innovation was gradually and differently adopted by companies of the industry. Some of the companies even rejected many of the changes and continued to produce in the same manner as they had always done, relying on the former traditional structure of competences of their quasi-independent workers, and keeping fuzzy firm boundaries. Other firms, most of them soon to become leaders of the industry (Ford, General Motors, Chrysler), elaborated a new structure of competences adapted to the development of the systemic innovation, and created a sophisticated organizational structure. The diversity of these different firms and their characteristics in terms of productive choices also had implications on market entry and exit, and hence on the definition of the boundaries of the industry.

Innovation and the evolution of the boundaries of the industry

In the domain of industrial dynamics, one key framework is the industry life cycle or ILC (Gort and Klepper, 1982; Klepper, 1997, 2002a, 2002b). The basic hypothesis is that innovative industries behave like biological organisms, and their characteristics evolve and change depending on the different stages of their life cycle. One of the major results of this body of literature is that market structure, i.e. the number of firms, is highly connected to the stages of diffusion of the innovation within the industry. Here again, business history studies show that this result can be discussed, especially when information problems are privileged to explain this phenomenon in a context of innovation.

The car industry is one of the specific domains of application of ILC models (Klepper and Simons, 1997, 2000). Empirical work in this industry generally brought new propositions into the conceptual framework and, in turn, theoretical models were tested in this sector. Using the database from the Federal Trade Commission for the period 1899–1960, for instance, we know the following facts. The growth rate of output increased considerably up to 1919 (25.8 per cent per year), and stagnated up to 1929 (11.5 per cent per year). In the period 1930–7 the growth rate decreased, and rose slightly at the end of the period. The ILC model is valid here, since the growth of output was high during the initial phases of the cycle, and then declined over time. The entry–exit process also evolved according to ILC recommendations. Entry was highly concentrated during the development phase of the industry since, during the period 1902–10, it reached on average 48 new firms per year, with a peak of 84 companies in 1907. After 1910, the entry rate fell: it reached 16 new entrants per year in the period 1911–21, and almost zero thereafter. In 1909, exits were greater than entry and thus a shakeout[11] occurred. This shakeout became more important during the 1920s and was at a maximum in the 1930s. Market shares fluctuated significantly initially and stabilized over time, as soon as the leader firms started to gain a dominant market position. In fact, in 1937, three firms (Ford, General Motors and Chrysler) accounted for 88 per cent of the market. These firms would keep their leadership until the 1960s. First movers survived and occupied leader positions in the long run. Entry was common, and there were five major cohorts of entrants (1895–1904, 1905–9, 1910–16, 1917–22, 1923–67). Entrants coming from these different waves had a similar survival rate during the first seven years, but after the seventh year, former entrants issued from the first wave clearly survived better than later entrants coming from the other four cohorts. A product substitution innovation process is also observed. Product innovation was at a maximum in 1905, and concerned major innovations in the definition of the basic structure of automobiles. Product innovation further declined and was progressively replaced by process innovation which continued to progress until the mid 1930s.

Business history studies here offer an alternative vision of the phenomenon of shakeout observed during the Great Depression. Aggregate economic data show that the shakeout confirms the basic teachings of ILC, while business history data seem to suggest that this is not necessarily the case.[12] The ILC model advocates that the industry was prospering and that there was suddenly a huge shock from the Great Depression. Business historians show, on the contrary, that the pattern of evolution was somewhat more complex.[13] Between the two peaks of 1929 and 1933, the total number of incumbent firms was nearly half the initial total, and entry stagnated at 10 per cent: there was clearly a shakeout. However a complete vision of what occurred involves a deeper investigation into what the firms looked like, what were the characteristics of those who survived between 1929 and 1933, who exited the industry, or emerged as new entrants in the same period.

The firms that disappeared were essentially different from the other two classes of companies. In 1929, when the Great Depression struck, automobiles were developed according to two different technologies. On the one hand, three major leaders (General Motors, Ford and Chrysler) were precursors in the development of mass production and modern manufacturing methods. On the other hand, other firms were using older technologies, which were more labour-intensive. The exit process is traditionally analysed by ILC in terms of the access to information and its impact on cost curves. This explanation is not appropriate here. The Great Depression cannot be considered as a period of transition in which less efficient firms disappeared. Rather it is a key period in which there was a profound mutation in the industry. Differences in cost curves are thus not central in the argument, since cost curves generally reflect production costs at a specific moment in time. The major element here to explain the massive exit process is in fact the sunk costs that some firms decided to engage, while others firms conserved a more flexible position. When the leading capital-intensive companies were faced with low levels of demand, they could not generate sufficient revenue, but more importantly they could not exit the industry voluntarily. Labour-intensive companies on the contrary could exit the industry without major losses. The rationale for the shakeout is thus the engagement in a systemic innovation involving high sunk costs and an internal reorganization dedicated to creating new competences, adapted to new productive challenges.

One could finally advocate that the choice of flexible labour-intensive companies was, at the end of the day, purely rational compared to the decisions of other firms that engaged high sunk costs and faced large losses during the Great Depression. However, this vision is also very partial. The leaders, by their irreversible choice, developed the conditions of their own development and viability. With the sunk costs of the investment in new production methods and new organizational structures, these companies were in a position to face the mass demand that emerged thereafter. These firms developed productive activities that corresponded to the market configuration, and controlled the articulation between the productive sphere and the market sphere. Other firms failed; they disappeared with the Great Depression and could never enter again.

Conclusion

This chapter has reviewed the literature on the possible links between business history and the organization of the industry. From the review, we show that a dominant trend considers economic models as a grid to structure historical facts, while an alternative vision leaves business history studies a larger space to refine basic economic frames on the organization of the industry. The chapter also shows that, in a context of innovation, the dominant trend is often inappropriate to deal with the question of the boundaries of firms and industries. This motivates the development of the second alternative to progress on the understanding of the theory of the firm and industrial dynamics.

Notes

1 See for instance 'Development of the American Economy' at NBER, 'History Friendly Modelling' at Bocconi and 'Innovative Enterprise and Historical Transformation' at INSEAD.
2 For a comprehensive analysis of the connections that exist between these different theories of the firm, see Chapter 2 of this book by Michael Dietrich.
3 See also Dietrich and Krafft (2005) for a related work on that point.
4 See, for instance, Hyde (1962); Wilson (1997); Jones (1997).
5 See Fisher (1991), but also Kaldor (1985) and Hayek (1937).
6 See also Lazonick (2002, 2003).
7 Again, according to Lazonick (1991: 242–4),

> in referring to Chandler's material on Swift, Williamson demonstrated his unwillingness (or inability) to comprehend the Chandlerian emphasis on high throughput and economies of speed. Paraphrasing Chandler on the reasons for Swift's ultimate success, Williamson argued that 'despite the opposition from the railroads and butchers, Swift's "high quality and low prices" combined with "careful scheduling" prevailed'.

Compare this statement with the quote from Chandler that I have just reproduced and emphasized. For Williamson, it was not worth mentioning the other factors – 'high volume and the speed ... of product flow' – that Chandler included in the same phrase as 'careful scheduling' (the factor that Williamson did quote) as ways in which Swift attained the 'high quality at low prices' that enabled him to win the market.
8 See also Chandler *et al.* (1997, 1998, 2000).
9 For Richardson, the process of production regroups the activities of conception, production, commercialization and distribution. This vision thus corresponds to an extended definition of the process of production.
10 See statistics and censuses on firms' payment schemes provided by the US Department of Labour, Bureau of Labour and Statistics, as well as the National Industrial Conference Board (Raff, 1995; Langlois and Roberston, 1995).
11 Klepper and Miller (1995) define the shakeout in the following terms: the industry is not in a situation of shakeout when the number of firms does not decline below

70 per cent of the peak or when, going below this threshold, the number of companies rises again to at least 90 per cent of the peak. With this definition, only 27 out of 46 firms studied initially by Gort and Klepper (1982) face a shakeout.

12 Data in this case come from the census of producers in 1929, 1931, 1933 and 1935. For this specific industry, and others, these census manuscripts survived in original or microfilm form with essentially complete coverage. The data is therefore suitable for panelization and analysis using sophisticated statistical methods.

13 Cf. Raff (1998) and Bresnahan and Raff (1991).

References

Bresnahan, T. and Raff, D. (1991), 'Intra-industry heterogeneity and the great depression: the American motor vehicles industry, 1929–35', *Journal of Economic History*, 5(2): 317–31.

Calomiris, C. and Hubbard, R. (1995), 'Internal finance and investment: evidence from the undistributed profit tax of 1936–37', *Journal of Business*, 68(4): 443–82.

Carlson, B. (1995), 'The coordination of business organisation and technological innovation within the firm: a case study of the Thomson-Houston Electric Company in the 1880s', in N. Lamoreaux and D. Raff (eds) (1995), *Coordination and Information: Historical Essays on the Organisation of Enterprise*, Chicago, IL: University of Chicago Press.

Chandler, A. (1977), *The Visible Hand: The Managerial Revolution in American Business*, Cambridge, MA: Harvard University Press.

—— (1992), 'Organizational capabilities and the economic history of the industrial enterprise', *Journal of Economic Perspective*, 6(3): 79–100.

Chandler, A. and Cortada, J. (eds) (2000), *A Nation Transformed by Information: How Information Has Shaped the US from Colonial Times to Present*, Oxford: Oxford University Press.

Chandler, A., Amatori, F. and Hikino, T. (eds) (1997), *Big Business and the Wealth of Nations*, Cambridge: Cambridge University Press.

Chandler, A., Hagstrom, P. and Orjan, S. (eds) (1998), *The Dynamic Firm: The Role of Technology, Strategy, Organization and Regions*, Oxford: Oxford University Press.

Davis, C. (1996), 'You are the company: the demands of employment in the emerging corporate culture, Los Angeles, 1900–930', *Business History Review*, 70: 328–62.

De Long, B. (1991), 'Did J.P. Morgan's men add value? An economist's perspective on financial capitalism', in P. Temin (ed.), *Inside the Business Enterprise: The Use and Transformation of Information*, Chicago, IL: University of Chicago Press.

Dietrich, M. and Krafft, J. (2005), 'The firm in economics and history: towards an historically relevant economics of the firm', ENEF Working Paper.

Fisher, F. (1991), 'Organizing industrial organization: reflections on the handbook of industrial organization', *Brooking Papers on Economic Activity: Microeconomics*, 201–25.

Gort, M. and Klepper, S. (1982), 'Time path in the diffusion of product innovations', *Economic Journal*, 92: 630–53.

Grieves, K. (1989), *Sir Eric Geddes*, Manchester: Manchester University Press.

Grossman, S. and Hart, O. (1986), 'The costs and benefits of ownership: a theory of vertical and lateral integration', *Journal of Political Economy*, 94: 691–719.

Hannah, L. (1983), *The Rise of Corporate Economy*, 2nd edn, London: Methuen.

Hart, O. (1995), *Firms, Contracts and Financial Structure*, New York: Oxford University Press.

Hayek, F. (1937), 'Economics and knowledge', *Economica*, 4: 33–54.

Holmström, B. and Kaplan, S. (2001), 'Corporate governance and merger activity in the United States: making sense of the 1980's and 1990's', *Journal of Economic Perspective*, 15(2): 121–44.

Hyde, F. (1962), 'Economic theory and business history', *Business History*, 5(1).

Jenkinson, T. and Mayer, C. (1992), 'The assessment: corporate governance and corporate control', *Oxford Review of Economic Policy* (3): 1–10.

Johnson, T. (1991), 'Managing by remote control: recent management accounting practice in historical perspective', in P. Temin (ed.), *Inside the Business Enterprise: The Use and Transformation of Information*, Chicago, IL: University of Chicago Press.

Jones, S. (1997), 'Transaction costs and the theory of the firm: the scope and limitations of the new institutional approach', in M. Casson and M. Rose (eds), *Business History*, special issue on 'Institutions and the evolution of modern business', 39(4).

Kaldor, N. (1985), *Economics without Equilibrium*, Cardiff: Cardiff University Press.

Klepper, S. (1997), 'Industry life cycle', *Industrial and Corporate Change*, 6(1): 145–81.

—— (2002a), 'Firm survival and the evolution of oligopoly', *Rand Journal of Economics*, 33(1): 37–61.

—— (2002b), 'The capabilities of new firms and the evolution of the US automobile industry', *Industrial and Corporate Change*, 11(4): 645–66.

Klepper, S. and Miller, J. (1995), 'Entry, exit and shakeouts in the United States in new manufactured products', *International Journal of Industrial Organization*, 13: 567–91.

Klepper, S. and Simons, K. (1997), 'Technological extinctions of industrial firms: an inquiry into their nature and causes', *Industrial and Corporate Change*, 6(2): 379–460.

—— (2000), 'The making of an oligopoly: firm survival and technical change in the evolution of the US tire industry', *Journal of Political Economy*, 108(4): 728–60.

Kocka, J. (1971), 'Family and bureaucracy in German industrial management', *Business History Review*, 45: 133–56.

Korczinski, M. (1999), 'Restrictive practices of capital: employer commercial opportunism, labour militancy and economic performance in the engineering construction industry, 1960–80', *Business History*, 41(3): 134–60.

Lamoreaux, N. (1991), 'Information problems and banks' specialisation in short-term commercial lending: New England in the 19th century', in P. Temin (ed.), *Inside the Business Enterprise: The Use and Transformation of Information*, Chicago, IL: University of Chicago Press.

—— (1998), 'Partnerships, corporations, and the theory of the firm', *American Economic Review*, 88(2): 66–71.

—— (2001), 'Market trade in patents and the rise of a class of specialized inventors in the 19th century United States', *American Economic Review*, 91(2): 39–44.

Lamoreaux, N. and Raff, D. (eds) (1995), *Coordination and Information: Historical Essays on the Organisation of Enterprise*, Chicago, IL: University of Chicago Press.

Lamoreaux, N., Raff, D. and Temin, P. (eds) (1998), *Learning by Doing in Firms, Markets and Nations*, Chicago, IL: University of Chicago Press.

Langlois, R. and Foss, N. (1999), 'Capabilities and governance: the rebirth of production in the theory of economic organisation', *Kyklos*, 52(2): 201–18.

Langlois, R. and Robertson, P. (1995), *Firms, Markets and Economic Change: A Dynamic Theory of Business Institutions*, London: Routledge.

Lazonick, W. (1991), *Business Organization and the Myth of the Economy*, Cambridge: Cambridge University Press.

—— (2002), 'Innovative enterprise and historical transformation', *Enterprise and Society*, 3(1): 3–47.

—— (2003), 'The theory of the market economy and the social foundations of innovative enterprise', *Economic and Industrial Democracy*, 24(1): 9–44.

Loasby, B. (1991), *Equilibrium and Evolution: An Exploration of Connecting Principles in Economics*, Manchester: Manchester University Press.

Ménard, C. (2000), *Institutions, Contracts and Organizations: Perspectives from New Institutional Economics*, Aldershot: Edward Elgar.

Raff, D. (1995), 'The puzzling profusion of compensation systems in the interwar automobile industry', in N. Lamoreaux and D. Raff (eds), *Coordination and Information: Historical Essays on the Organisation of Enterprise*, Chicago, IL: University of Chicago Press.

—— (1998), 'Representative firm analysis and the character of competition: glimpses from the great depression', *American Economic Review*, 88(2): 57–61.

Raff, D. and Temin, P. (1991), 'Business history and recent economic theory: imperfect information, incentives, and internal organisation of firms', in P. Temin (ed.), *Inside the Business Enterprise: The Use and Transformation of Information*, Chicago, IL: University of Chicago Press.

Reader, W. (1975), *Imperial Chemical Industry: A History*, Oxford: Oxford University Press.

Richardson, G. (1960), *Information and Investment*, Clarendon Press, Oxford; 2nd edn, 1990.

—— (1972), 'The organisation of industry', *Economic Journal*, 82: 883–96.

Schleifer, A. and Vishny, R. (1997), 'A survey of corporate governance', *Journal of Finance*, 52: 737–83.

Shelanski, H. and Klein, S. (1995), 'Empirical research in transaction costs economics: a survey and assessment', *Journal of Law, Economics and Organisation*, 11: 335–61.

Sunderland, D. (1999), 'Objectionable parasites: the Crown Agents and the purchase of Crown colony government stores, 1880–1914', *Business History*, 41(4): 21–47.

Teece, D. (1986), 'Profiting from technological innovation: implications for integration, collaboration, licensing, and public policy', *Research Policy*, 15: 285–305.

Temin, P. (ed.) (1991), *Inside the Business Enterprise: The Use and Transformation of Information*, Chicago, IL: University of Chicago Press.

Tirole, J. (1988), *The Theory of Industrial Organization*, Cambridge, MA: MIT Press.

—— (2001), 'Corporate governance', *Econometrica*, 69(1): 1–35.

Wiggins, S. (1991), 'The economics of the firm and contracts: a selective survey', *Journal of Institutional and Theoretical Economics*, 149: 603–61.

Williamson, O. (1985), *The Economic Institutions of Capitalism*, New York: Free Press.

—— (1989), 'Transaction costs economics', in R. Schmalensee and T. Willig (eds), *Handbook of Industrial Organisation*, North Holland: Amsterdam.

Wilson, J. (1968), *Unilever, 1945–1965: Challenge and Response in the Post-War Industrial Revolution*, London: Cassell.

—— (1997), *British Business History – 1720–1994*, Manchester and New York: Manchester University Press.

11 The firm in history: city–industry relations

A case study of the engineering sector in the UK economy during the interwar years

Sue Bowden, David Higgins and Christopher Price[1]

Introduction

All models of economic growth stress the importance of capital investment for long-run growth. Whether the emphasis is on the quantity of capital (Solow, 1956) or the quality of capital (Romer, 1994) there is consensus within the economics profession that the economy that best sustains its investment is the economy that will best prosper. Investment in capital, however, requires finance. If we can understand intrinsically the importance of investment at the macroeconomic level, then how do we explain the mechanics whereby, at the micro level, firms raise the necessary monies to finance investment?

How does the firm raise monies both to establish itself and to finance growth? The majority of small-scale enterprises throughout history were financed largely through the largesse (and risk-taking) of the firm's owner and friends, family and business acquaintances. This indeed continued to be the model most commonly applied during industrialisation in most parts of the world. Working capital – the monies required to support the on-going day-to-day activities of the firm – and investment capital – those monies required to finance long-term development – tended to be 'personal'. Friends and family provided the monies to establish the firm, and retained profits were used to finance working capital and future investment.

Matters became more complex with the growth in scale and scope of the firm. Investment in larger-scale plants and associated technology required funds beyond the remit of the personal network. Increasingly, access to alternative sources had to be sought. The solution came with use of monies from the financial markets, largely banks, for working capital requirements and through the stock exchange for long-run investment purposes. With industrialisation, firms increasingly raised money from the financial markets through equity capital and bonds. Through the primary market firms were able to raise capital through the sale of bonds, equities or other securities (the secondary market deals with trading in existing securities by investors). For the first half of the twentieth century, firms on both sides of the Atlantic sought, and did not always obtain, working capital from merchant and clearing banks; new money was raised via bonds and equities and other securities (Chandler, 1977, 1990, 1991; Hannah, 1980, 1983).

By the beginning of the twenty-first century the size of the world bond market was $31 trillion (this compares with $36 trillion value for world equities). The United States has become the world's largest bond market; its nearest rivals are (in descending order) Japan, Germany, Italy and France. Historically, the main issuers of bonds have been governments. By 2000, government bonds accounted for 53 per cent of US bonds – and 72 per cent of Japanese bonds. Globally, the trend is for most countries to have larger equity than bond markets: there are, however, important exceptions: namely, Japan, Germany and Italy where the bond market is larger than the equity market. At the other extreme, in the United Kingdom the bond market is only a third of the size of its equity market. Why? The relative importance of the two markets largely reflects macroeconomic policy and in particular the size of the public sector: countries with larger public sectors and more nationalised industries tend to have larger bond markets. On a micro level, those countries with bank-based financial systems placed more emphasis on debt than equity finance – which in turn encouraged the growth of larger corporate bond markets. Examples of this would include Germany, Japan and Italy (Dimson *et al.*, 2002: in particular Chapter 2).

The question of risk is important as this applies to all firms in industrialised capitalist economies. The evidence suggests that the financial markets were willing and able to supply monies to established firms, with good credit history and the potential for growth (Capie and Collins, 1992). From the banks' perspective, this would appear to reflect rational economic judgement. The problem arises if risk aversion acts to deter entrepreneurial drive and constrains the dynamic growth which underpins long-run economic success. This does appear to have been a problem in the United Kingdom where small and medium firms experienced difficulties in raising capital from the financial markets throughout the twentieth century – the so-called Macmillan Gap (Committee on Finance, 1931: 173–4; Henderson, 1951; Cottrell, 2004; Ross, 2004). The problem then was not one of supporting existent firms, but of support for those who wished to 'begin' and those who wished to develop from initial beginnings to sustained growth – the engines, so-called, of long-run dynamic change and growth. It is easy to support the successful – less so to take risk in supporting the unproven.

Firms also raised finance through equity – and hence stock markets. We should note here that stock exchanges have a very long history: the earliest founding of stock markets dates from 1611 in the Netherlands, 1685 in Germany and 1698 in the United Kingdom. By the end of the eighteenth century, they had been established in France, Austria and the United States (in 1724, 1771 and 1792 respectively). By the beginning of the twenty-first century 111 different countries had stock markets, and the combined values of shares traded on those markets exceeded $36 trillion (Dimson *et al.*, 2002: 20, 11, Table 2.3).

Mature industrial capitalism on both sides of the Atlantic witnessed the growth of limited liability companies and the resort of firms to capital through the issue of equity. By the end of the nineteenth century, 783 companies had their shares traded on the London Stock Exchange. Initially in both the United States and the United Kingdom railroads dominated, but by the mid twentieth century chemicals, brewing, tobacco and retailing had all grown in importance; chemicals and retailing were to continue their strong profile throughout the rest of the century (Dimson *et al.*, 2002: Chapter 2). In the second half of the twentieth century equity finance became dominated by financial institutions: in the United States, the United Kingdom, France, Germany and Japan, to name but five leading economies where this applied (Charkham, 1994; Dimsdale and Prevezer, 1994; Roe, 1994).Whereas the first half of the twentieth century witnessed a transition from the owner-managed firm to limited liability and ownership in the hands of individual private shareholders (Hannah, 1980; Payne, 1984), the second half witnessed a switch in equity holdings from the private to the institutional investor, made possible by the growth of the pension and insurance industries. The rise of the institutional investor was premised on the assumption of a steady steam of dividend income (Bowden, 1990).

The literature on the interwar period, as far as equity finance is concerned, has tended to concentrate on the negative implications of the re-capitalisation boom of 1919–20 (Dowie, 1975), with particular emphasis on cotton textiles (Higgins and Toms, 2001, 2003). The wider issues as to the raising of finance by other industries and sectors has, to some extent, been overlooked (Bowden and Higgins, 2004).

To summarise, first the literature sees the evolution of the firm as being premised on the ability to finance short-term working capital requirements and long-term investment needs through the financial markets. Second, there is a long-run explanation which sees new and small firms as having difficulties raising external finance. Third, the literature has described the evolution of the divorce of ownership from control through the raising of external finance through the equity markets. Finally, there is an implicit if not explicit view that this was a smooth evolutionary process which gradually occurred through the twentieth century.

This chapter seeks to explore some of these issues using new datasets from ESRC-research-funded projects. The emphasis is on the interwar years, on the equity markets and on firms which were quoted on the London Stock Exchange. Appendix 11.1 lists the relevant variables contained in the *Stock Exchange Official Year Book* that have been used in this research.

The next section presents new evidence which considers the growth of equity finance in the period 1918 to 1939 as measured by the number of firms seeking quotation in these years. Following this we consider the key characteristics of those firms seeking quotation: which firms sought equity finance? Were they new entrants or did existing quoted firms seek additional funds? In the next section we open up the analysis by presenting our findings on debt finance. We sought to establish whether only older-established firms with 'risk-averse' track records obtained quotation on the Stock Exchange. The final substantive section places our findings in a longer-run perspective. We consider the lessons learnt in terms of the survival of those firms which sought equity finance. Who were the shareholders, and more importantly what were the effects of this increase in share ownership on the investing public? Finally conclusions are drawn.

Growth of equity finance 1918–39

Why would anyone believe that the interwar years – surely a time of depressed international economic environment – should witness an enhanced tendency to seek external finance to fund long-term investment? The answer lies in the 'dual' economy with old staple industries in export-dominated sectors being depressed, but with the new growth industries dependent on a growing and buoyant domestic market (based largely on the improvement in the standard of living of the middle classes and more affluent working classes). Two such industries were electrical engineering and vehicle engineering. In hypo- thesising an increase in corporate capitalism in the electrical and vehicle engineering sectors, there is additional evidence which demonstrates increased investment in these sectors in the interwar years. Between 1924 and 1937, electrical engineering recorded an annual percentage growth of 2.4 per cent in capital stock whilst that for vehicle engineering was 3.1 per cent. These were the two highest sectoral increases in the period (Matthews *et al.*, 1982: 240, Table 8.7). By 1935, investment in plant and machinery in the motor vehicle industry amounted to £12.4 million and constituted 77 per cent of investment in plant and machinery in the vehicle sector (Census of Production, 1950: 9–10).

Our research identified a significant increase in public quotation in terms of the number of listed companies in *all* sub-sectors of these two industries. If we take the interwar years as a whole, by 1938 the number of firms listed had grown, since 1917, by 30 per cent in the vehicle sector, and by 40 per cent in electrical engineering. Much of that increase occurred in the 1920s, and, within that decade, in three particular years: namely 1920–1, 1924–5 and 1927–9. The growth in the use of external – equity – finance, in other words, was largely a feature of the 1920s (see Figure 11.1).

The growth in the use of external equity finance was a function not only of the number of listed firms but also of the capitalisation value of each of these quoted firms. All our three sub-sectors in engineering participated in

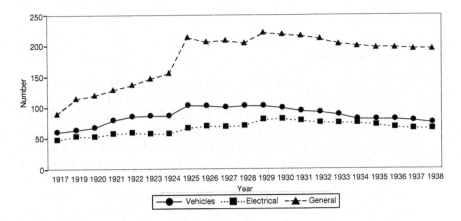

Figure 11.1 Number of companies listed on the London Stock Exchange, 1917–38.
Source: *Stock Exchange Official Year Book.*

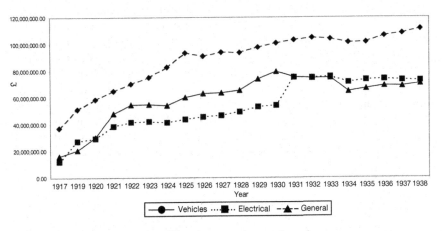

Figure 11.2 Total book value of listed companies: engineering.
Source: *Stock Exchange Official Year Book.*

significant increases in capitalisation, this being a trend particularly associated with the 1920s (Figure 11.2). Prima facie our results suggest that the
total book value of equity of engineering firms increased markedly in the
interwar years. Very significant increases were recorded in all sectors
between 1917 and 1919 and 1919 and 1922. There were, however, important
differences between the sectors. Vehicle engineering experienced the largest
growth in capitalisation, with a marked upsurge from 1917 to 1922 and again
between 1925 and 1930. The increase in general engineering was no less
substantial – but there the increase was more of a steady trend throughout
the 1920s. The electrical sector, again in contrast, experienced its greatest
growth in capitalisation from 1928 to 1933.

Our research has thus identified an enhanced propensity amongst firms to seek external finance through the equity markets in the interwar years.

Firms and equity finance

The upsurge in the book value of equity in vehicle engineering between 1919 and 1922 was accounted for by increases in capitalisation among *existing* (that is quotation before the war) motor vehicle companies. Table 11.1 details re-capitalisation amongst existing motor vehicle firms in the early postwar years. The data are organised in descending order of value of capitalisation. Of particular note are the re-capitalisation undertaken by Austin Motors, Leyland, Wolseley, Crossley, Rover and Rolls Royce. In these terms our findings confirm the hypothesis stipulated in the previous section that equity finance in the initial postwar years was sought to finance investment in productive capacity to exploit the predicted middle-class market.

Whilst the increase in capitalisation in the motor vehicle sector derived from *re*-capitalisation by *existing* firms between 1917 and 1922, increases thereafter were affected by inclusion of entrants and by the entry onto the listings of four significant players: Briggs Motor Bodies (£1m in 1936); Morris Motors (£5m in 1926), Chrysler (£6.2m in 1933) and Ford (£7m in 1929). In these terms, our findings confirm our previous hypothesis that firms desirous of exploiting the growing middle-class market for cars sought equity finance to underpin expansions in productive capacity. By 1938, Morris's total net assets of £11,464,000 were the highest among the major car-producing companies, with additions to net assets achieved by this company between 1934 and 1938 being valued at £3,617,000 (Bowden, 1991).

Table 11.1 Capitalisation (book value £), motor vehicle firms quoted on the London Stock Exchange in 1917

£s	1917	1919	1920	1921
Austin Motors	650,000	1,650,000	1,650,000	5,000,000
Leyland	400,000	500,000	1,850,000	1,850,000
Wolseley	600,000	600,000	1,800,000	1,800,000
Crossley	300,000	600,000	600,000	1,250,000
Rover	200,000	200,000	700,000	1,050,000
Rolls Royce	200,000	1,000,000	1,000,000	1,000,000
Joseph Lucas	500,000	500,000	500,000	800,000
Sunbeam	320,000	700,000	700,000	700,000
Vulcan	150,000	150,000	150,000	620,000
Vauxhall	300,000	400,000	400,000	600,000
Riley	50,000	100,000	100,000	350,000
Triumph	130,000	290,000	290,000	290,000

Source: *Stock Exchange Official Year Book.*

In contrast, the increase in capitalisation in electrical engineering derived less from re-capitalisation by existing firms between 1917 and 1921 than the *entry* to the London Stock Market of firms between 1928 and 1930 (that is firms seeking external equity finance for the first time). The latter coincided with the launch of the National Grid. Of particular note in this respect (Table 11.2) were Associated Electrical Industries (first listed in 1929 at £6,395,000), Electrolux (first listed in 1928 at £1,000,000), Phillips Incandescent Lamps (£20m in 1931); and Tube Investments (first listed in 1928 at £1,550,000). In 1930, General Electric re-capitalised, increasing its equity finance from £6m to £7.6m.

In contrast to both vehicle and electrical engineering, general engineering was characterised by both new entrants and by re-capitalisations. Significant re-capitalisation in general engineering was carried out by Ingersoll Rand (US), (increasing its capitalisation from £4.1m in 1922 to £7.2m in 1923), United Shoe Machinery Corporation (increase from £10.3m in 1923 to £15.4m in 1924) and Radiation (increases from £2.75m in 1920, to £4m in 1921 and £5m in 1928). The most active re-capitalisations, however, were the province of two companies: British United Shoe Machinery and British Oxygen, who regularly re-capitalised throughout the period.

To summarise, our research has identified an increased tendency to raise external finance through equity markets in the engineering sector in the interwar years. We found that this was a function of firms seeking equity finance for the first time and of new issues by existing quoted firms. The emphasis, however, differed between sub-sectors. In the motor engineering sector, the latter was more important, whilst in the electrical sector, the former dominated. General engineering was characterised both by new entrants and by re-capitalisation. Taking the interwar years as a whole, our research suggested that the 1930s was a decade of relative stability in terms of the number of quoted firms in all three sectors, with the significant exception of the increase in the number of firms quoted in the vehicle sector.

Table 11.2 Significant entrants to London Stock Exchange listing, general engineering in the 1920s: date of first listing and book value (£)

	Date of first listing	*Amount*
Worthington Pump and Machinery Corp.	1919	7,407,407
Amalgamated Dental (manuf of dental mats)	1925	2,850,000
Radiation	1920	2,750,000
Armstrong Whitworth Development Co.	1920	2,000,000
Morgan Crucible Co. Ltd	1920	1,500,000
Tweedales and Smalley (1920)	1922	1,250,000
Kynoch	1919	1,000,000
Parkinson and Cowan	1923	1,000,000
Glenfield and Kennedy	1922	750,000
Crittal Manufacturing Co.	1925	150,000

Source: *Stock Exchange Official Year Book.*

Our analysis of the number of firms in the engineering sector quoted on the London Stock Exchange equally revealed a significant increase in public quotation during the 1920s, some exit from public quotation in the period 1929–31 and relative stability in terms of the number of firms quoted on the London Stock Exchange thereafter. In all, the number of firms listed during the 1930s was greater than the number listed in both 1917 and 1919. In these terms we found evidence to support the growth of corporate capitalism in the interwar years.

In addition, our research evidence suggested that firms in each sub-sector responded rationally to the economic environment in which they operated. The increase in listings and in capitalisation in electrical engineering coincided with the launch of the National Grid, whilst those in motor vehicles reflected the growth of demand for cars in the domestic middle-class market. Our research indicated that firms sought to raise equity finance – but only if and when the economic environment in which they were operating suggested the viability of expansion.

Firms and debt finance

In this section we address three questions. First we consider the balance between debt and equity finance. In this respect, we were particularly interested to explore the effect of the rises in the bank rate in the 1920s and the decline from 1933 on such choices. It might be expected that the significant rise in the early 1920s and the significant declines from 1933 would influence firms in their choice of finance instrument, favouring equity in the former period and debt in the latter period. Second, we tested the Thomas hypothesis that debt was associated with longer rather than newly established firms (Thomas, 1978). Finally, we examined the effect of the bank rate on debt and equity.

We first present our findings on the balance between equity and debt in each of our three sub-sectors. Table 11.3 details finance by year in which external finance was raised, differentiating between new debt, new listing or re-capitalisation, Figures 11.3 to 11.5 illustrate the amounts involved. In electrical engineering (Figure 11.3) we found overall that debt levels were low and falling, whereas equity levels were high and growing: firms in electrical engineering raised long-run finance through equity rather than debt in the interwar years.

In vehicle and general engineering (Figures 11.4 and 11.5) we found an even larger gap between debt and equity, but that equity levels were high and grew substantially, particularly between 1917 and 1930 in the case of vehicle engineering.

We have in the case of general engineering (Figure 11.6) identified a switch in the kind of debt used – namely a reduction in long-run debt and an increase in short-term debt in the form of overdrafts: a finding which is the subject of on-going research.

Table 11.3 Choice of finance instrument

	1919	1920	1921	1922	1923	1924	1925	1926	1927	1928	1929	1930	1931	1932	1933	1934	1935	1936	1937	1938
Vehicles																				
Number of firms entering listing	3	5	13	6	3	2	18	4	2	3	8	2	0	1	1	1	1	3	1	1
Number of firms re-capitalising	15	15	17	2	1	1	7	4	3	6	4	7	3	2	3	3	2	6	13	7
Number of firms raising new debt	4	1	6	1	2	1	6	4	1	1	1	0	0	0	3	5	1	0	0	0
Number of firms seeking external finance	22	21	36	9	6	4	31	12	6	10	13	9	3	3	6	9	4	9	14	8
Electrical																				
Number of firms entering listing	8	1	3	1	0	2	0	0	0	1	1	1	1	3	6	1	0	1	1	0
Number of firms re-capitalising	10	5	9	2	1	1	8	2	4	3	10	0	1	0	1	1	0	0	0	0
Number of firms raising new debt	0	0	7	4	0	0	2	3	2	1	5	6	7	0	2	4	4	4	5	6
Number of firms seeking external finance	18	6	19	7	1	3	10	5	6	5	16	7	9	3	9	3	4	5	6	6
General																				
Number of firms entering listing	25	8	12	9	9	11	51	8	6	6	19	5	3	0	1	2	2	3	1	0
Number of firms re-capitalising	7	11	20	8	1	5	6	8	9	4	4	7	12	3	1	4	5	5	11	11
Number of firms raising new debt	5	2	1	1	7	4	0	3	1	3	0	0	0	1	1	0	4	4	0	0
Number of firms seeking external finance	37	21	33	18	17	20	57	19	16	13	23	12	15	4	3	6	11	12	12	11

Source: *Stock Exchange Official Year Book.*

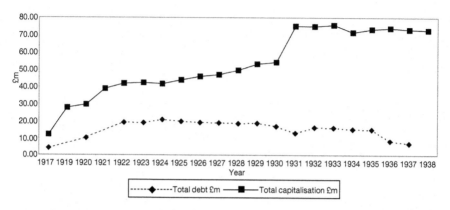

Figure 11.3 Electrical engineering: debt and equity.

Note: The vertical column (£m) indicates the amounts involved.
Source: *Stock Exchange Official Year Book*.

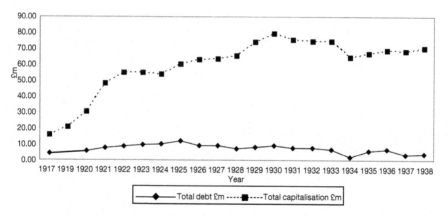

Figure 11.4 Vehicle engineering: debt and equity (total) in the interwar years.

Note: The vertical column (£m) indicates the amounts involved.
Source: *Stock Exchange Official Year Book*.

Thomas hypothesised that debt was associated with longer rather than newly established firms (Thomas, 1978). To test this hypothesis, we examined the debt equity balance of two cohorts of firms: those which were registered before 1900 and those registered between 1900 and 1914. In defining our cohorts by registration date we also include firms which ultimately were listed by 1920.

For electrical engineering (Table 11.4), we found little evidence that long-established firms were more likely to seek debt rather than equity funding. On the contrary, we found a propensity amongst our two cohorts of firms to have no debt and to seek finance through listing and through re-capitalisation between 1919 and 1921. We also discovered a propensity to reduce debt

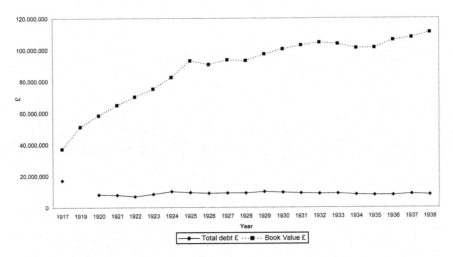

Figure 11.5 General engineering: debt and equity book values.

Note: the vertical column (£) indicates the amounts involved.
Source: *Stock Exchange Official Year Book*.

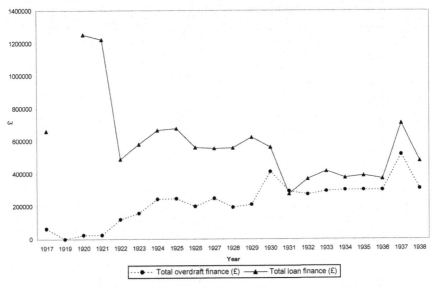

Figure 11.6 General engineering: the move from loan to overdraft finance.

Source: *Stock Exchange Official Year Book*.

during these years. For vehicle engineering (Table 11.5), we identified a similar propensity to seek equity rather than debt finance.

Further, it is clear from our analysis of the firms in vehicle engineering that firms did not chose *between* equity and debt; rather they used *both* forms of finance. Greater numbers of firms sought equity but this decision was not to

Table 11.4 Electrical engineering: finance by debt and equity of pre-1900 and 1900–14 cohorts of firms

	Pre-1900 cohort	1900–14 cohort
Total number of firms	28	36
1917 position		
Number not listed	10	15
Number of non-listed firms with debt		0
Mean average size of debt	£112,000	0
Median size of debt	£40,000	0
Number listed	18	
Number of listed firms with debt	13	10
Mean average size of debt	£216,455	£127,953.50
Median size of debt	£175,000	£75,000
1920 position		
Number of firms who acquired listing	8	3
Number of firms who acquired listing with debt	4	1 (as bank loan)
Debt as percentage of equity for the four firms in 1920 [pre-1900] / for the one firm which acquired listing and with debt [1900–14]	8.7%, 30.8%, 42.9% and 35.4%	10%
Number of firms which re-capitalised 1919–20	8	6
Number of re-capitalising firms with debt in 1917	5	4
Number of re-capitalising firms with debt in 1920	6	3
Median size of debt of re-capitalising firms in 1917	£300,000	£110,000
Median size of debt of re-capitalising firms in 1920	£475,000	£200,000
Number of re-capitalising firms who increase debt between 1917 and 1920	3	0
Number of re-capitalising firms who reduce debt between 1917 and 1920	2	1
Debt as percentage of equity of the re-capitalising firms by 1920	67%, 33%, 54%, 50%, 60% and 87%	3%, 5%, 64%

Source: *Stock Exchange Official Year Book.*

Table 11.5 Vehicle engineering; finance by debt and equity of pre-1900 and 1900–14 cohorts of firms

Pre-1900 cohort		1900–14 cohort	
Total number of firms	31	**Total number of firms**	58
1917 position		*1917 position*	
Number not listed	8	Number not listed	26
Number of non-listed firms with debt	5	Number of non-listed firms with debt	0
Mean average size of debt	£94,250	Mean average size of debt	not relevant
Median size of debt	£90,000	Median size of debt	not relevant
Number listed	23	Number listed	32
Number of listed firms with debt	19	Number of listed firms with debt	12
Mean average size of debt	£198,814	Mean average size of debt	£91,691.40
Median size of debt	£150,000	Median size of debt	£75,000
1920 position		*1920 position*	
Number of firms who acquired listing 1917–20	2	*Number of firms who acquired listing 1917–20*	7
Number of firms who acquired listing who also had debt	0	Number of firms who acquired listing who also had debt	1
Number of firms from 1917 cohort which re-capitalised 1919–20	12	*Number of firms which re-capitalised 1919–20*	16
Number of re-capitalising firms with debt in 1917	3	Number of re-capitalising firms with debt in 1917	7
Number of re-capitalising firms with debt in 1920	3	Number of re-capitalising firms with debt in 1920	8
Median size of debt of re-capitalising firms in 1917	£75,000	Median size of debt of re-capitalising firms in 1917	£70,000
Median size of debt of re-capitalising firms in 1920	£75,000	Median size of debt of re-capitalising firms in 1920	£75,000
Number of re-capitalising firms who increase debt between 1917 and 1920	1	Number of re-capitalising firms who increase debt between 1917 and 1920	3
Number of re-capitalising firms who reduce debt between 1917 and 1920	0	Number of re-capitalising firms who reduce debt between 1917 and 1920	0

Source: *Stock Exchange Official Year Book.*

the exclusion of all debt finance. The evidence on vehicle engineering disputed the idea that long-listed firms sought debt rather than equity finance; it also disputed the idea that firms chose exclusively between the two. What our findings did show was that there was an overall tendency to seek increasing amounts of funding from the equity markets by a growing number of firms in vehicle engineering.

The question then arises as to what determined the finance instrument of choice. We suggest two explanations. The first relates to the cost and perceived risk of debt. Whilst firms might reasonably expect that wartime interest rates would not continue, we expected the escalation in bank rates in the early 1920s and the marked fall in the rate from 1933 to have affected the choice of finance instrument. To this extent we expected to find a negative relationship between debt and the interest rate and a positive relationship between the interest rate and equity finance in the early 1920s and from 1933.

Our research identified two specific time points when the bank rate did appear to have had a significant effect on the take-up of debt: in the postwar boom years when the sharp increase in interest rates prompted a fall in the take-up of debt, and the significant decline in the bank rate from 1933 which appears to have prompted firms to obtain debt finance. Prima facie, firms were responding in a rational manner to two specific points of time characterised by significant changes in the interest rate.

In addition to the above, our research identified another factor. We tabulate (Table 11.6) actual rates levied on debentures for companies in each sector. The major deterrent to debt finance, we suggest, was the rates levied on new debt finance. Our findings suggest a risk premium for firms in vehicle as well as electrical engineering throughout the 1920s. It is significant that from 1924 general engineering was considered less of a risk than vehicle or electrical engineering, as evidenced by interest rates.

By the mid 1930s, however, the tables had turned – general engineering was considered more of a risk than electrical or vehicle engineering. The data suggest that by the 1930s there was more of a level playing field, although the absence of new loans in this decade warns against too firm a judgement.

Survival and perspective

What did firms learn from this period? How many of these firms actually survived? We begin with an assessment of firm survival during the Great Depression. We found that exit (that is, no longer being listed) in each sector was associated with newly quoted, low-capitalised firms. In electrical engineering, only eight firms left the listings between 1929 and 1932. Of the eight, six were newly listed firms.[2] In vehicle engineering, 18 firms ceased listing between 1929 and 1931; of the 18, only four had been listed before the end of the war: the remainder had entered through the 1920s, including two which were first listed in 1929.[3] The same applied in general engineering: 16 firms

Table 11.6 Interest rates levied on long-term debt

	General %	Vehicle %	Electrical %
1919	6	6	5.5
1920	6	5	6
1921	8	8	8
1922	n/a	8	7
1923	6.5	6.25	6
1924	5	8	6
1925	n/a	7.5	n/a
1926	5.5	6.5	n/a
1927	6	6.5	n/a
1928	6	7.5	7.5
1929	n/a	n/a	n/a
1930	5.5	4	5.5
1931	n/a	n/a	5.5
1932	6	n/a	5
1933	4.5	5.5	4.6
1934	n/a	5.5	4.5
1935	5.25	4.5	n/a
1936	4.5	n/a	4
1937	n/a	n/a	4.5
1938	n/a	n/a	n/a

Source: *Stock Exchange Official Year Book.*

ceased listing between 1929 and 1931 and all but one had first achieved quotation during the 1920s.[4] Our research shows that those firms that exited in the Depression were short-lived firms with low capitalisation values. The Depression, in other words, appears to have had its greatest impact on those firms that were newly capitalised and had low capitalisation values.

We found (Table 11.7) that whereas the 1917 cohort of firms in each sub-sector was relatively long-lived, those firms that had acquired listing status between 1919 and 1921 were less likely to survive. This phenomenon was more noticeable in vehicle and electrical than in general engineering. The results are stark: those firms which acquired listing status in the 1919–21 floatation boom years, particularly those in vehicle and electrical engineering, were less likely to survive than those which had acquired listing status before the beginning of the interwar years.

Our second question referred to the effects of the 1919–21 re-capitalisation boom on survival. We found (Table 11.7) that in electrical, general and vehicle engineering, firms that re-capitalised were most likely to survive, whether or not they were listed after or before the end of World War One.[5]

Conclusion

To summarise, we found that companies showed a growing preference for equity finance in the interwar years. In this respect, the need to raise external

Table 11.7 Re-capitalisation and survival

	Number of companies which re-capitalised 1919–21	%	Number of companies which did not re-capitalise 1919–21	%
1917 cohort				
Electrical engineering	18	40.91	26	59.09
Vehicle engineering	33	53.23	29	46.77
General engineering	26	29.21	63	70.79
1919–21 cohort				
Electrical engineering	2	11.11	16	88.89
Vehicle engineering	3	14.29	18	85.71
General engineering	10	22.73	34	77.27
1917 cohort *Number who survived*				
Electrical engineering	15	50.00	15	50.00
Vehicle engineering	23	62.16	14	37.84
General engineering	22	34.38	42	65.63
1919–21 cohort *Number who survived*				
Electrical engineering	2	15.38	11	84.62
Vehicle engineering	2	18.18	9	81.82
General engineering	6	20.00	24	80.00

Source: *Stock Exchange Official Year Book.*

finance to fund investment in capacity to raise production for the new growth industries in electrical and vehicle industries did encourage an enhanced propensity to seek equity finance. In addition, our research found that companies did not experience any difficulties in raising funds (debt and equity) to finance expansion, brought about by the new industries. It would therefore seem that companies in the vehicle and electrical firms were deemed to have good investment potential and, as a result, the City and financial institutions were prepared to make finance available. In these terms, our research supports the work of Capie and Collins.

In this respect we would note a strong contrast with experience in the depressed staple industries. In relation to firms in these industries, banks were compelled to lend to preserve their previous lending during the 1919–21 boom. This does not appear to have been the case for vehicle and electrical engineering, where the evidence suggested voluntary provision of finance. Our research suggested, in contrast to the cotton textile industries, that re-capitalisation was not important in vehicle and electrical engineering.

This, however, is not to claim that debt finance was not used. Indeed, we found that, throughout the period, companies in each sector used debt finance. To that extent, we did not find evidence of reluctance on the part of the financial institutions to supply debt finance. Indeed, we found, and in particular in the case of general engineering, a growing propensity to hold overdrafts. We also found evidence to dispute the theory that older established firms sought debt finance. Our research indicated that both established and new firms used debt. In this respect we did not find evidence to suggest an aversion on the part of the financial institutions to supply debt finance to only 'safe' long-established firms.

Why did firms seek equity finance? We suggest that the interwar years were characterised by a preference for equity over debt finance, a preference we explain in terms of the prevailing interest rates (and in particular actual rates) and a perception that shared ownership did not constitute a real loss of control. The latter, we argue, was a reflection of the absence at this time of the exercise of either voice or exit by shareholders. This in turn reflected the local and personal nature of shareholding. The majority of our firms were 'owned' by a small number of personal investors. At this time, the presence of the financial institutions was limited.

How did this affect the evolution of the firm and of corporate capitalism? For a start, personal shareholding was always a problem insofar as funding was limited, particularly in an era when other 'safe' asset investments were available – namely houses. It was, second, a problem insofar as many personal investors 'burnt their fingers' in the negative effects of share pushing which took place in these years. In this respect we find the interwar years to be a transition process: important steps were taken in the evolution to the growth of equity markets, but the period was still reminiscent of the character of shareholding in the late nineteenth century.

In essence, however, we find that the interwar years were characterised by a preference for equity over debt finance, a preference we explain in terms of the prevailing interest rates (and in particular actual rates) and a perception that shared ownership did not constitute a real loss of control. The latter, we argue, was a reflection of the absence at this time of the exercise of either voice or exit by shareholders. This in turn reflected the local and personal nature of shareholding.

Notes

1 This paper presents preliminary overview findings of our work on the engineering industry in the United Kingdom during the interwar years. The research was funded by ESRC Research Grant.
2 Aeonic Radio was first listed in 1929; it ceased listing in 1931 with a capitalisation value of £450,000. Automatic Equipment (first listed in 1929) ceased listing in 1931 with a capitalisation value of £150,000. Burndept Wireless, first listed in 1927, ceased listing in 1932 with a capitalisation value of £200,000, whilst MPA Wireless, first listed in 1929, ceased listing in 1931 with a capitalisation value of £100,000.
3 That is, Ascot Motors. This firm was first listed in 1929, but ceased listing in 1931 with a capitalisation value of £400,000. Lewis and Crabtree Motors, first listed in 1931, ceased listing in 1931 with a capitalisation value of £60,000.
4 That is, Machine-Made Sales which was first listed in 1929 and ceased listing in

1931 with a capitalisation value of £225,000; Turner Automatic Machines, first listed in 1929 and ceased listing in 1931 with a capitalisation value of £250,000.
5 Of our 1917 cohort, 83 per cent of firms in electrical engineering who re-capitalised survived; 58 per cent of those who did not re-capitalise survived. The results for vehicle engineering were 70 per cent and 48 per cent respectively. Those for general engineering were 85 per cent and 67 per cent respectively.

References

Official papers

Board of Trade, *Census of Production*, 1924, 1930, 1935, 1948 and 1951.
Board of Trade, *Share-Pushing; Report of the Departmental Committee appointed by the Board of Trade,* PP. 1936–37, XV.725, Cmd 5539.
Committee on Finance and Industry, Report, 1931, Cmd 3897.
Committee on Industry and Trade, *Factors in Industrial and Commercial Efficiency,* Being Part I of a Survey of Industries, London, 1927.
Committee on the Working of the Monetary System (1959), *Report,* August, Cmnd 827.
Committee to Review the Functioning of Financial Institutions (1977), *Progress Report on the Financing of Industry and Trade.*

Primary sources

Public Record Office (Kew)

Secondary sources

Bowden, S. (1990), 'Credit facilities and the growth of consumer demand for electric appliances in England in the 1930s', *Business History,* 32: 52–75.
—— (1991), 'Demand and supply constraints in the inter-war British car industry: did the manufacturers get it right?', *Business History,* 33: 241–67.
Bowden, Sue and Higgins, D. M. (2004), 'British industry in the inter-war years', in Roderick Floud and Paul Johnson (eds), *The Cambridge Economic History of Britain since 1700,* vol. 2, Cambridge: Cambridge University Press, Chapter 14, pp. 374–402.
Capie, Forrest and Collins, Michael (1992), *Have the Banks Failed Industry? An Historical Study of Bank/Industry Relations 1870–1990,* London: Institute of Economic Affairs.
Chandler, A. D. (1977), *The Visible Hand: The Managerial Revolution in American Business,* Cambridge, MA: Harvard University Press.
—— (1990), *Scale and Scope,* Cambridge, MA: Harvard University Press.
—— (1991), *Strategy and Structure: Chapters in the History of the American Enterprise,* 17th printing, Cambridge, MA: MIT Press.
Cottrell, P. L. (2004), 'Domestic finance 1860–1914', in *The Cambridge Economic History of Modern Britain,* vol. II: *Economic Maturity, 19760–1939,* Chapter 10, pp. 253–79.
Dimson, Elroy, Marsh, Paul and Staunton, Mike (2002), *Triumph of the Optimists:*

101 Years of Global Investment Returns, Princeton, NJ: Princeton University Press.

Dowie, J. A. (1975), '1919–20 is in need of attention', *Economic History Review,* XXVIII: 429–50.

Hannah, L. (1980), 'Visible and invisible hands in Great Britain', in A. D. Chandler and H. Daems (eds), *Managerial Hierarchies,* Cambridge, MA: Harvard University Press.

—— (1983), *The Rise of the Corporate Economy,* second edn, London: Methuen.

Henderson, R. F. (1951), *The New Issue Market and the Finance of Industry,* Cambridge: Bowes and Bowes.

Higgins, D. M. and Toms, J. S. (2001), 'Capital ownership, capital structure, and capital markets: financial constraints and the decline of the Lancashire cotton textile industry, 1880–1965', *Journal of Industrial History,* 4: 48–64.

—— (2003), 'Financial distress, corporate borrowing and industrial decline: the Lancashire cotton spinning industry, 1918–1938', *Accounting, Business and Financial History,* 13: 1–26.

Matthews, R. C .O., Feinstein, C. and Odling-Smee, J. (1982), *British Economic Growth, 1856–1973,* Oxford: Oxford University Press.

Payne, P. L. (1984), 'Family business in Britain: an historical and analytical survey', in A. Okochi and S. Yasuoka, (eds), *Family Business in the Era of Industrial Growth,* Tokyo: University of Tokyo Press, pp. 171–206.

Romer, Paul (1994), 'The origins of endogenous growth' *Journal of Economic Perspectives,* 8: 3–22.

Ross, Duncan M. (2004), 'Industrial and commercial finance in the interwar years', in *The Cambridge Economic History of Modern Britain,* vol. II: *Economic Maturity, 19760–1939,* Chapter 15, pp. 403–27.

Solow, Robert M. (1956), 'Contribution to the theory of economic growth', *Quarterly Journal of Economics,* 70: 65–94.

Thomas, W. A. (1978), *The Finance of British Industry 1918–1976,* London: Methuen.

Appendix 1: *Stock Exchange Official Year Book* database – variables collected for the database

- Year of registration
- Book value of capitalisation (for each year)
- Dividend rate (for each year)
- Profit recorded (for each year)
- Debentures raised: amount, interest rate applied and date of raising of debt
- Loans: amount and date of raising of debt
- Overdraft: amount and date of first listing

Index

Note: numbers in **bold** are illustrations.

Printed in the United States
by Baker & Taylor Publisher Services